NEVER A HOME
OF MY OWN

Also by William J. Nicol:

Against the Grain:
An Autobiography of William J. Nicol,
doctor, surgeon, Minister and
pilgrim with Avril

ISBN 0-595-40040-X

Another Story:
A Tale of a Son and a Daughter
of Two Villages

ISBN 978-1-907294-37-2

NEVER A HOME
OF MY OWN

An Autobiography of William J. Nicol, Doctor,
Surgeon, Minister, Author, Pilgrim with Avril and
ever-searching with Margaret

by

William J. Nicol

DIADEM BOOKS

Published by Diadem Books

For information, please contact:

Diadem Books
8 South Green Drive
Airth, Falkirk.
FK2 8JP
Scotland UK

www.diadembooks.com

The views expressed in this work are solely those of the author and do not necessarily reflect the views of the publisher, and the publisher hereby disclaims any responsibility for them.

ISBN: 978-0-244-30230-6

The front cover is a view from our home in Kelso showing the ruins of Kelso Abbey in the background and part of our walled garden in the foreground.

For Avril and Margaret

There are decisions we make in life which are really made for us. Though we're responsible for making them, and must stand or fall by them, we're very often compelled by something or someone beyond ourselves directing us, pointing us on our way.

– **William J. Nicol (*Against the Grain*, 2006)**

Wrestle, gracious God, with each of us, that we may cling on to you.

– **William J. Nicol (*Another Story*, 2010)**

'A Silent sentinel at the mouth of the Firth of Forth, the Bass Rock can be seen equally well on a clear day from Buckhaven and West Wemyss. Gazing almost due east over the sheltered waters of the Firth to the restless North Sea beyond, the Rock is, in one sense, a barrier, an impenetrable protection proclaiming the security of home in the Kingdom of Fife. In another it's a stimulus demanding the quest of what cannot be seen on the other side, a magnet to exciting seas beyond, the God-goal of our lives. The same Bass Rock that we viewed from our student-day homes in Buckhaven and West Wemyss aroused different emotions in each of us, Margaret and me, then, and still does'.

– **William J. Nicol (*Another Story*, 2010)**

ACKNOWLEDGEMENTS

Thank You! Thank You! Thank You! – to all my family and friends who have, over the years, consoled me with the reassuring words of encouragement, 'Why are you doing this? There's no need for it. You've already done it. Why? Why? Why?' It's these assumptions that have prompted me to respond 'against the grain' and bring this book to press today. To everyone, your efforts have been invaluable.

But acknowledgements beyond the call of duty go to my Editor, my good friend, Charles Muller and, above all, to my Proof Reader par excellence, Margaret Thomson, much more to me, of course, than just a literary critic.

For the perceptive Foreword to this book written from your heart, Charles, it touched mine. For your infinite patience with me at every stage in bringing it to publication, thank you. Your constant reminders of the many details required to bring it to life were always much appreciated. My best wishes to you and yours, Charles, for sharing with me in some of the highlights of your life, not least enhancing our common love of your birth place, South Africa.

But my last acknowledgement is reserved, and more than just reserved, for Margaret, for her attention to every detail from the smallest cedilla to the biggest, boldest, most sensational printing feature unearthed in her meticulous proof-reading of this book, *Never a Home of my Own*. Thank You! Thank You! Thank You, Margaret! And love and kisses to go with it, now and always.

William J Nicol (February, 2017)

TABLE OF CONTENTS

FOREWORD

We are told that no man is an island and indeed we are not insular no matter how much we might think we are; we are not isolated individuals after all – but spiritual and social beings with many connections – and invariably we have extended families – but the basic marital unit sends out many binding roots and feelers. This new book by Bill Nicol reminds us of this – and it's a blessing too, that we are not alone for it's a warming thought that our lives have a destiny with a higher power in control. The epigraph that appeared in his preceding autobiographies is still so apt: *'There are decisions we make in life which are really made for us. Though we're responsible for making them, and must stand or fall by them, we're very often compelled by something or someone beyond ourselves directing us, pointing us on our way.'*

Bill suggested that instead of divisions into 'Chapters' in this book, there should be 'Acts' – not a bad idea since each chapter enacts the development of the author's life at a different stage, in keeping with Shakespeare's parable of the seven stages of a man's life – from the cradle to death. This begs the question – who is the Director of this play in seven Acts? – again, a question that evokes thoughts of each man's destiny. The Rev William Nicol's life has surely been shaped and inspired by a higher Destiny – for why else would there be such a dramatic *volte face* in his life, that at the height of a career of successful hip-replacement surgeon he made the remarkable transition to a higher calling – that of a church minister. And that led him to a path that was different yet contiguous with his former path, taking him back to South Africa where previously he had fulfilled his calling as a surgeon and doctor, this time as a minister of the Gospel. I am pleased that he has included his remarkable sermon in this book, which he had included in his previous Memoirs – the sermon on the hip joint which highlights the need for a regeneration inspired by God, who takes the initiative to wrestle with us to bring us closer to his divine plan and purpose for each one of us.

Indeed it has been a privilege to have been, once again, the editor and portal to publishing for Bill's new book – for a man who has become a much valued friend. It has always been an uplifting experience to read his books, and certainly a regenerating experience to be in his company. His enthusiasm and zest for life come through, whether it be listening to him in his spiritually-charged home in the shadow of the Abbey in Kelso, or in each of his books where one walks in the shadow of an unseen Third Man – a spiritual presence. He is indeed the 'son of the manse' so it should not be surprising that the manse is woven into the fabric of his book – and his life.

It feels like an uncanny providence that Bill elected me to be his editor, for reading his life story there are so many points of contact between his life and mine. The time he and his wife Avril spent in the Transkei in South Africa coincided with my years at the University of Natal in Pietermaritzburg and it's a pleasure to think that all these events so vividly recreated in the Transkei were taking place not far off from where I was at the time. Strange to think that it would be almost half a century later that our contingent paths would eventually touch each other, in the Highlands of Scotland, when I became the editor for Bill's first autobiography *Against the Grain*. Of course it's not surprising that I could relate to and empathise with his time in South Africa, in the Transkei and then again especially when he came, in the capacity of a Minister, to Pietermaritzburg, the town of my old Alma Mater.

Their time in the Transkei coincided with a time of seminal change in the country, when the first rumbles of the political earthquake began that eventually shook the country to pieces. What is so impressive is the degree to which the author has imbibed the spirit of the Transkei in South Africa, and his knowledge of the landscape, the topography, the roads, the isolation, the mealie fields – it is all so true, so authentic, as I can testify, having been part of that world myself – for the then Northern Transvaal where much later I was a Professor of English was not very different from the ethos of the world he describes in the Transkei, where the Zion Christian Church was also a vital presence for the Northern Sotho population. His descriptions and evocations of that landscape and society I found quite nostalgic. I even discovered that we shared voyages, though on different occasions, on the Union Castle Line *SS Oranje,* which brought me to Britain in 1967. Another of those quirks which seemed to have loosely knit together the contingent paths of our lives, of author and publisher, is apparent when I moved from the Highlands of Scotland to Kennoway in Fife, just a stone's throw away from Buckhaven, the home of Margaret, his first love! And this of course facilitated the new meetings that took place between author and publisher – and once again it was my pleasure to be present at the launch of his second book *Another Story.*

The author's life has been a pilgrimage, as he puts it – and it has been a pilgrimage with two 'help-meets'. The letters written by Avril, especially those from the Transkei days, are real gems, and in their lives together the reader is very aware of the bonds of love that held their nuclear family together, through thick and thin, wherever their home was transplanted to. But after the sad loss of Avril another gem in his life reappeared, and the new story of how he sought out 'the sweetheart of his student days in St Andrews, the girl at the bus stop at the top of Wellesley Road in Buckhaven,'is very touchingly told. As the author puts it, 'My life with Avril has been a Pilgrimage, with Margaret a journey to an unknown future.' But it is a secure and happy future as this volume testifies, a future in which, as he says, 'We behave as though we belong to each other because we do belong to each other.' Margaret was present when he gave his uplifting sermon on the hip joint – and one is tempted to say that from that point onwards the two of them were joined at the hip – though more aptly, joined in heart, united in love.

When the author attended the First National Conference of the Bangladesh Orthopaedic Society, he was struck by the motto of the Orthopaedic Society emblazoned on a banner behind the podium – 'Expect great things from God. Attempt great things for God.' In this book he has demonstrated how well, in fact, he has fulfilled this mission – although it was not a conscious aim of the book to do so. Now with Margaret by his side, he has gone forward, a change of direction once again, you might say – but forever expecting great things from God, and attempting great things for God.

Charles Muller
MA (Wales), PhD (London), DEd (SA), DLitt (UFS)

INTRODUCTION

I **AM BY NATURE** a non-conformist. For most of my life I've lived against the grain of convention, questioning the popular norms of society wherever I've lived. In 2006 I recorded the highlights of my boyhood days, my time in the Army, as a medical student and doctor, a family man and a father and, above all, the days most dear to my heart, my time with my wife, Avril, the inspiration of the best in me in my autobiography, *Against the Grain*, two years after she died. Till then I faced many conflicting attitudes to life, the ideologies of the leaders of nations like our own and South Africa in the apartheid days, the professed beliefs of people from a variety of cultures, professions, and ramifications of the church, all with their specific outlooks on one another, from my own, no doubt, fixed perspective. I knew, I thought, what I cherished and what I disapproved of. I knew what I liked about life and what I didn't, and when I relive events of the past in my mind today I find my feelings as fresh as ever. I might have mellowed with the passage of time but the passions that made me tick in yesteryear still set me alight today.

But life has moved on, and so, I hope, have I. What saddens me about today's world is the confrontational relationships that seem to pervade almost all aspects of life, not least of all in the political arena. The bitter way in which any outlook different from our own is demonised has been a growing worry to me. So much so that my inherent hopeful nature has been threatened by the danger of my anxieties giving way to a depressing obsession.

Relationships have never been so much an integral part of life as they are today. We're all being forced to relate to one another, to talk to and acknowledge those we like and those we don't. No more 'against the grain' alone, or 'with the grain' alone, but 'across the grain' more and more. That's what this book was to be all about until I moved from 'our house', 'our home' in Abbey Royd to 'Grandad's Deluxe Apartment' down below in Abbey Royd in August 2013.

This is a copy of a circular letter that I wrote to all my friends on my Christmas card list in 2010. It serves as an introduction to this book, not now *Across the Grain* but *Never a Home of my Own* and is a summary of what lies between the pages you are about to read.

'Dear......
I never had a house of my own, my own home, and I don't know if I really want to.

> *'All the world's a stage,*
> *And all the men and women merely players:*
> *They have their exits and their entrances;*
> *And one man in his time plays many parts,*
> *His acts being seven ages. ('As you like it', act 2, sc. 7)*

> *At first the infant,*
> *Mewling and puking in the nurse's arms.*
> *And then the whining schoolboy, with his satchel,*
> *And shining morning face, creeping like snail*
> *Unwillingly to school'*

As an infant, a child, a boy at school, my home was my family's. The house I lived in was 'our house'.

> *'And then the lover,*
> *Sighing like furnace, with a woeful ballad*
> *Made to his mistress' eyebrow.'*

Try as I have I have been unable to relate to Shakespeare's image of lover. For me the relationship of lover transcends all ages, from the very first breath of life to the very last and even beyond.

> *'Then the soldier,*
> *Full of strange oaths, and bearded like a pard,*
> *Jealous in honour, sudden and quick in quarrel,*
> *Seeking the bubble reputation*
> *Even in the cannon's mouth.'*

In the Army, as a Medical student and as a young doctor, my home was with my parents, my fellow-students and later fellow-colleagues. When I married Avril, the inspiration of my life, and we moved into our first home in Dornoch, it was not 'my house' we moved into, but 'our house'. And it was the same with all the many homes we lived in with our growing family over the years in Dundee, South Africa, Halifax, and many other places, the longest stay, by far, in one home being 'Abbey Royd' in Kelso. 'My home' or 'my house' was always 'ours'.

> *'And then the justice,*
> *In fair round belly with good capon lined.'*

The prime of my days in Orthopaedics and the Ministry came and went as we passed from the fifth to the sixth age.

'Sixth age shifts into the
Lean and slippered pantaloon,
With spectacles on nose and pouch on side,
His youthful hose well saved a world too wide
For his shrunk shank.'

It was Avril who gave 'Abbey Royd' its name – 'Abbey' from the town Abbey over the wall from our treasured walled garden, and 'Royd', a Yorkshire term meaning 'a clearing', 'our bit', or 'mine', a place of belonging'. And so it was throughout her days in it. In the last few weeks of her life she surveyed the grounds, fondly claiming 'Abbey Royd ' for herself and me, but looking beyond to posterity, including in 'our home' as much our children and our grandchildren as ourselves enhancing the sense of belonging in its name.

I've never had a house of my own. Even on my own now in the too-big rambling house with the too-big, unmanageable garden which is 'Abbey Royd', it's not mine alone because our family is as much part of it as their parents, and it's not even 'Grandad's house' alone because it is as much part of our grandchildren as his.

And since Margaret reappeared in my life four years ago to rekindle cords of affection which grew almost instantaneously into bonds of love, transforming our lives into a treasured relationship of uninhibited interdependence, the last scene of the seven ages of our lives has been delayed, if not banished for ever.

'Last scene of all,
That ends this strange eventful history,
Is second childishness, and mere oblivion,
Sans teeth, sans eyes, sans taste, sans everything.

Margaret is now as much part of our home in Kelso as anyone else. She plays her part, in her own way in making 'Abbey Royd' 'our home'.

'But sentimentality,' I continued in my Christmas letter of 2010, 'must be tempered with practicality.' As a rapidly approaching octogenarian it finally dawned on me that the homestead in Kelso was getting too much for me to cope with. I bowed to my better judgement and the sensitive advice of well-wishers. I'd pack up, I reasoned, sell out, and move on to a more manageable house, a smaller place of my liking, easily kept and easily run. A house of my own at last!

The process of purchase was well underway. The dice was in my hand, ready and eager to be cast. Responsible me, I would do what any prudent person in my position would do. My own house beckoned.   But something in me stirred. Perhaps a whisper of the quotation from my autobiography, *Against the Grain*, that appears on the front fly-leaf of it and again in my second book, *Another Story*, rippled through my flesh and blood till my bones began to rattle in their skin. **'There are decisions we make in life which are really made for us. Though we're responsible for making them, and must stand or fall by them, we're very often compelled by something or someone beyond ourselves directing us, pointing us on our way.'**

What I want is what I've got, not 'my house' or 'my home', but 'ours'. All my dearest friends, the reality of their presence or their memories make 'my house' 'our' house', 'my home' 'our home'. There's always room in 'Abbey Royd' for someone else.

Luke tells us that *'there was no room for him at the inn'. (c2, v7)* It's my prayer, as it is, I hope, yours also, that 'there's room in this inn', that there's room in the inns of our hearts this Christmas and for many New Years to come.

With love and every blessing from W.J.N.'

ACT ONE

'At first the infant,
Mewling and puking in the nurse's arms.'

I **AM A SON** of the manse, which may well in some way account for my looking upon the homes I've lived in ever since the day I was born into this world in the 'upper front room of 234 King's Park Avenue, Glasgow S4, Scotland, at 10 P.M. on 26th November 1930' (Ref. *Against the Grain*) not solely as 'my home', or even my family's home alone because the parish people in the community around us could also with some justification lay claim to a small corner of their manse, 'our home', as theirs as well. In the same way in my earlier years as a doctor some of my patients looked upon their doctor's home as with an open door, never closed to anyone in need. An exclusive home of my own seemed always a less naturally appealing concept of home to me than one of 'our home', 'our house'.

Though I never lived in Glasgow for any appreciable length of time, my grandparents' home there, where I was born, was always the home I kept returning to as a boy and young man. It was always to me 'our home'. I was always part of it but it was never mine. Apart from the birth itself in Glasgow, the first five years of my life were spent in Canada, in Southampton, Ontario, where my father was minister of a Presbyterian Church of Canada, but I have no real memories of those days. My recollections of having an older brother, Douglas, then and a sister, Mary, born in Southampton and marked by frostbite one severe winter out walking in the snow, and of a red apple in an apple tree in the garden may have some basis in reality but are more likely the result of anecdotes of our home in Canada and a photo or two which persisted through the years. What we children were not aware of but what came across to us in the way our parents described our days in Canada, was the vaguely intangible feeling of inadequacy which in time overwhelmed the local church at the height of the General Depression of the '30's. The impoverished congregation could no longer support its minister. Our return to Glasgow, 234 King's Park Avenue, in 1936 was sealed. 'The mewling and puking in the nurse's arms' age of my life had come to an end. 'The whining schoolboy, with his satchel, and shining morning face, creeping like snail unwillingly to school', in Guiana, in Glasgow, and in Fife had started.

ACT TWO

'And then the whining schoolboy, with his satchel,
And shining morning face, creeping like snail
Unwillingly to school'.

'SCHOOL DAYS** are the happiest days of your life', some say, and for them and many others that may be so. But not for me. I was seldom really unhappy and often satisfied, content, fulfilled, successful to a point but never to the extent of achieving success for the sake of achievement in itself, always spurred on by what my mother came to repeat over and over again in her precious time in my life – 'Try again! You'll try again, Willie, won't you?' And she'd look at me with a look that left no other way I could reply to but, 'Well, Yes!' And I did. Whatever else my school days taught me they taught me as much, if not more, about 'home days', not 'my home' days but 'ours', not 'me' but 'us', than the cold virtue of education for the sake of knowledge in itself. It was in my school days that the concept of 'our house', 'our home' took root in me as I became aware of more and more people coming and going through 'our home' wherever it was. Our home was always 'ours', never 'mine', alone. In the coming and going of life in my school days our home seemed to attract an unending flow of people all in their own ways part of my life in 'our home', 'our house'. Where were they all coming from? Where were they all going to? Where was I coming from? Where was I going?

BERBICE

A year or two before the outbreak of the Second World War in September 1939 my father was accepted for the ministry in the Church of Scotland and sent, through the Colonial and Continental Department, to a church, 'All Saints Church' in New Amsterdam, Berbice in British Guiana. Our home, in the manse, for the next seven years would be what was once a Dutch governor's residence. I can't remember much about the rooms except for the study with a wicker waste-paper basket with our parakeet perched on it, an open room with a large dining-table with silver knives and forks and spoons which our maid had to keep highly polished along with all the brass ornaments on it, and finger bowls to wash your fingers in after eating mangoes on it as well, and a Berbice chair to lounge on and look out of the window, over the verandah, into the garden beyond. The yard underneath the house was a mud bath in the rainy season but trampled down to form a hard-baked, uneven floor in the dry season. The rafters between the thick wooden stilts which supported the house and the house itself were, one night, stuffed with half-eaten newly baked loaves of bread which my mother and our cook had made, and the yard strewn with stacks of silverware, ornaments, personal jewellery, things of little more than sentimental value to us, when a well-known gang of naked and heavily greased thieves were disturbed by my mother who woke to find one of them rummaging through her dressing table. 'Is that you, Douglas?' she asked, but it wasn't.

What I remember about New Amsterdam, Berbice, is patchy. It's where our home was, where we lived. It was for a short, passing phase of my life, its centre. It was where I went to my first school, Miss Cummings' Kindergarten School. The tightly plaited hair on the back of black girls' heads left a lasting impression on me, as did my first slate on which I first formed letters into words and numbers into sums. Of my parents in those early years, what sticks in my memory about my mother is her telling me about one sultry Sunday morning in church when a regular maiden lady worshipper fainted and my mother went to help her. When she undid the top buttons of the lady's dress to give her air, she was surprised by the tide-mark where the heavily floured upper part of the 'white' lady's neck met the dusky lower part which was her natural skin colour. For many years of the poor woman's life she had been seen in public, like coming to church, always well dressed with colourful hats, her face partly concealed by a fine- meshed net, a high collar, her arms with laced elbow-length gloves, her legs with brightly coloured stockings and neat close-fitting shoes. Like some other 'black' people she longed so much to be 'white'. Of my father, what I remember is that he sometimes wore a dog collar and preached in the Church, that he named our dog 'Bonzo' after 'pro bono publico', and that a special friend of the family, a kind man, a minister or pastor of some kind, I think, with disfiguring marks and holes on his face and unsightly deformed hands visited us from time to time. He had spent several years in a leper colony but was eventually safe enough to live outside and to mix with other people.

As 'the whining schoolboy', creeping still like a snail but not so 'unwillingly to school', began to become more and more aware of his environment in Berbice, his discernment grew apace. Often at the week-ends we would go for a run in the country. A car would arrive and take my sister, Mary, and me along with other 'European' children in the neighbourhood, to play on one of the nearby sugar estates, like Blairmont, and bring us back at night. I enjoyed the runs through the open countryside and cane fields with the occasional East Indian indentured worker cutting grass at the roadside, to the owner's home or the club house with its welcome swimming pool, and gradually became aware of what lay behind it all, the sugar cane industry. There were occasional hushed stories of unfortunate accidents like a worker falling into a vat of molten sugar, and trouble with the labourers. Among the administrators and supervisors was a particular group of men called 'Overseers' who came for a while and then went back home. When they came out from the 'old country' they had young, fresh faces and lily white arms and knees, and spoke with a public-school accent, but they soon grew in confidence as they rode their horses through the cane fields and cracked their whips when necessary in the course of their work overseeing gangs of cane cutters. Their arms, knees and faces soon turned to bronze and they confidently demanded, often with disdain, assistance from a servant to remove their field boots after a hard day's work. Many became involved with women, even black or brown women, and some had to be sent home in a hurry.

QUEEN'S COLLEGE of BRITISH GUIANA

Then at the age of nine it was off to join my brother, Douglas, at school in Georgetown, Demerara, to 'The Queen's College of British Guiana' for me. My family nest, 'our home' in New Amsterdam, was suddenly substituted by an unknown, uncertain place of belonging. 'Our home' was for the first time in my life questioned. This was understandably a turning point in my early childhood life, but it was cushioned, by the reassuring presence of my brother, Douglas, and a new mother figure, a Mrs Ezekiel, whose home became 'ours' for our remaining years in Guiana.

Queen's College was '*the*' boy's school of British Guiana. It had a long history of excellence and it accepted boys of any race, from many backgrounds but with a common parental interest in their sons getting on, having instilled into them the hallmarks of a good English education, moral values and social graces, and being well prepared for University entrance examinations. From my years at QC the foundations of an all-round education were laid. I excelled in nothing but absorbed something from everything. My spelling and writing were never very good, but I tried. With the aid of my fingers, Maths wasn't too bad! I was proud of taking Latin and French, but was hopeless at both. When I returned home after the first term in my new school and I excitedly told my mother that I knew the Lord's Prayer in Latin and in French her response took me by surprise. 'Well done, Willie!' she replied, smiling, 'But that's funny. You never knew it in English.'

My lasting memories of everyday life at QC are the animal house with several ring-tailed monkeys, a talkative multicoloured macaw and a few snakes; the tuck shop with its popular sticky buns and sorrel and mango drinks; the sports ground associated with proud athletic achievements; the head's office the thought of which even today still makes me wince at the nightmare thought of the black and blue, greenish-yellow, fading but still painful stripes, the legacy of a humiliating and smarting caning; and the names of outstanding scholars of the past, some on active service then, some who had been killed in action in the war, on the roll of honour in the assembly hall.

Looking back at my childhood days in Guiana it was there that I must have first formed some kind of sense of belonging. In New Amsterdam 'my home' was 'ours' in a local, homely environment. In Georgetown, at home in the expanding awareness of 'my home', 'our family', in my new home with the Ezekiels, the cosmopolitan mix in the cauldron of life in the colony's capital with The Queen's College of British Guiana at its centre, the schoolboy, less whining as he grew, was beginning to identify with his environment and to thrive on it. It was there that I first heard about the Battle of Bannockburn.

My pale, bespectacled face was one of a class of many other boys, black, white, brown, yellow, pink and intermediate shades, all with bright eyes and attentive. Our history teacher was a popular West Indian product of Queen's College who had studied in England on a scholarship and returned to teach English and History in his own school. He must have known about my Scots parentage and I must have been the only, or one of only a few, Scots boys in the class. He seemed to be looking straight at me and speaking only to me with passion as he described Bruce's ragged Scots band defeating the mighty English Army. His personal convictions and his sympathy for the oppressed underdog were passed on to me. I drew in a deep breath and stuck out my chest with pride. My teacher gave up teaching soon after, returned to England to take a Law degree, and returned to Guiana as a barrister for a short time before entering politics. He was Forbes Birnham, who later became the first Prime Minister of independent Guyana. His great-great-grandparents had been slaves and he had, burning inside him, what it meant to struggle for freedom.

A year or so before the end of the war our time in British Guiana came to an abrupt end. The war of the North Atlantic had passed through the years when German U-Boats could pick off Allied cargo and passenger vessels more or less as they liked, to the time when well organised, protected convoys were ferrying more and more provisions, essential war materials, and personnel from the United States to Britain in preparation for the long-awaited D-Day which would soon bring the war to an end. Cargo ships were beginning to sail again from BG and some also took a few passengers. In the interests of security, sailing dates and dates of arrival weren't disclosed until the very last minute, and then only to those directly involved. So it was that we had our passages booked, sold our non-essential belongings and hastily packed the rest, bade a few close friends farewell, and sailed on a small freight and passenger vessel from Georgetown in the summer of 1944.

The excitement and novelty of a long sea voyage home was, for me, a welcome adventure. For my parents there must have been mixed feelings of sorrow and relief, of doubts and uncertainties, satisfaction and frustration, of foreboding and expectation, but also of anxiety and even fear, in exposing themselves and their children to the hazards of a long sea trip during the war. But whatever they were, they concealed them well from their children and returned us all safely to our native land.

234 KING'S PARK AVENUE, GLASGOW

After the 'Guiana' experience of our small Nicol family, each of us ploughing our own furrow in our own way (my parents absorbed in their Church work and we children, Douglas, Mary and me in our own worlds of play and school), the Glasgow experience of almost two years which was to follow was quite different. From wondering where I belonged, where my home was in the cosmopolitan diversity of Guiana in which we were but only a drop in the ocean, I found in my birthplace, Glasgow, to which I had returned, an all-embracing extended family with one source, from one stalk, my Granny and Grandad Dallas whose home was also ours though the bricks and mortar of 234 King's Park Avenue belonged to them.

Though we were known as 'the Nicols from British Guiana' by most of my new found friends for many years I became more and more identified with Glasgow.

Without a doubt it was my Grandfather of all my relatives, apart from my parents, to whom I owe the most. I firmly believe that he was, from the day I was born and certainly from the day '234' became 'our home', 'our house' as well as his on our return to Glasgow in 1944, an ideal roll model. He went to sea as an apprentice carpenter and sailed for many years as a 'chippie' on the eastern run from the Clyde before marrying, embarking on a family he was always proud of, and working tirelessly to establish a 'blinds' business, 'Dallas and Forrest', in Bridgeton Cross, in Glasgow before following my progress through school and eventually university but died a year before I could call myself a doctor. He knew in his heart, if not his bones, that his secret aspirations for himself would be realised in his grandson, me, and they were. He taught me how to play draughts, and how to carve animals like cart horses, to use a chisel and make model yachts and sail them, how to plane a bit of wood, about knots and how to deal with them, and how to make a good dove-tail joint. Joint Surgery came naturally to me in later years.

My Grandad was a keen gardener. His pride and joy was his hothouse. His grapevine and tomato plants were diligently pollinated at the critical time for pollination using a rabbit's tail tied to the end of a stick. He enjoyed reading about people and things, what they thought and how they worked, and took a keen interest in new breakthroughs in Science and Medicine. When he developed Pernicious Anaemia in his later years he took particular delight in demonstrating the raw liver which he took regularly as the most up-to-date treatment for his Vitamin B12 deficiency. Behind a practical business-like approach to life was sensitive compassion; behind a staunch sense of loyalty to what he considered right and wrong was a listening ear and an understanding heart; behind a confident assurance in himself were aspirations for his family extending to new horizons beyond himself.

It was the semi-detached house at 234 Kings Park Avenue in Glasgow, my Grandparents' home, that I first came to look upon as 'our home' more than 'my home', 'our' home more than 'mine' because my Grandad made it so.

Though I warmed to the sense of belonging in my new extended family life in my native Glasgow, to identifying myself with my grandparents and to the excitement of a new kind of life that included a paper round, scouts, and happy family outings to pantomimes in theatres in the city centre on Boxing Days, – though I adapted reasonably well to all these aspects of my new life in Glasgow, the cultural shock of school days at King's Park Senior Secondary School inflicted scars on my sensitivity that still rear their heads today.

The classrooms and corridors, the stairs and the concrete playgrounds, and the 'boys' toilets and the 'girls' toilets and cloak-rooms were all so different from QC. They seemed crowded and noisy, and the accents of pupils and teachers so strange at first. But the biggest cultural shock to me was the girls. Girls and boys in the same school was too much for me to cope with. My confidence was shattered. My inherent shyness overwhelmed me. I was reduced to incoherent mutterings. I blushed crimson whenever any girl looked at me and was thrown into confusion whenever anyone spoke to me. With the words of my last memories of BG still fresh on my lips, 'No more Latin, No more French, No more sitting on the old school bench', my whole timetable was disrupted. There was no more Latin. I dropped it and never took it up again. 'No more French.' I continued with French but it seemed quite different from my previous French. I began to hate the subject and dislike my teacher. The Geography of Guiana was no help in placing the Grampians or the Cheviots on a map. History, even of the Battle of Bannockburn, seemed unrelated to the state of Europe at the start of the First World War. And the 'old school bench', and the memory of my first slate, were nostalgic in the unfamiliar reality of modern, individual desks at the new King's Park Senior Secondary school.

It took about a year for me to begin to settle into school life in Glasgow and even to begin to enjoy the 'Gay Gordons' and the 'Dashing White Sergeant' in the dreaded dancing classes that had hitherto struck terror into me in the run-up to Christmas. In early 1946 my father received a call from St Adrian's Church in the mining village of West Wemyss and we moved from the Glasgow to which I was beginning to feel I belonged – to *The Kingdom of Fife* where the remaining years of school days would see me transformed from a 'whining school boy' to a 'soldier, full of strange oaths'.

FIFE

With our move to Fife our family was once more united. We were a single unit again. My father returned to full-time permanent work as minister of St Adrian's Parish Church, West Wemyss. He was again the breadwinner for his family in his own house, the manse. My mother assumed the supportive role of minister's wife and the 'lady of the manse'. Their three children came together again under one roof, which was to be our family home until my father retired in 1965. From being a Dallas in Glasgow, I became a Nicol in our Nicol family in West Wemyss.

As I had reacted to the cultural shock of girls in the same school as me in Glasgow, so I reacted to my new role of minister's son in West Wemyss. My self- consciousness became an obsession. I was confused and embarrassed whenever I walked down the street with my father or mother, and forbade them to speak to me for fear of drawing attention to us. I loathed going to Kirkcaldy in the bus with my father when he wore his clerical collar because we'd have to wait in a queue for the bus with other people from the parish and, invariably, someone would speak to him and he'd reply in what seemed to me to be too loud and too posh a voice. I breathed a sigh of relief when we finally boarded the bus and I was left on my own to look out of the window and speak to no one.

Most of us live our lives, to a greater or lesser extent, in compartments. One face is seen in our workaday lives, another in our home environment, and others in different situations depending on our varying interests and concerns. My clearest and most visibly maturing face during my schooldays in West Wemyss was, of course, my school face. My home face ran a close second but, because it was subdivided into Sunday and weekday activities, events in West Wemyss itself and interests which took me further afield, it wasn't so clearly defined.

As far as Sundays went, I attended most services reasonably regularly for a year or two after we had moved to Fife, but less frequently as school and homework intensified with the approach of the Highers. Very often I'd arrive with my mother at the side door of the church as my father was about to make his entrance from the vestry and, as we took our seats facing the laird's pew on the opposite side to ours, we'd hear the sexton, or beadle, say to my father, 'Your folks are here. You can go in now.' I listened attentively to most of the sermons, sang the hymns, psalms and paraphrases with conviction, and took my turn, at times, pumping the organ for 'the laddie', our medical student organist who I was to meet in different circumstances a few years later. In time I came to join the Church 'by profession of faith' and could then take part in 'the Sacrament of the Lord's Supper'. I cherished my membership but was anything but fanatical about the Christian faith I professed.

My daily routine school face appeared each morning from Monday to Friday during term time when I bade my mother 'Cheerio!', pocketed my buttered jam 'piece', and set off for the school bus with jotters and books for the day in my schoolbag; and it disappeared when I arrived back home in the late afternoon, threw my bag into the front porch, and set out to chat to gardening friends in the allotments, collect 'messages' or chicken feed, help gather sea-coal, or just walk idly by the harbour before returning home for supper, homework and bed. Most of the children on the bus in the morning were bound for the Secondary Modern School in East Wemyss. The others, who'd passed the Qualifying Examination and proved they were High School material, or, like me, were in-comers from another system, remained on the bus after it reached East Wemyss and continued along the road to Buckhaven, to Buckhaven High School. Its pupils came from the towns and villages in a wide area around Buckhaven as well as the town itself.

In my first year at the High School I think I justified the standard non-committal comment on my progress report, 'Settling in'. I continued the subjects I was taking in Glasgow, but took also practical subjects like Woodwork (washing tongs and pencil cases) and Metalwork (name-plates and ornamental animal heads) which I enjoyed most of all. Maths and Science came reasonably easy. I had a fascination for using theorems to solve Geometrical problems and delighted in ending them with Q.E.D. I got carried away with details when I wrote an essay in English. My grammar and comprehension weren't bad, but my spelling and writing were poor. I was covered with embarrassment every time I had to speak French in the French class. I found History and Geography not much trouble and making linocuts in Art interesting.

But from the start, it was the Scripture or R.E. class that I never fitted into. My teacher was the stereotype of a bitter, frustrated, spinster woman. I hated reading aloud in any class, but especially from the Bible in the dreaded Scripture class and my teacher knew that. And she knew also that I was a son of the manse and kept reminding me, and the whole class, about it. When I made a mess pronouncing some obscure biblical name she'd delight in commenting, 'And you a minister's son!' I was reduced to a walking nervous wreck in her class, and there was more to come. She couldn't resist moralising. One day when the potato holidays were approaching, a time when schoolchildren were allowed off school, around September, for 'tattie howking', our teacher raised the question. 'Hands up,' she asked, 'those who are picking potatoes for the national effort in the potato holidays?' Most hands shot up, but not mine. 'And why are you not going, William? Do you think you're too good to pick potatoes?' I lost my cool. 'Because I'll be digging our garden at home, and building our hen-house,' I blurted out, red-faced and fuming, 'and I don't need an old besom like you to tell me when to howk tatties!'. Things were never quite the same again.

The last two years at school were my best. I knew where I was going, worked hard, and could feel that I was getting there. There were, of course, times of uncertainty. English was a constant struggle but was improving all the time. French was a constant mystery. I enjoyed History, but there was nothing critical at stake. To pass at the Highers would be a bonus. To fail wouldn't be the end. Art was a fun subject and the only subject I was completely relaxed in. I did enjoy it. There was nothing better than sitting in a holed boat on the shale beach in Buckhaven with a sketch pad, drawing and painting red-tiled houses on the shore in the foreground and the sea and clouds and sky in the background. I enjoyed the task at hand as well as going off with my artistic friends for ice-cream in the summer term in a popular coffee shop with slot machine and a jukebox. We were able to dream about the future, about East Fife winning next week, girls in the year and whether or not they were improving, and all of this at the same time as trying to get the objects in our drawings in proper perspective. And I worked hard to keep my Maths and Physics and Chemistry up to scratch.

'The more you do, the more you do' has been a stock expression in our family for as long as I can remember. Just when it started I can't recall, but its seeds most likely go back to my last two years in Buckhaven, when I got down to serious studies for the Highers and found that, far from narrowing down my interests, this seemed to stimulate a wider outlook on, and participation in life around me. I found that I was relating better to my peers. I was able to share in their experiences and share mine with them. I lost my fear of girls and began to enjoy their company, especially during school outings to the theatre or ballet during Festival time in Edinburgh. I started playing the mouth organ at the time that Jimmy Shand was becoming a celebrity, and my medleys of Scottish dance tunes, and folk and national songs, soon became a feature of the bus and train journeys to and from Edinburgh. A busload of pupils and teachers would be singing lustily to my efforts on the mouth organ on the last lap of the way back home until we reached the West Wemyss toll and it was time for me to get off. As I did so I could still hear the echoes of 'Auld Lang Syne' and 'We're no awa' tae bide awa' ringing in my ears as I headed down the road in the silent darkness of the night.

I had my moments of glory also on the athletic field, and relive them every time I become engrossed in any sport on TV even now. When I see an athlete limbering up for an event I see myself in him and am overcome by the smell of wintergreen in my nostrils. I was best at the quick dash of a sprint but was an all-round trier. Humiliation was tinged with pride when the Gym teacher singled me out at school assembly the day after I came in last after being lapped by the winner in a mile race. It was supposed to illustrate determination and grit, and the greater value of competing than winning. I did a reasonable modified Eastern Cut-off high jump, and in our school games in my last year won the long jump with a leap of 17 ft. but was unable to repeat it in the interscholastic sports a few weeks later.

Then came the Highers in 1949. I failed English and French, and without them my other subjects weren't good enough. My mother was disappointed, but responded as she was to respond many times in the future. 'That's a pity,' she said, 'but you'll try again, won't you?' Her answer to temporary failure was always, 'Try again.' The name of my uncle's fishing boat in Gamrie was also *Try Again.* It must have been in the family, and it was also in the ethos of Buckhaven High School, which I must have absorbed unknowingly because it was only then that I realised the full significance of the school motto, 'Perseverando'. I spoke about leaving school then but my headmaster took me to one side and gave me the advice I needed to harden my resolve to embark on a Medical career. 'William,' he said, 'you'll have to come back to school for another year. If you don't you'll never do Medicine.' So I returned, for two months, but couldn't stand sitting in classes without my usual friends, going through the same ground that I had already covered. I left school to start two years National Service in The Royal Army Medical Corps. 'The whining schoolboy', with his satchel from the manse in West Wemyss, Fife, had metamorphosed to 'a soldier, full of strange oaths, and bearded like a pard, jealous in honour, sudden and quick in quarrel, seeking the bubble reputation even in the cannon's mouth.'

ACT THREE

'And then the lover,
Sighing like furnace, with a woeful ballad
Made to his mistress' eyebrow.'

IN MY EARLY youthful schoolboy days at King's Park I was pathologically shy, dreading the dancing classes in the Gym in preparation for the Christmas parties everyone seemed to be getting excited about, but, in spite of myself, I was harbouring a secret that in no way ever approached a sighing furnace or a woeful ballad made to anyone's eyebrow (if I could ever have located it). Nevertheless I was beginning to enjoy a Gay Gordon's and a Dashing White Sergeant. In my last few weeks in Glasgow I was inspired to put pen to paper in an English class with these words that I think Robert Burns would have been proud of but have my doubts about William Shakespeare:-

> 'O Margaret McPhee,
> You dance like a flea.
> But, O Gee!
> It's you and me.'

On the subject, ponder on these immortalised words of the bard from his Sonnet CXVI:-

> *'Let me not to the marriage of true minds*
> *Admit impediments. Love is not love*
> *Which alters when it alteration finds,*
> *Or bends with the remover to remove:*

O, no! it is an ever- fixed mark,
That looks on tempests and is never shaken;
It is the star to every wandering bark,
Whose worth's unknown, although his height be taken.
Love's not Time's fool, though rosy lips and cheeks
Within his bending sickle's compass come;
Love alters not with his brief hours and weeks,
But bears it out even to the edge of doom.
If this be error and upon me proved,
I never writ, nor no man ever loved.'

ACT FOUR

'Then a soldier,
Full of strange oaths, and bearded like a pard,
Jealous in honour, sudden and quick in quarrel,
Seeking the bubble reputation
Even in the cannon's mouth.'

FROM THE DAY I left the familiarity of my home in the manse in West Wemyss, Fife, to report at Queen Elizabeth Barracks, Crookham, Aldershot for service in the Royal Army Medical Corps as '22197222 Private Nicol' on Thursday 3 Nov. 1949 until the day of my marriage to Avril on 11 August 1960 'I never had a house of my own' for very long. Communal living was to be the kind of life for me; first, in the Army, then as a Medical student in Halls of Residence or in hospital accommodation as a House Officer and even in temporary rented houses for short but eventful periods at home in this country or in South Africa until settling into a house of our own, our own family home, in *Wheatstone*, Skircoat Green Road, Halifax, West Yorkshire, in 1973.

ARMY DAYS

My mother made sure I had with me the few things I was to take with me, and especially, a large sheet of strong brown paper, some string, and a self-addressed label, which were to be used to wrap up my jacket, flannels and other civilian clothes and post the parcel home as soon as I had been issued with my Army kit. From then on there would be no more

27

civilian clothes for me or my new friends, except when on leave. As the day came to an end we gathered our newly issued gear, including our blankets and sheets, and official papers, and personal things like my mouth organ, a Bible and a few textbooks to be hardly ever opened, and a few photos and addresses together on our beds in the barrack room or 'spider' of B4 Squad, B (Rec) Company to start our three months Basic Training. Having my own possessions, on my own bed, in my part of the 'spider' was, to me, in the hostile regimentation of Army life, both reassuring and comforting. I was, at one and the same time, gathered unceremoniously into the wide world of the Services in general and the Royal Army Medical Corps in particular, and given a minute patch, the territorial area around my bed, with my own belongings, where I could retreat into a secret life, personal only to me. I was to become more and more aware of this balanced relationship between being part of a wider world and being completely on my own in the intimacy of my personal, spiritual, social and family life in a variety of situations in many parts of the world.

TEMERLOH – CENTAL PAHANG
MALAYSIA

ime in the Army was a _hlanders, when I was sent on detachment from the 21st Field Surgical Team to the 1st Seaforth 'A' Coy in Temerloh as their Regimental Orderly. I had a small tent to myself where I lived and ran daily clinics for the men returning to camp from patrols with leech bite sores, ringworm and pressure sores and abrasions gone septic, as well as dysentery, fever, heat exhaustion and dehydration. The setting of the camp in thick jungle surroundings, the smell of paraffin lamps lit up at night, latrines a discreet distance from the tents, and fetching drinking and washing water from a well a few hundred yards along a grassy path were what I expected in an actively engaged infantry unit in one of the most heavily infiltrated and hostile parts of the country. The memory of lowering a bucket down the well, pulling it up filled with cool fresh water, having a long drink from it and then washing in the water before filling the bucket again and returning with it along the muddy path are as vivid now as when I first visited that well. And the sight and sound of the Company piper playing a lament as the sun dipped into the surrounding jungle canopy still stirs my Scottish blood.

As 1950 drew to an end it brought with it a contrasting combination of events and issues which highlighted the high points and the low points, the happy satisfying times and the worrying sad times of my life then, and prepared me for the complexities of life that lay ahead. We never live in a vacuum for very long. Extremes are never far away and its how we cope with them that makes us what we are. Dedication, conviction, faith, trust, responsibility, concern – call it what you wish – they all dictate how we 'switch on' and 'switch off' in facing our responsibilities to ourselves and to others. I was pleased with my achievements. I had successfully completed my NO III training and had the thrill of putting it into practice, and I still had, in my sight, the burning ambition in me to be a doctor driving me on to use my experiences of the day towards this end. I was content with my situation.

Then came the day in September when I looked out my heavy Army greatcoat, packed up my belongings and bade farewell to my mates. On the way back home we shouted 'Get your knees brown!' to a passing troopship in the Suez Canal. The words held a deeper meaning for us then than they had when we first heard them being shouted at us going out.

MEDICAL STUDENT DAYS

Soon after returning home from the Army I had to think seriously about my future. Not without some difficulty and considerable stress I made good the necessary requirements for University entrance to study Medicine and was offered a place at the University of St Andrews starting in 1952. Having been conditioned by the regimental institution of Army life it seemed natural for me to favour a Hall of Residence with other students to live in in term time rather than digs with a landlady or a flat with a few other students fending for themselves. My three pre-clinical years were spent in the men's residence, Hamilton Hall, overlooking the Royal and Ancient Golf Club, and the three final years in Airlie Hall in Dundee.

Though there were students from other disciplines at St Andrews, most of my Medical student colleagues, like me, confined themselves to themselves. Our days were full. From 9 to 5 almost every day there were lectures, tutorials or lab or dissection room sessions to attend. I didn't socialise much and went home most weekends to avoid the distraction of noisy gatherings of revellers putting there own words to the well known ballad, 'The Ball of Kirriemuir', reminding me that 'The minister's wife, she was there', and get some work done. But I went to the Students' Union enough to play a reasonable game of billiards and found a partner from my year to take to the Hamilton Hall annual ball once. In the summer term of the first year I played my part in the Rag weekend. Most students were able to balance the need for sufficient work to pass examinations and the thirst for social engagement.

As the first term progressed I got into a routine of getting the bus home on Friday evening, swatting all the weekend with

30

only Saturday afternoon at the football as a break, and returning to St Andrews on Sunday night.

It was, as you, perceptive reader, may not be surprised to learn, on these return journeys, changing buses at the bus stop in Buckhaven, that I met the girl who was to play a major part in my life over the next five years, and very much later in our present lives. Margaret was finishing a BSc and would follow this with a year's teacher training before starting a lifetime of teaching Mathematics. We had similar interests and soon fell for each other. Our friendship developed, we met our families, became engaged, and fell into a routine. In the first year we'd meet for a game of tennis in St Andrews one evening during the week but be taken up with our own studies apart from this, and we'd meet in Buckhaven on a Saturday afternoon after I'd been to the football, have tea and go to the pictures. In St Andrews and in Dundee almost up to the time of my finishing in 1958 I became known as someone with 'a girl at home'. As time passed we talked about marriage and settling down as a family doctor with his wife. Margaret was practical and conventional. I was a dreamer with a dislike of conformity. Margaret was a home bird. I had my sights on work abroad in challenging situations in a mission field. Routines become comfortable and are hard to break. So it was with Margaret and me. A growing fear of inhibiting conformity came to overwhelm me. We broke off the relationship, then tried again, and finally recognised that we were not for each other.

By the time the finals came round my fingernails were down to the quick. The marathon of written papers in the three core subjects, Medicine, Surgery and Obstetrics and Gynaecology, clinical assessment of patients on the wards, side room examination of X-Rays, specimens of urine, faeces and blood, and orals in each subject with both internal and external examiners extended over three weeks. There were highs and lows. One moment there was hope, the next, none. Late in the afternoon of the last examination the results came out. We assembled in a lecture theatre and the names of those who'd passed were read out in alphabetical order. I listened only for one name and when I heard it I was in another world.

JUNIOR HOSPITAL DOCTOR

Six years as a medical student take their toll in conditioning you to soaking up as many facts as a sponge you use to wash which absorbs molecules that react with soap and washing liquid to generate endless bubbles of s of knowledge have been sown but the sensi ptions of the art and practice of Medicine have yet to come. Plodders and eggheads alike have still to put their skills to the test. Ambitions and aspirations born in student days have yet to be realised. Disappointments and setbacks have still to be faced and put into perspective. But the metamorphosis from student to doctor is as sudden as the instant a new-born baby takes its first breath and a new life becomes a reality. Within a few weeks of completing the final MB, ChB examination I could feel the conglomerate of hastily assembled fragments of knowledge at my fingertips that had satisfied my examiners, slipping from my grasp. I was Dr Nicol but had not yet done my doctoring.

In my six months of Medicine and six months of Surgery at DRI I learnt, above all else, to develop a sixth sense in confiding in my patients and those most concerned about them, to respect the confidentiality they placed in me, to dispel feelings of despair and futility and instil, even in the face of hopeless terminal illness, something beyond the present and beyond our comprehension of it. From my senior Medical Consultant I picked up many practical tips but above all, an honest appraisal of my competence and confidence, which goes with knowing one's limitations. From my Consultant Urologist boss so engrossed in peering up a cystoscope that he was oblivious, one day, to a trickle of urine becoming a river in full spate cascading down his fresh red face I learnt to keep my silence out of dutiful respect and not burst into raucous laughter. From six months at Bridge of Earn Hospital where the seeds of bone and joint surgery which were most likely sown in my school days in Glasgow and Fife germinated under the supervision of senior colleagues into a fascination for Orthopaedics (meaning 'straight children') which has never diminished throughout all the acts in the stages of my life to date. But my destiny at the 'Brig' (Bridge of Earn Hospital) was not fashioned by Orthopaedics alone. No, far from it. The centre of excellence was a hotbed of dramatic intrigue, of emotional heart-searching, of compassion and passion, of decision and commitment, of love and envy far surpassing even the words of the bard,

> *'Jealous in honour, sudden and quick in quarrel,*
> *Seeking the bubble reputation*
> *Even in the cannon's mouth.'*

It was in this cauldron of ardour that the love of my life was to germinate and blossom.

From the day I first arrived at Bridge of Earn, one of my tasks was to arrange for emergencies like open fractures or, most commonly, fractures of the neck of the femur in elderly patients to be operated on, or fractures of the wrist (Colles fractures) or the ankle (Potts fractures), to be manipulated under general anaesthesia. This meant arranging things with the Anaesthetist on call. It was after I had arranged a case one night, reduced the fractured wrist reasonably well, put on the plaster, been comforted by the check X-ray being satisfactory and written up the notes, that I was gently but firmly corrected. I'd spelt the Anaesthetist's name wrongly. 'It's not McIntosh. It's Mackintosh. Dr Avril Mackintosh. Remember!' I've never forgotten. In the following few weeks we did a few more cases together and in the six months I was at the Brig we spent many a night together, me often assisting my Senior Registrar trying to site a guide wire in the centre of a fractured neck of femur under X-Ray control, and Avril sitting at the head of the operating table patiently keeping an eye on everyone, including the patient, as the anaesthetic gasses bubbled through her machine, keeping the patient peacefully unaware of everything. It didn't take me long to notice the best pair of ankles below her red velvet skirt. Their presence and her sparkling eyes above the mask that obscured her smile of reassurance, stirred me to confidence in what I was doing and much more. We began to take longer to arrange cases and found that we needed to discus the post-operative care in greater detail. We often returned to the doctor's dining room for coffee and to share an omelette after a case in the middle of the night or long after the routine work of the day was over. Our professional relationship grew to an affinity, our affinity to affection, and our affection to a deeper understanding of ourselves and each other that amounted to love.

The next six months for me at Craigtoun Maternity Hospital in St Andrews and for Avril as Senior House Officer in Anaesthetics in Dundee flew past. Work, of course continued, but meeting families and parents, arranging details for the wedding in Avril's hometown in Hull and the next stage of our lives together in Dornoch, in the Highlands where I would be trainee assistant to the local doctor took centre stage in the priorities of our lives.

After the wedding and a traditional honeymoon in Grassmere in the Lake District and in North Wales we were on our way to Dornoch in Sutherland in the Highlands. On a bend on the main road north at its junction with the road down to Dornoch, in the village of Evelix, was, and may still be, a cottage, *Corner Cottage*, which we rented, fully furnished, from the daughter of the Wee Free minister. It was to be 'our house', 'our home' together for the first year of our married life.

DORNOCH

From the wrought-iron gate in front of *Corner Cottage* a short path, flanked on each side by a small green, led to our front door that opened into a small hall. On the right, a living room with an adjoining kitchen opened into the back yard. On the left the 'good room' looked on to the main road and surrounding mountainous countryside. At the end of the hall a narrow stairway led upstairs to the two attic bedrooms and a small bathroom and toilet. The furniture was basic but all we needed. When the fire was lit in the living room and we had moved in, spread our things around, boiled the kettle and made ourselves a cup of tea, and sat back in an armchair each on either side of the fire, we were in paradise, alone with our own thoughts in our own home and with each other, free from the inhibiting responsibilities which were to become more and more part of our life in years to come.

I enjoyed my year as a trainee assistant. I liked the country life, my patients and my colleagues and grew in confidence as I picked up invaluable practical tips from my trainer and attempted to follow them up and apply myself to the work of the Medical Practice but something in me kept nudging me back to something else in another setting, some kind of mission setting in some far-flung place where Avril and I would fulfil a common calling.

For Avril our time in Dornoch was largely a time of waiting. Within a few months in the fresh air of the Highlands we had sown the seeds of our first baby. We were thrilled and overjoyed as were our parents and waited patiently through the winter months into spring and early summer. After a long, distressing labour our first boy, Jim, arrived. 'Our home' would never be just the house where Avril and I lived, let alone 'my home' where we lived, but an expanding 'our home' which now included Jim and would soon include David and our other children over the years. I had resolved to set my sights on a career in Surgery and to help prepare for the long uncertain years of training jobs and exams ahead had obtained a post as an Anatomy Demonstrator at Dundee University for a year when my time in Dornoch was completed.

ANATOMY DEMONSTRATOR

We were lucky enough to find a modern cottage on Strathmartine Road to rent for the better part of a year before moving to an old semi-detached house on Broughty Ferry Road, opposite the docks, for the remaining few months of our stay in Dundee. After our first idyllic home together in *Corner Cottage* in Dornoch the very temporary houses we lived in, in Dundee were to set the scene for many of our homes in the years to come. Our first home in Dundee was in open countryside with plenty fresh air for the new baby, Jimmy. Our

as good an account of our time in our home in Sulenkama as I could give in a recall of past events between 1962 and '65. The images are as vivid today as then but time has moved on and so have we, both you, my perceptive reader, and me.

Chapter titles include 'Sulenkama – Red Blankets, Kraals, Stick fights and Dancing feet. An oasis in a world on edge' (p97); 'Unrest in the Homelands. A different Christmas. Our Third Son, John' (p110); and 'The end of a Mission Hospital era. Bantustans' (p135).

These are the quotations:-

'Donald, the accountant from the Nessie Knight Hospital, was in Durban to meet us off the flight from Johannesburg and take us the 250 odd miles by car to Sulenkama. It was hot and humid. We piled into the car and were glad to get moving. Out of town the warm breeze from the Indian Ocean on the Natal coast was refreshing. After a short break for lunch it was back into the car and on and on for most of the day on a National tarred road heading south, first through sugar cane plantations in Natal, then through good farming land around Kokstad until the lush countryside rapidly changed to barren, eroded undulations sparsely populated with huts more concentrated at times into *kraals* or villages surrounded by mealie fields outlined with aloe hedgerows. This was the Transkei, the homeland or *'bantustan'* of the Red Blanket, Xhosa people. Colourful hoardings advertising things like 'Joko Tea' told us we were approaching larger trading towns and as we passed through them we could see and hear the people close at hand. Red blankets predominated. Animated conversations frequently punctuated by the characteristic clicking of spoken Xhosa often ended with emphatic exclamations like *'Eke!'* or *'Yho!'*. On the more open stretches of the road we could see from the

39

windows of the car the cloudless blue sky, open hills dotted with huts, smoke from fires at meal times, laughing children in ragged clothes, bare-breasted red blanket girls and stick-carrying youths identical to the scenes on post-cards we had been shown in Dundee. We sped up long steep slopes of road in third gear, down mountainsides to dried river beds and over 'one way only' iron bridges over larger rivers. We gazed in silence for long periods at the countryside around us which was to be our home in the Transkei.

'It was a long weary day. The boys were getting restless as we turned off the National road where the signpost pointed right to 'Sulenkama' just before darkness descended. Several huts had been bulldozed down to clear the corner and we'd noticed the same thing earlier along the road where the huts stretched to the roadside. 'That's for security reasons,' said Donald when we asked why. 'A little while ago, because of all the trouble, the Police and the Army had to clear the roads so that they could get quickly from one trouble spot to another.' The road from then on was a dirt road, rutted even after being graded in the dry weather, a mud-bath, often flooded and impassable, when it rained. It passed close by and through villages sometimes, mostly with little signs of life for miles around. It was soon dark. Only a few lights and fires could be seen in the distance. Our headlights pierced the darkness as we raced along. Then, as we came over the brow of a hill, in a valley beyond, with other smaller valleys converging in a common basin, was a denser cluster of lights in bigger buildings, the village of Sulenkama, that means 'The Meeting of Many Waters'. We would come to know it well in a short time, but in the darkness, lit only intermittently by a full moon appearing from behind low-lying clouds, little more than shadows could be made out. When we drove into the hospital and up to the part of the Staff House that had been prepared for us, the brief, but warm welcome we received turned it at once into 'our home', a place where we lived and where we belonged.

'A few weeks after our arrival in Sulenkama, Avril was able to write home:-

'We are really getting settled in now and feel we have been here for months. We are enjoying the life very much and Bill is kept hard at it in the hospital. Last Saturday was a great day for me as I was called in to anaesthetise a patient for laparotomy in the afternoon. It is a very well equipped theatre here, and the staff very efficient. The operation was a success and the patient is alive to tell the tale. It was grand to get the smell of ether in my nose again. Derek is a very competent surgeon. I hope to anaesthetise tomorrow again. It is nice to have another interest again and I am lucky to be able to take an interest in the hospital.'

and a week later:-

'Everything is still very new and interesting here – the gorgeous sunshine and the queer folk you see. The locals wear an abundance of clothes in the heat. The men have a queer assortment of things, usually topped by a long gabardine mac, an old trilby hat and a large black umbrella – and bare feet. A lot of them ride horse-back and trot along, holding up the umbrella – with the wife walking along behind with a baby on her back and a bucket on her head. They always stare at us and laugh at Jimmy in his pushchair, but never think that they look funny themselves.'

'Sulenkama was at once the answer to our dreams. Avril saw the funny side of life around us in the same way that the

Xhosa, Red Blanket, people saw the funny side of us. We experienced an instant affinity with our new friends and never lost it. We were never able to speak the Xhosa language and were, therefore, always on the periphery of their thoughts, unable fully to share their thoughts with them, but through interpreting nurses, empathising glances, body language, and surprising mutual respect, established many friendships. From the State Registered Sisters and Staff Nurses and the Auxiliary Nurses in the hospital we were to be given a lesson on hard work and justifiable achievement in a society primed to produce manpower for the mines. Professional men like doctors, teachers or solicitors among the Africans were far too few in number to offer any significant choice of intellectual male companionship for well trained women in the nursing profession. From the seventy nurses in training for the Auxilliary Nurse Certificate from the South African Nursing Council we were still to learn the value of dedicated efforts at education with limited schooling. The official languages of South Africa in the early sixties were English and Afrikaans in that order of common usage. Most white people spoke one well and the other indifferently. Most of the girls who came to train for two years in hospitals like the Nessie Knight Hospital had never spoken to any white people other than their local storekeeper. They came from kraals with no running water and no electricity. When they started training they were shadows, physically and mentally, subservient, inhibited, lost. The native language they spoke and wrote naturally wasn't used, though they could speak and understand English and Afrikaans as well as Xhosa. When they switched a light on and light appeared if our generator was working, and when they turned a tap on and clear water came out if the pumps were working, or they flushed a toilet and it worked if the septic tank wasn't blocked or the septic ponds system not overflowing they stood back in amazement, puzzled, at the marvels of modern technology.

Yet, within a few months, the same girls, looked upon by most white South Africans as inferior 'girls', like their 'boy' counterparts, were assisting reliably at operations most medical students would never be asked to do. Their application of English and Afrikaans to their work, integrating them with their native Xhosa to give an understanding of nursing practical relevance put most English and Afrikaans speaking whites to shame.

'After daily ward rounds and a cup of tea came the Out Patient Clinic. People would gather from over twenty miles around. Men would carry their ailing parents on their backs for miles. Women would drag themselves, debilitated with TB, or with haemoglobins off the records, or carry babies almost dead from dehydrating diarrhoea or afire with fever, on their backs for many hours or even days, to sit and wait on the steps of Outpatients to be seen. On the long hot summer days they'd follow well-worn paths along and over dried-up dongas. In the short cold winter days they'd brave lashing rain and bitter winds, often snow-filled, blowing fiercely from the not too distant Drakensberg Mountains. (meaning Dragon's Back.) When it rained heavily for any length of time the barren red earth was turned to mud, making transportation of patients in ox-drawn wooden sledges easy. In the hottest weather most people wore their traditional Xhosa Red Blanket, and in the coldest, the same single Red Blanket. The youngest and the oldest were, naturally, most vulnerable to extremes of weather conditions which, on top of generalised malnutrition and prevalent Tuberculosis, accounted for many deaths.

'Then it was Christmas, something really special for Avril to write home about:-

'The celebrations started on Christmas Eve with carol singing by the nurses. Bill and Derek went, too, carrying lanterns on poles and they walked right up to the village to sing there and all round the hospital wards and grounds. The singing is really fantastic. Beautifully harmonised and 'Silent Night' sounded just perfect – you know how difficult the last line is to get up to. They have wonderful voices and really enjoy singing. I stayed at home and made my mince pies and some shortbread and tried to get organised for the next day.

Christmas day was lovely and warm and sunny. The Doyle girls were hammering on the front door with their gifts at 7.30a.m. and Jimmy was rushing about with his tube of Smarties clad only in pyjama top to receive them! The morning service was held at the front of the hospital – seats arranged around Dr Patterson's memorial and Derek taking the service from the top of the steps. After the service the patients all got their presents and the nurses all went wild, jiving in and out of the wards with Derek and Bill doing Xhosa dances for the benefit of the patients, reducing the nurses to near hysterics. All the men got hankies for their heads and tobacco and the women pieces of cloth. It was quite pathetic to see them sitting up in bed, both hands outstretched for their gifts. They were all so grateful and were singing and clapping as the doctors did the rounds with the gifts. After that, Bill and Derek were carving turkeys for patients and nurses, maids, gardeners etc. and were serving them till after 2 in the afternoon. We didn't bother with the usual Christmas dinner ourselves but had a good relaxing day with the Doyles later on, including the nurses' Nativity Play in the evening, which was a hoot. (Referred to by Flora as the 'Activity Play')'

'As we came to terms with our busy, but little, world in the hospital in Sulenkama and the outlying clinics, I started developing a special interest further afield, taking on patients from the Cripple Care Association who had had surgery recommended by a Specialist in the Frere Hospital in East London, in the Ciskei, for treatment nearer home in the Transkei. I'd go through to Umtata with an ambulance and a nurse and examine the referred patients in the Out Patient Department of the Bantu Hospital which was confusingly unfamiliar to me then but would become, in later years, almost a second home to me, and bring them back to Sulenkama for surgery. What started with only a few patients soon gathered momentum. I'd do my best to correct deformities from poliomyelitis, spastic contractures, tuberculosis of bones and joints, and eventually the spine. Fusion of the knee joint is a simple operation that I was to perform on several patients, including our telephonist, Hirum, who I was to meet up with again in very different circumstances a few years later. Many of the 'Cripples' were biblically deformed, crawling on their hands and knees, reduced to begging pathetically, or, like the paralysed man who Jesus healed (Matt.9.1-8; Mark2.1-12; Luke5.17-26.), dependent on being carried around everywhere.

'As we began to get about more we became more aware of what was happening in the country. Letters from home and passing visitors reinforced the image we developed of the 'troubles in the Transkei'. Reassurances to our parents at home and friends in Johannesburg were sincere. They and we had nothing to worry about, we assured them, but Avril was glad to see me in from a clinic before dark. Rumours of traders being attacked and even killed became a reality but life in general continued on an even keel.

'On 18.3.63 Avril was able to write home in general terms:-

'Jimmy has found a new friend among the gardeners. His name is Jim Nojoko and he is 'wanting a foot' and he is just about the most dour of all the workers; but they have struck up a friendship and Jimmy has to get his watering can out as soon as he sees 'Joko' appear. 'Man, Man,' he says and he's off. It is funny to see them, side by side, solemnly watering the flowerbeds. Jim Nojoko talks to him in Xhosa, and Jimmy trots behind him to the tap to get his wee can filled up alongside the big one. I think Joko is quite pleased in his own dour way that Jimmy has broken down his barrier of reserve.'

'But on 10.4.63 she had another tale to tell:-

'How funny you should have seen Umtata on T.V.
I don't know just how much is in your papers etc. about the state of affairs here, but there has been some anxiety these last few days and we think it is as well to tell you – especially if you are reading about it in the newspapers, and let you know we are well prepared for trouble and not living in a fool's paradise. On Sunday, the police called here, to say they had issued a state of emergency all over the Qumbu district and that they had been tipped off that the Poqo were planning a raid in the next few days in our area. All the white traders were evacuated from the outlying stores and the forestry people in outlying districts went to Qumbu Hotel for a night or two. The traders all went up to our Sulenkama store and stayed there. This meant that the police patrol could cut down on their mileage of patrolling the roads at night as they didn't meander miles away out to the stores from which the folk were evacuated, but concentrated round here and into Qumbu. Donald was summoned back urgently from a few days off with his parents in Durban. We were glad to see him and he moved

46

in with us and has been staying here overnight since Sunday. We have made our own fortifications in our own house, and Donald and Bill have been keeping watch in shifts through the night. We have the necessary firearms and fire extinguishers, and a good big light fixed in place on the verandah to light up the stoep and the ground in front of us, but keep the house and windows dark.

You'll probably have a fit when you read all this – but don't worry, as Bill said to me the other night, after I'd sat watching them load their rifle and pistol – 'Lock all the doors, extinguish all lights and put Prince the boxer to sleep on the stoep as watchdog'. Not worry! I was planning which cupboard I'd go into with the boys and everything, before dawn finally broke.

The emergency is over in our district, now, with no incidents, but the Poqo have been busy in East London and there have been a lot of arrests.'

Looking back, when we first heard about the Nessie Knight Hospital in Dundee, we'd heard about Macmillan's 'Wind of Change' blowing through Africa, and about the Sharpville incident, we'd noticed the bulldozed huts on the roadside on the way to Sulenkama, especially at the turnoff from the main National road, and we'd heard vague rumours, and more than rumours, from traders about unrest, and warnings in letters from home, but none of these indicators seemed to be particularly worrying and certainly any cause for anxiety. The Poqo scare was a wake-up call for us but soon settled down.

'The arrival of two Medical Students from Cape Town in June 1963 brought with them a welcome breath of fresh air. Sulenkema was, for them, unbelievable. Brought up in the white environment of Cape Town, of Jewish origin, keen and enthusiastic to learn as much as they possibly could, they questioned everything and everyone. The spectrum of pathology they encountered at the Nessie Knight Hospital was a microcosm of their Medical course. They were the first of many final year students who visited us on placements and took advantage of the opportunity to do as many procedures as they could. They tapped chests and abdomens, they did lumber punctures and took bloods, they put up drips and assisted in theatre whenever they could, they sat in at clinics and prompted us to hold teaching sessions on the wards, and they delivered babies at the drop of a hat, stitching up the episiotomies they had performed. Socially they were fascinated by the nurses and other workers, their only previous contact with 'Blacks' being with the 'boys' and the 'girls' in their homes. Now they knew the kind of place they came from. Our first students and several who followed gave hints of dissatisfaction with conditions at home. Though Jewish, they were comfortable with our degree and mould of 'mission', they sensed our Christian dream of something better, our hope for a better future, and they empathised with it because they had the same themselves. They confessed that their parents had reconciled themselves to their lot in the South African way of life but that they would most likely go, as soon as they could, to the developing State of Israel to serve their time working as required on Kibbutzim, identifying themselves with the ideology of the Jewish Nation.

'Soon another Christmas day was fast approaching and Avril would write home with pride:-

'When it came to Christmas day it was another scorcher. We were up at the crack of dawn and opening stockings to find water pistols, false faces and the like and then, after breakfast, we had a big clean up of faces and hands to go to the outside service held, as usual, at the front of the hospital. The routine

was the same as last Christmas with the addition of the Nativity Play. The first performance in the evening on Christmas day was a resounding success. The next day, Boxing Day, it was even better with crowds of people coming in cars and vans from all around. One store-keeper where a clinic is held commented afterwards, 'Next year I will bring a bus.'

'But what Avril did not mention in her letter home was that one of the angels in the Nativity Play was all but at the end of an anxious pregnancy having lived through a nightmare, alone, tortured with guilt and uncertainty, working on hoping no-one would notice, knowing that she would have the baby any day. Before the Christmas day celebrations started the police found a dead full-term new-born infant wrapped in a nurse's green uniform behind the Nurses' Home. In a break in the hectic festive activities I left the hospital and spent an hour or two with the poor girl. I remember clearly to this day presenting myself at the Police Station in Qumbu, explaining who I was and who I wanted to see, being ushered into a small, stark, cell with a bed in it and a nurse I knew curled up on it. She looked up, blank, impassive. I put an arm round her shoulders and mumbled something. After a while we said some practical things. I tried to smile to convey compassion. I held her hand for a while and left. Of all the Christmases I've lived through, it's that Christmas that touched me more than any other.

'Administrative and political changes in South Africa in general, and in the homelands like the Transkei where we lived and made 'our home' in Sulenkama, were gathering momentum. The days of traditional mission hospitals were coming to an end. Many still clung to an element of individualism along denominational lines, and were still, to a greater or lesser extent, patronising. They persisted with familiar codes of conduct in rapidly changing surroundings and were confused by manipulative policies with which they found it hard to come to terms. Others adapted to the inevitable. Our hospital was singled out for upgrading and survival. For weeks on end builders and electricians kept coming and going, digging trenches, laying cables, plastering, painting, renewing old parts of the hospital and building extensions. A new X-Ray Unit and more efficient generator were installed. The flow of students from Cape Town increased as word got round that a few weeks at the Nessie Knight Hospital was well worthwhile. When an Assessor from the teaching staff of Cape Town University came to see first hand what we had to offer his students we were officially recognised for teaching purposes.

'Soon after our second Christmas in Sulenkama we spent a week or two on a visit to our friends in Johannesburg which was followed with the news that a new member of our family was on the way. Whooping-cough dogged the pre-natal days and agonising gall-stones requiring gall-bladder surgery the post-natal period, but the delivery itself, after a false start, went well. John William, another boy, had arrived. Avril's mother, who flew across to be with us over the gall-bladder surgery, was, of course, a great help, but also, the precious comfort her daughter needed in the postpartum days. She was with us as part of 'our home in Sulenkama' for John's baptism in the hospital chapel and shared in the celebrations along with all our now many friends from all backgrounds and many shades.

'All too soon Avril's mother was away and back home. It all seemed a dream but one that continued through Christmas into the New Year. In being drawn more passionately into the work of the hospital and at the same time empathising more strongly with the people, I was being faced with a dilemma. While the work was satisfying, it was all consuming. The demands of the daily routine left no time to do justice to serious studies to say nothing about time with the family. I still longed to specialise in the branch of medicine dearest to my heart, Orthopaedics, and it became a compulsion, not unlike a call that some people have to some religious order or to the ministry. Without saying much to each other, both Avril and I were becoming restless. It was time we moved back to the thick of the competitive reality of medicine if I was to realise my ambition. The precious experience of Sulenkama was coming to an end. When I was accepted for a three-month course in Edinburgh in preparation for the Primary Fellowship Examination, the date was fixed. We'd start saving for our return home in time for me to start the course in January 1966.

'As quietly and as quickly as we arrived we took our leave. Piled high with luggage, our three boys packed among it, Avril glanced at me and we nodded. Through the settling dust on the windscreen we could see the bulldozed huts at the end of the dirt road from Sulenkama. We headed north to Durban and the trip home. Our boys caught our subdued excitement at the thought of returning to Scotland but it couldn't hide the sensitivity in their sadness in leaving their friends in Sulenkama which reflected our affinity for the Xhosa people of the Transkei.'

'SATISFIED THE EXAMINERS'

For three months I steeped myself in the books. The course was concentrated and comprehensive. It was just what I needed to focus the mind. I lived a Spartan life in Edinburgh. Breakfast on my own in the Guest House saw me through to a snack lunch with some of my new postgraduate friends, or on my own, and after an afternoon of lectures, tutorials, or free time in the library, I'd wend my way back home along the Bridges calling into a chip shop for chips and a pie on the way. While the room warmed up I'd make myself a cup of tea to take with my 'healthy' supper, then get back to the books till the small hours. I became conditioned to the work and let the rest of the world pass me by. When I saw the family in Dunblane every two or three weeks they seemed unreal, and I seemed unreal in their presence. My mind was fixed on one thing and one thing only, getting the Primary this time. I lapped up every scrap of knowledge thrown at me, and must have been one of the dullest, most boring, self-centred, single-minded students on the course, anti-social and humourless.

Towards the end of the course I got a job as Registrar in Orthopaedic and Accident Surgery at Stirling Royal Infirmary, only a few miles from Dunblane. It came up at the right time for us as it was to start as soon as the course came to an end and the Primary Fellowship Examination was over. I braced myself for the exam. Then came the results. I knew the routine. Waiting in silence in the gathering of anxious candidates outside the Royal College in Edinburgh, time seemed to stand still, till a secretary appeared and the crowd closed in. She had in one hand a large pile of large envelopes and in her other hand a small pile of small envelopes. We were each handed an envelope with our name on it. Fortunately, mine was one of the small ones. The larger envelopes included an application for re-examination, the smaller envelopes a simple statement, 'Satisfied the Examiners'. I'd start my new job with the Primary, able to direct my thoughts uninterruptedly to my chosen speciality for a short time before starting to prepare for the Final Examination.

'OUR HOME', 'OUR HOUSE', IN STIRLING
Associations with 'MORVEN' and 'BERBICE'

Stirling days were, in many ways, idyllic. For me the self-imposed monastic days in 'Newington Guest House' in Edinburgh had paid off with success in the Primary. For Avril and the boys the vigil of confinement in the home of loving parents and equally loving grandparents deprived of physical contact with precious new lives in their charge for a short while had come to an end with my arrival back home. The doctors' families who moved into newly built hospital houses in Randolph Road with us had never had it so good. Our boys thrived on meeting new friends, and so did we. Like me, all the other middle-grade doctors had their stories to tell. They had proved themselves competent for specialisation, were enthusiastic and dedicated, but still had a long way to go. Many years of low pay, increasing family commitments, professional anxieties and uncertainties lay ahead. They had consultant posts in their sights but were still raw and lean.

Avril's parents were frequent visitors to Randolph Road. Whenever they arrived the entire gang of street children would follow them from their car into our living room. Grandparents thrilled to their grandsons' milestones passing by. The Tufty Club gave the boys the basic principles of road safety in a friendly way. Sunday- School in a barn of a Church behind our house reminded them, and us, about something else. My parents were less frequent visitors. Just before we left Sulenkama my father retired from St Adrian's Church in West Wemyss. 'Granny and Grandad in West Wemyss' were no longer in West Wemyss. They'd moved to Blair Atholl, in Perthshire, to a bungalow they'd had built for them for their retirement, and called it 'Berbice', in memory of their days in New Amsterdam there, in British Guiana.

As the Primary Fellowship course had proved successful in preparing me for the examination we felt, after a year in Stirling in an environmentally family friendly life, that it was time to concentrate on the books again, this time with a view to the Final Fellowship examination. I applied for study leave and enrolled for an eight-week course in Edinburgh. It was back to the Newington Guest House and a Spartan, self-centred life with only occasional weekends at home. I was as well-prepared as I'd ever been for any exam when I put pen to paper and I coped confidently with the orals and small cases. When it came to the long case in Kirkcaldy I was over confident and too talkative at a critical point in my clinical examination and paid the price. I knew the result but hoped I was wrong. In my despondency my fears were confirmed. Luck or fate or coincidence, or some guiding hand wasn't far away. Among the candidates waiting for their results, I met a student friend from my St Andrews days and as we chatted he told me where he was, in Halifax, in Yorkshire, finishing a job at the Royal Halifax Infirmary, as Senior Casualty Officer in the Accident Department before starting a Senior Registrar's job in the teaching hospital in Leeds. He talked enthusiastically about life in Halifax, the wide variety of work he did, the good standard of life he could support on relatively good pay, good colleagues, the stimulation of a greater volume of work and the competitive edge which came from it. In comparison my good life in Stirling was dulling my intellectual outlook. Within a week I was in Halifax, looking round the Casualty Department, and confirming my decision to take my friend's job when he moved to Leeds. It's strange how, when one door closes, another opens.

HALIFAX – 'MUCK' and 'BRASS'
FRCS Ed.
AILSA MARY NICOL

From the brim of the Calder Valley basin surrounding it, we looked down on Halifax, our new home in the heart of 'Muck and Brass' Yorkshire. There was nothing to be seen. It was shrouded in a dense dark cloud of smoke, the product of a host of competing mill chimneys, belching their polluting toxins skywards. A rented furnished semi-detached house on Green Park Road was our first home in Halifax before we moved for a short time into the first house of our own only a few doors away and identical to it. From the luxury of Randolph Road in Stirling the contrast of industrial Halifax was stark. We could only echo the fears in John's innocent question, 'When are we going to go home?' but hope for something better. We were to know good times and bad times, experience disappointments and achievements, come to love and respect Yorkshire people as Halifax became, first, our temporary home and later the home our family grew up in during their formative years, to form and cement many relationships, and to share in many passing changes with many passing friends in our association with Halifax over two decades.

I thrived on being, if anything, over-stretched and soon learnt that I was unlikely to become stressed from working long hours doing what I enjoyed. It would be the frustrations of inactivity and being thwarted from doing what I knew was needed that would get to me. I threw myself into my work and our family, and Avril, who had become a Family Planning Trainer after having been trained herself, did the same. The books, and the Fellowship examination still to pass, haunted me. Every spare minute when the day came to an end, when the routine hospital work was over, when our family ploys were over and the boys fast asleep for the night, after we'd had a few minutes to ourselves and Avril had retired to bed with a good book to transport herself into another world of her own I'd get down to the books for a few hours and get up for a few hours more before the start of another day and apply myself unstinting to the academic task at hand.

There are some examinations when nothing goes well and others when almost everything goes well, but not quite enough to satisfy every critical examiner. Occasionally everything goes well and every examiner is satisfied. It was like that for me, waiting patiently for the results after a concerted effort at the Final Fellowship Examination in Edinburgh. The lady with the envelopes came out and invited a few of us to go in. I'd passed. With other blank, unbelieving, faces I was ushered into the President's Room and given a glass of sherry. Never before or since has sherry tasted so sweet. Hand-shakes from examiners, college dignitaries pointing to portraits of college fathers and recounting an appropriate witty story for each, the President himself giving a potted history of the Royal College of Surgeons, one time College of Surgeons and Barbers of Edinburgh, reverend nods of homage, smiles and grins, and the occasional tear, it all seemed as in a dream. When I arrived home early the next morning Avril and the boys were still asleep. They'd had a long day the day before. Routine games and stories, and baths and feeding had to continue normally. Avril's secret fears of failure again, hopes of success this time and jubilation when she heard my faltering voice on the phone telling her that 'It's all right this time!' were submerged in the routine of domesticity. I nudged her as I crept into bed. She grunted a grunt of relief, turned over and fell into a deep sleep. So did I.

Back in 'our home', 'our house', in Halifax we had our work cut out. Avril combined her work in Family Planning with keeping us all on an even keel as well as deciding when and how to break her news that an additional member of our family was on the way. As she always put it, 'Every child a wanted child! – planned or not.' The boys grew increasingly excited at the prospect of a baby sister or even another boy. I started the hunt for one of the few Senior Training posts in a Teaching Hospital which would prepare me for a Consultant appointment and, as it turned out, a Senior Registrar post came up in my home ground in Dundee, and I got it. Everything seemed to be going our way.

A few weeks before we left Halifax we gathered round the font at St Andrew's Church at a morning service and Ailsa Mary, – 'Ailsa' after her Auntie Ailsa, Avril's sister, and 'Mary' after my sister, Mary, as well as my mother – was baptised after a relatively unremarkable pregnancy and delivery. With our many new friends we sat around after the service eating cake and drinking coffee, receiving congratulations, sharing stories and playing games with the children, at one with our extended family of congenial friends, till it was time to leave. Our Goodbyes were the start of many over the following week ending with our final parting. We had found a house in Broughty Ferry, outside Dundee and a buyer for our Halifax home. A new chapter in Dundee was to open. Our brief attachment to Halifax was coming to an end. We'd always have fond memories of it. What we didn't know was that our association with the town, it's 'muck and brass', its down-to-earth, compassionate but unflattering people, was to be rekindled a few years later and fanned into the warmth which our family has shared for Halifax ever since.

DUNDEE PRE-CONSULTANT DAYS.
WITH FAMILY COMPLETE IN KATE'S ARRIVAL
PLAIN SAILING TO A SETTLED LIFE.
BUT STILL THE CALL OF THE TRANSKEI

The modern semi-detached two good size bedrooms with spacious through and through lounge and bright eating area including a well fitted kitchen which Avril had chosen from a few other properties for sale on the fringe of a housing estate on Blake Avenue, off Claypots Road, was all that we could have wished for. It was handy for small shops, a haven for families like ours with prams and bikes, dirty-faced toddlers and jammy-piece-eating schoolchildren cluttering the neighbourhood, and well placed for a good new Primary School that our three boys soon settled into.

Back in the DRI again since my earliest days as a pre-registration house officer on the Medical and Surgical wards, it seemed, at first, unreal. I should have known the familiar Infirmary but I didn't. It was the Orthopaedic Unit I was on now. The familiar faces of my student days and my first year as a doctor had gone. People and places move on. I knew most of the Consultants on the Unit from my Bridge of Earn days and enjoyed working with them all, learning from them, discussing new techniques, running trials, teaching and supporting our House Officers and Registrars, and organising regular postgraduate meetings and clinical conferences. In the two years I was to be the Orthopaedic Senior Registrar in Dundee I was to gain in confidence, recognise my limitations, learn from my mistakes, wrestle with ethical issues like the care of irreparably mutilated casualties, and support and be supported by medical and nursing colleagues in our joint responsibility for the care of terminally ill patients and children with congenital and hereditary disabilities. I thrived on the mix of work and the opportunity to stand alongside people, patients and their loved ones, bringing ordered objectivity out of confusion and bewilderment, giving hope even in the face of the most traumatic injuries, tranquillity in the recognition of impending death, introducing an element of humour into the most serious of conditions. Laughter is often the best medicine, provided it is not at anyone's expense. From my teaching Consultants and the opportunities to attend specialised courses the seeds of hand surgery, hip arthroplasty in a sterile environment, and the art of prosthetics were sown. I was introduced to new innovations in the field of Orthopaedics. Silastic implants were on the way in. Joint Replacement Surgery was taking off. The benefit of Bone Tumour Registers was being recognised. Interest in all these developments, in research and the preparation of articles for publication was encouraged. I spent hours in the library checking on every relevant reference and statistic relating to the subject of a paper that I had published in *The British Journal of Surgery* soon after we left Dundee.

Whether it's 'mine', or 'yours', or 'ours', 'Home', the 'house' we live in and the place we belong to for a life-time or a transient few months is enriched by the happy harmonising of coming and going of people in deepening relationships. Blake Avenue was all of this. Avril's parents came and went as often as they could, each visit adding to the quality of our mutual affection. My parents came and went less frequently, each precious visit no less meaningful, but their faces betrayed the anxieties of fading health, especially my mother's. When the time came, she was admitted to hospital, the DRI, ironically on the same Medical Ward that I did my first Junior House Officer job on. The beds and the layout were the same. I went once or twice with my father to see our patient then yellow-faced from jaundice, peaceful from hypnotics. On the last night I sat with my mother, on my own, in silence, our thoughts alone the only bonds of communication before she smiled a distant smile and died. A few days later she was buried in Blair Atholl.

Early on in our time in Blake Avenue I wrote, just for curiosity, to the South African Department of Health in Pretoria outlining my experience and asking what they would require of me for recognition as an Orthopaedic Specialist in South Africa. Back came the answer in a few weeks – 20 months in a Teaching Hospital like Dundee Royal Infirmary. We put the thought to the back of our minds for a year or more, till our fifth child, Kate, was on the way, then wrote again to Pretoria, this time in an ultra-confident tone. Would they not think of creating a Specialist post in the Transkei appointing me to develop an Orthopaedic Service in their first, model, Bantustan? A few letters with questions, promises and undertakings, formal documents dropped into the South African Embassy in London by a passing friend during the Post Office strike of 1971, and it was fixed. In spite of warnings about burning our boats a second time, the decision was made. Rather than a conventional consultant appointment at home, the challenge of the post of Principal Orthopaedic Specialist at the Sir Henry Elliot Hospital in the Transkei, in spite of its unpredictable nature, seemed more natural for me. There are decisions we make in life which are really made for us. Though we're responsible for making them, and must stand or fall by them, we're very often compelled by something or someone beyond ourselves directing us, pointing us on our way.

Kate's arrival in the labour ward at Dundee Royal Infirmary on February 9th 1971 was different from any of our previous babies because I was there, on the spot, for the event. I was the first to see that our baby was a girl, Katharine Anne, Katharine spelt with a 'K' and an 'a', 'arine', and Anne spelt with an 'e', after no one in particular, because Avril liked both names. She was to be 'Katie' till she was old enough to tell us that it was to be 'Kate' when she started Grammar school. A few weeks later Jimmy, David and John stood self-consciously but dutifully round the font at St Steven's Church, off Broughty Ferry Road, holding Ailsa by the hand, taking in the mystery of the baptism of their sister, our Katharine Anne Nicol.

THE TRANSKEI IN TRANSITION.
HELPING IT ON IN UMTATA
AND THE BEDFORD ORTHOPAEDIC CENTRE

The voyage from Southampton to East London on the Union Castle Line *SS Oranje* was a tonic for us all. In, what seemed no time at all it was over and we were in South Africa again. Avril's first sketchy note home describes the picture:-

'We docked at East London at about 8 a. m. and were having breakfast when an Immigration Official joined us to welcome us to South Africa and say there was a hospital van waiting beside the Customs shed to drive us to Umtata immediately. That was a great relief, as we thought we'd have to stay in East London overnight and get the slow train to Umtata the following day, which takes about 14 hours! So we were whisked away into the 'Combi', plus all our trunks and pushchairs etc. and were in the hospital at 1 p.m.'

From the moment we drove through the open gates of The Sir Henry Elliot Hospital in Umtata to the red stoep-polished steps of the front offices and were warmly welcomed with the news that 'our home' which had been allocated to us was three rooms in the Nurses' Home the tone was set for every day of our second, short-lived, stay in South Africa, the aspirational home of our dreams. It was confrontation, confrontation and more confrontation, but with the thrill of accomplishment that went with the confrontation transforming the totality of the experience into an act of faith fulfilled.

The acting Medical Superintendent, an energetic, clinically orientated and competent man as dedicated to the development of Specialist Services in the Transkei as me, was a natural friend from the start, but he had his administrative responsibilities to exercise. He apologetically showed us what had been arranged for us at the Nurses' Home. The first night over and our apprehension aroused, my new friend was round to see how we had fared. He was keen to show me round the hospital, discuss my duties, and his aspirations for expanding the health service. My enthusiasm for, and interest in, the work I had come to do matched his but I found that, for the first time in my working life, I was consumed by aggression. It was frightening. I refused to set foot in the hospital or talk about my work until more suitable housing was found for my family. There was none available. We talked and paced around. In desperation I spotted an empty blue house in the grounds and exclaimed, 'What about that one?' 'No!' was the blunt answer, firmly, 'That's the Medical Superintendent's. Yes, it's been empty for a while, but it's for the new Medical Superintendent when he's appointed.' 'It'll do!' was my reply, and it did, for almost six months.

'Well,' wrote Avril, *'everyone was aghast at this, as this house had to be kept for the new (still to be appointed) Medical Superintendent, but we insisted and they said, 'Right – we'll move you tomorrow!' Well, it's a super house – two storeys and an enormous garden the boys can get lost in. It is next to the hospital grounds but we have our own gates and loads of*

trees around so we are on our own. Monday morning, everyone was set to work and the house was cleaned and necessary furniture moved in from various sources so we could start living in it. All there was in the kitchen was an electric stove but we have beds, bedding, 2 wardrobes, two dressing tables, a dining table, 6 chairs and a kitchen table – and that's all! We have a sitting room, dining room, kitchen and pantry downstairs and three enormous bedrooms and a dressing room and bathroom upstairs. The boys are all in together, but they have to shout over to each other's beds, and Ailsa is all alone in a room with one bed and a wardrobe! It is a great picnic but we feel we are very lucky getting in here. Houses are hopeless to come by in Umtata and if you go away for a weekend you are liable to come back and find it occupied by someone else. We feel we have our foot in the door here, and as they will be hard pressed for somewhere else for all of us – I think we'll stay!

'The furniture removal and house-cleaning was done by a squad of prisoners supervised by a poor white colonial type overseer seated firmly in a tatty wicker chair scowling fiercely at his charges and smiling benignly at us whenever we passed, all this much to the awed fascination of the boys (not to mention mine) and we didn't take long to move in and take possession. I have a maid, Nancy, who was the first of a long string looking for employment and she is very good so far. She speaks good English and is fond of the children already.'

The one thing, and that above all else, which struck us forcibly about the South Africa, or at least the Transkei, we had returned to, could be summarised in the term 'Afrikaanerisation' on everyone's mind and on their lips. If it took me the better part of a week to appreciate this and to begin to grasp the undercurrents in relationships between the differing cultural interests and spot the major changes that had occurred since our time in Sulenkama just under ten years before, it took Avril only a few minutes shopping in town. Where she could easily find a tin of 'Baked Beans' in the supermarket, BV Bazaar, before, they were now no longer to be found. 'Where are the Baked Beans?' she asked a white check-out attendant in English. The garbled answer she got in Afrikaans meant nothing to her. No one would speak to her in English. The advice of an Italian doctor's wife she was given on our arrival sprung to mind. 'The best thing to do is to be as off hand and as rude as they are, and don't feel hurt by their manner.' The beans were there all right, but the tins had been turned round. Their 'Baked Beans' labels were no longer on display. They had been replaced by 'Boontjes', Afrikaans for 'beans'.'

With the teething problems of accommodation settled for the moment, the family settled happily into the 'Viege house' (So named after the previous Medical Superintendent with whom I had corresponded when we were in Dundee and developed a healthy respect for, but who retired just before our arrival back in the Transkei) and the boys enrolled in the English High School where Afrikaans was a compulsory subject spoken fluently by staff and pupils alike, my energies were directed to my work. I relished every aspect of it. At the alternatively named 'Umtata' or 'Sir Henry Elliot' Hospital I'd walk across each morning from our home in the hospital compound, enter through a side door and find my way to the wards for 'rounds' or the operating theatre to see what was on what I was used to calling the 'list' but was known in Umtata as the 'slate'. An occasional gem of knowledge, a subtle joke or astute observation fell from my lips on the attentive ears of my hospital doctors and our more silent, submissive but perceptive Xhosa nursing staff. 'Hot' trauma cases, many the result of horrific road traffic accidents and 'Cold' cases ranging from more unusual things like hydatid cysts and congenital anomalies of almost every conceivable bone or joint to common conditions like tuberculous paraplegia found their way on to my slate. I'd then retreat to my office in a small room near the administration offices at the entrance of the hospital, to deal with the usual paperwork of my department, especially correspondence with the Department of Health in Pretoria. From the beginning, I set my sights on establishing an Orthopaedic Service for the Transkei with recognition of Umtata and Bedford as centres for the training of doctors and nurses in the speciality of Orthopaedics. The response from Pretoria was, initially, encouraging and as I became known a few doctors befriended me, a life-long friendship soon developing with my nearest Orthopaedic neighbour, Dick Lancaster, in East London.

Orthopaedic Clinics soon got under way. More and more patients appeared from near and far as the peripheral hospitals, many of which I knew well from my previous time in South Africa, got to hear about the new Orthopaedic Specialist. A car was set aside for my use visiting several outlying hospitals coming to terms with changing from 'Mission' to local 'State' administration. And I started visiting a small Government General Hospital at Butterworth, between East London and Umtata, holding clinics and even carrying out a few operations.

But of all the resources at my disposal it was the Bedford Orthopaedic Centre which was to prove itself most helpful. Off the road to Queenstown five miles out of Umtata, along a narrow, seldom graded, dirt road, over a cattle grid and through the gates proudly boasting 'The Bedford Orthopaedic Centre ', the buzz of the hive of activity on the Convent Farm, pioneered originally by a German order of nuns over a hundred years earlier, has remained as palpable through the years as it was striking when I first set foot on it. The compound with its stone Church and Presbytery, Sisters' and Novitiates' Centre, kitchens and workhouses, its School for orphaned coloured children with appropriate large cold-in-the-winter, hot-in-the-summer classrooms, dormitories and staff houses, outside farm and farmer's house, and a few wards for convalescent and long term tuberculosis patients spoke of a timeless something beyond itself. Black and white nursing and religious sisters and a varied staff supervised the care of their patients conscientiously. Nothing was too much for them. The senior staff ran a small dispensary and X-Ray Department and turned their hands to corrective plasters that they put on in a small plaster-room not much bigger than a broom cupboard. Little did we imagine at the time that from that plaster-room a full-blown theatre facility in a Regional Orthopaedic Centre would evolve. To begin with I started with a few simple manipulations, then, with Avril giving reliable anaesthetics, I became more ambitious. Debridement of infected wounds became possible and simple corrective procedures such as lengthening of the Achilles tendon and the release of contractures followed. The transfer of tendons in an attempt to rectify muscle imbalance and operations for clubfoot and other congenital anomalies became common practice. Inspired by what he saw, an enterprising local doctor, Don Luswaze, started assisting me more and more with our operations at Bedford and was soon able to be left on his own with Avril encouraging him to stop and think, as I would do, when he got into any trouble. Our mutual respect for each other grew with our friendship. Over the operating room table in Bedford Avril and I were able to discuss our frustrations with Don and he confide his fears with us. As it turned out Don was to specialise in Surgery and emerge as the single hope for continuing the Orthopaedic Service for the Transkei in the immediate years to come.

Looking back, as we often did, on our time in Umtata, it was like a dream and a nightmare packed with meaningful events that warmed the heart one minute and turned it to ice the next. No sooner was the initial trauma of having to live in the Nurses' Home put behind us with our moving into the Medical Superintendent's house than a top level, on the spot, meeting was called with the national Secretary for Health to clarify, as I thought it did, several emotive issues and aspirations. It was confirmed where I was staying with my family and that there appeared to be no other acceptable accommodation and the Secretary seemed to understand and to sympathise. We then discussed my aspirations for a Physiotherapy Service at Bedford, the development of a Limb-Fitting facility, and plans for regular visits to Butterworth and several of the mission hospitals as well, of course, as the Bedford Orthopaedic Centre. The Health minister appeared enthusiastic. We were on a common wavelength. I was assured of every co-operation, inspired to set to work to develop the Orthopaedic Service of my dreams for the Transkei.

In a few weeks the dream seemed to be becoming a reality. Our family affairs in order, the boys settling into school, the different aspects of the work beginning to knit together – we could identify ourselves with what we'd come to Umtata for. Reassured and encouraged, we adopted a more positive outlook, looking to the future with optimism. But the unsubstantiated suspicions about the significance of Afrikaanerisation and, above all else, the horror of housing began to haunt us. We couldn't either rationalise or minimise our fears.

'My home is your home,' said Dick the first time we visited him in East London, our three boys nestled in the camp beds in his garden summer house, Ailsa and Katie asleep in an adjoining children's room off ours as we sat back on his stoep chatting about his pioneering years in South Africa with his wife Norah. Their welcome was as from their hearts as it was to be in changing circumstances in years to come. They'd met in Alloa just after the war when Norah was a Theatre Sister in the hospital there and Dick an Orthopaedic Registrar. Married in Stirling, they set off for South Africa to settle in East London and make a happy home for themselves and their six children. Our commonality was striking. Orthopaedics was our lives. Our roots sprung from Scotland and took us to South Africa and the Xhosa people, Dick to the Ciskei, me to the Transkei on the other side of the River Kei. Our hobbies and interests outside our work revolved round our families and our homes. Learning about our precarious position in Umtata, we discussed the possibilities of a job for me in East London. It might be good to work with Dick. Life in the seaside town of East London was attractive, and, soon after, I was offered similar jobs to the one I was doing in Umtata as Principal Orthopaedic Specialist in a hospital near Pietermaritzburg and even as far afield as Windhoek in what was then South West Africa. Each had its own temptations but none was ever seriously considered. We had come to South Africa to work in the Transkei and nowhere else.

Away from the close-knit, tension-packed working environment of Umtata, able to talk freely with friends, share mutual family concerns, to look beyond our little world to a wider world beyond, our visit to East London did us the world of good. We returned to Umtata refreshed, ready for whatever lay ahead, and with an additional member to our family, a lovely creamy white Maltese poodle puppy with brown ears and a cute face like a lamb. 'Cindy' would be part of our family for many years.

Back in Umtata I was soon caught up in my work as well as the hunt for a house to resolve our predicament. In the hassle of life the natural blend of humour and pathos in my patients was a constant factor which I found both encouraging and soothing. I thought I remained fair-minded and objective, sympathetic and compassionate when called for, firm and persuasive when necessary. Above all I strove to retain my natural optimism, to look forward with hope. I was aware that my protective instincts were tested, that I had to fight for my family and what I wanted for my patients, that survival had become very real to me but didn't for a minute think I was becoming belligerent. As it turned out our immediate future improved when, at last, an acceptable house was identified for us and plans set in motion to modify and upgrade it to a sufficient standard for the hospital to buy it and rent it out to us. I retained my sanity. I could laugh, with Avril, at myself. She was perceptive enough to see the humour in the dignity of life around us and to see, also, the traces of bitterness creeping into me.

For a short time, at what proved to be the zenith of my busy Orthopaedic life in the homeland, when the Department for Health was capitalising on the prowess of one of its innovative Specialists at work with the Xhosa people it served, a light aircraft was made available for me to visit the most remote outlying clinics. Seated, early one morning, beside the pilot in a twin-seater with space behind for a stretcher for a patient, we were soon airborne, scraping the treetops as we circled above the hospital complex in Umtata. I looked down and there it was, the distinctive blue 'Viege house', 'our precious home', 'our house', 'our most memorable family home' for the short time we lived in it, – there it was, 'ours', and in the garden, our boys, setting off for school, Avril with Katie in her arms, waving excitedly up at me, Ailsa pottering among the shrubs.

69

Waving back as we circled, the figures were soon specks. I was on my way to a new Government Hospital specially commissioned for the treatment of patients with tuberculosis in a remote part of the Wild Coast, so remote that it proved inaccessible for both patients and staff. As I recall, the only patient requiring my services was a young man with an injured arm. Undaunted by either the prospects of surgery or the anxiety of a flight in a fragile aircraft, my patient gathered his red blanket around him, tied his few belongings up in a hanky, and marched purposefully to the plane, but not before stepping smartly aside to empty his bladder. You'd think he flew every day and knew what to do and when.

Then the waiting was over. The new Superintendent had arrived. The day started peacefully. Faithful Nancy, our maid, was warned to let us know the moment anything untoward happened. The boys were off to school, Katie asleep in her pram at home, Avril and me at Bedford relaxed in the silent concentration of our work, she rhythmically inflating an anaesthetic machine bag with her right hand and writing a note home with the other, me dissecting a resistant clubfoot, Ailsa asleep in her pushchair in the yard. The phone rang. 'He's coming in!', screamed Nancy, distraught, deference thrown to the wind. The clubfoot well-moulded plaster scarcely set, we were on our way racing over the red dirt road back to Umtata. What stands out in my memory, even today, is weaving through a logjam of crates and baggage packed solid from the front door to the back, and a little later, in his office, the measured words of my new colleague. 'You've put me in an embarrassing position, having to dismiss you on my first day here. My wife and baby are still in the car outside, our three dogs in the trailer.' He needed the space in the fenced garden around the house for his three Alsatian guard dogs. 'If you're embarrassed, how do you think I feel,' I replied, strangely calm and collected, 'with our family of five in a hostile country miles from the comforting familiarity of my home?' 'Move out!' you insist, 'How can we? We can't move a thing for your boxes jamming us in, even Katie in her pram!'

The day the three Alsatian dogs arrived the 'Viege house' was no longer 'our home'. Though we stayed on in it for a few days until our new home was almost ready for us it no longer felt like our home. In the end it was a relief to make the move.

We had known George from our previous Sulenkama days in the Transkei and were very much looking forward to meeting up with him again and integrating his work with the local Presbyterian churches with mine establishing an Orthopaedic service for the Transkei. George was expected back in Umtata with his wife, Margaret any day and my enquiries about just when he would be back were well known. Time passed. We waited and waited with our own affairs enough to keep us going. Then an end to the period of waiting came as suddenly if less dramatically but equally forcibly as the arrival of the Medical Superintendent and his three Alsatian guard dogs. At the end of a clinic at the Umtata Hospital a week or two after moving to our new home, I gathered my case notes together. From the back of the concrete-floored, wooden-benched waiting room a solitary figure emerged. An elderly lady came forward nervously, looking around, checking that we were on our own, and spoke quietly. 'Dr Nicol?' she asked to check my credentials, and when satisfied, continued, 'I'm a friend of George and Margaret, like an 'auntie' to their children, Barbara and George. I've been trying to see you for a while.' We left together. My new friend declined getting into the front seat of the car beside me. It would be better for her to be in the back. The short drive home was in silence but when we were indoors, over a cup of tea, with Avril chatting cheerily, attentively first to our account of our meeting, then, her pent-up suspicions removed, wrapped for a moment in hopeful anticipation about George, our guest telling us about happy times with George and Margaret and their children, her close relationship with the family, asking about ours, listening with repeated shakes of her head as some of our recent experiences unfolded, nodding thoughtfully at times at our ramblings about plans for the future in Umtata, fed with one chocolate biscuit after another from Ailsa, 'cooing' over Katie now crawling on the floor, 'auntie' was soon at ease laughing, chuckling, carefree and uninhibited at first, then seriously solemn. The object of her visit was short and to the point. It was good to meet George's friends but the news she had for us was this, 'They're not coming back. Don't ask too much and don't talk too much about it.' She gathered her things together, joked about coming the next time to see us selling fruit with a basket on her head, and walked off through the now darkness of the night, the chirping of crickets at play the only sound in the air. We were to see George again next in his home in Edinburgh but never again in South Africa. He was too much of a security liability to be granted a Permit of Permanent Residence and our association with him would place us in the liability category as well.

My contacts through my work, and especially from my trips to the scattered Missionary Hospitals preparing for the impending hand-over to local direct control from the Transkei Legislative Assembly, brought me in touch with how my friends felt about the political and social changes they were living through. Apartheid was being consolidated throughout the country and Separate Development in the Bantu Homelands was part of it. We drew comfort from the few close friends we found ourselves gravitating towards, confiding in them as they did in us. Small though our circle of friends was, their support was invaluable. Foreboding shared can be controlled. In isolation it can so easily become overpowering. From our everyday dealings with the hospital authorities and local government officials as well as many of our colleagues it became clear that our closest friends, the ones who thought and felt as we did, were viewed with suspicion, not in the apartheid set of the day. Our friends, black and white doctors, ministers of religion, priests, pastors, nurses, teachers and old time missionaries trying to move with the times had all one thing in common. They were being kept under surveillance. Most had had their passports restricted or withdrawn, work permits confiscated or limited, and many had been visited by the Security Police or been detained pending charges against the State. We could feel ourselves being drawn into a struggle with only one end. It would only be a matter of time before our allegiances would catch up on us.

The cultivated pine forests on the hill slopes around Umtata thrived on the heat and rain of the summer months. A brief break in Kambi Forest just beyond Bedford was always popular. Avril's letter home describes the scene, but she had something else to add after one visit:-

'Yesterday,' she wrote, *'we took a picnic up to a forest near here and had a lovely afternoon at a picnic spot with tables and chairs and fireplace for cooking in a clearing. It was so nice and shady and cool under the trees and Jimmy found a porcupine quill. Cindy had a great time running wild round the place. When we got back, just after 6 p.m., it was obvious the house had been broken into.'*

From the obvious forced entry through the back door, food strewn around the kitchen, and signs of ransacking in the living room, it looked as if the culprits were after whatever valuables they could find and ready cash. We were immediately angered at what we found but froze at the thought of a possible connection with an incident we'd encountered soon after moving to our new house on Wesley Street. We had not made much of it for the sake of the family, and Avril had not written home about it. The first time had been more of a mysterious, unaccounted for incident than a more definite break-in. Looking through some papers in a desk one day, Avril and I each accused the other of leaving it untidy. 'You might have put your papers away when you finished with them. Don't leave important documents lying around in an open desk,' I was admonished. My lame excuses went unheard until we both realised that neither of us had been at fault. Someone, a careful, methodical rifler had been at work. Throughout the house our desks, a book-case, a briefcase with passports, permits, employment documents, letters and notes, even some of the boys' school books had been ransacked and scrutinised. No signs of a broken lock on a door or window were to be found. There were no traces of a robbery. Our suspicions were aroused. It looked very much as if someone had been searching for any kind of subversive literature, evidence of association with undesirable organisations, a list of names. Secret police and Security agents could well have been involved. We dismissed these thoughts from our minds and didn't report our mysterious intruder to the police, but we did report the more recent, obvious break-in.

Soon after the removal from 'our home', 'our house', in the 'Viege house' which we felt most at home in to an adequate house on Wesley Street that never really felt like our home we started thinking more consciously than unconsciously about abandoning our dream of work in the Transkei. Avril conveyed our feelings to her parents in a letter home on 1.2.72.:-

'Things seem to be folding up here altogether now. The biggest worry is lack of doctors in the hospital as the more experienced have left or resigned and there are just three housemen trying to do everything. There should be 9 or 10 of them. They have had to close OPD to everything but Casualty as there are no doctors to cope with the perpetual streams of people. Bill has never had a houseman yet and it looks as if he never will. Anyway, this gives me a chance to do 2-3 evening sessions a week of anaesthetics to relieve one poor doctor. The whole future of this place is very dicey for everyone and no one could care less. Morale is rock bottom. There is less and less done at the general hospital here. It is impossible to operate when there are no doctors for after-care. And Butterworth hospital has virtually had to close as well. But the work at Bedford is, if anything, increasing, mainly because Bill has his own private anaesthetist, me, to keep him going. So, when we grumble, we've just cause and the housing problem being meanwhile settled has not reduced the worries.'

Six months later, on 11.7.72, Avril broke the news to her parents that *'We have decided to take a calculated risk (another one) and return to the UK at the end of the year. We have realised since the end of last year that the future here holds little promise and things have got worse and worse during the last six months as regards the work.'*

In a strange way, when the decision to leave Umtata was made it came as no surprise. It seemed almost inevitable. Our closest friends who shared our anxieties and felt as we did, our many associates at work who didn't feel as we did, the Security Police whose attention had been drawn to us, and the State Health Department that had employed me in the hope of projecting an image of a benevolent regime doing its best for the Bantu under its care only to find the project expanding far beyond its expectations and much more comprehensively than planned seemed, if anything, relieved at the news. Concerned about our leaving, a few local businessmen invited me to speak at the Umtata Rotary Club outlining the kind of work I was doing and explaining why I had finally decided to give it up. At the end of the talk came the questions, some from a few newspaper reporters in attendance. My feelings of disappointment, dashed hopes and frustrated ambitions, family loyalties and responsibilities to my patients must have come through. The reporters left with something newsworthy but were stopped on the way out. 'Tear it up!' they were warned, and knew better than go to press with a story that could cause trouble. A shrewd observer's comment, though probably true, didn't help. 'You've got the wrong name. That's your problem. If it was 'van-Nicol' you'd have had no trouble. If you had compromised a bit, conformed with the ideology of the National Party success would have been guaranteed.' But even as he spoke I knew that our short-lived efforts would not be in vain. The seeds of an Orthopaedic Service had been sown. They'd sprout, be nourished by our friend Don Luswazi, and grow in some yet unknown way in years to come. In leaving I'd be leaving behind an inspired Dr Luswazi.

In some jobs, or perhaps more accurately, with some people in some jobs, running down or even switching off, coming to a standstill, is achievable. Disillusionment spells discontent, and discontent the withdrawal of responsibilities. The work dries up. It was not like that with us. Though Avril's analysis of life and conditions in Umtata in her letter home on 1.2.72 – *'Things seem to be folding up altogether now.'* – was in no way inaccurate it was certainly not like that for us in our last few weeks. In fact the tempo of my work continued, intensifying with every passing day. I forced myself to take stock of my work and inject some kind of order into the records of our developing Orthopaedic Service in an effort to leave a base from which my immediate successor might build and my short-lived efforts grow.

The search for jobs at home started. There was nothing in Dundee or Stirling – only Good Luck and Best Wishes. Surprisingly, one day, a letter came from one of the London hospitals. The Umtata address in South Africa on my application couldn't have registered for the reply was an invitation to join other prospective candidates on a Saturday morning for coffee and drinks in the boardroom before being shown round the hospital and meeting potential colleagues. Flattered at being considered, I was more disappointed at missing out on the drinks. Several similar opportunities came and went until enquiries at the Centre for Hip Surgery in Wrightington proved more hopeful. There was a vacancy on the training rotation for six months, starting in January 1973. John Charnley, the Director, who I had met when I attended a conference there during my time as Senior Registrar in Dundee, would be happy to have me join the unit if I made a formal application. Back though it would be to a trainee Registrar grade, albeit in a highly specialised, prestigious centre of excellence, it was a chance too good to miss. The application was posted the next day and in due course a post was offered at the Centre for Hip Surgery. The authorities at the Centre confirmed the appointment with the comment, 'We'll be glad to have you join Mr Charnley's team in January.'

Our passage home on the *Edinburgh Castle* was booked, shipping of our crated belongings organised, and the Animal Shipping Service, 'Spratt's Patent Ltd.' engaged to ship our Maltese Poodle dog, 'Cindy', to kennels outside Edinburgh where she would serve the necessary Quarantine period of six months before rejoining our family at 'Morven' in Dunblane.

As the weeks passed the pent-up excitement mounted. Avril wrote:-

'We have just five weeks to go and are working hard at Bedford just now. Bill has so many patients lying around he feels he should do and not leave too much for Luswazi as more come in from the clinic each week.'

But I was, of course, leaving much more than just a handful of outstanding operations to my friend. We talked at length about our mutual aspirations. I confided in Don my fears for the future as well as my hopes. He responded with his conviction that, one way or another, things would change. The political status quo could not remain. Our open discussions could no longer be disguised. They were frankly subversive. Shortly before we left we attended a gathering of 'friends' at Don's home – well-educated, articulate, confidently critical but prudent men and women, couples and people on their own, mainly Xhosa with a handful of Zulu, respectful but not patronising, all concerned about the educational welfare of their children. Their objective was the best available environment for their families in an environment different from the apartheid they'd endured themselves. It was a privilege to be with friends like these. We ate and drank well and talked plenty. In a strange way, the only white couple at the meeting, Avril and I, were more relaxed, more at home, than we had been at any time since our arrival in Umtata. Bonds of trust were struck which would endure through the years to come.

In her last letter home from Umtata Avril's description of our last days included:-

'On Sunday, we had a wonderful farewell concert for us at Bedford. Words couldn't describe the warm feelings of all the staff here and the time they had taken over all the preparations. Among many gifts we were presented with was a large collection of bead-work denoting the status of women in the community.

'This is our last full week of work and I am at Bedford just now. Bill is busy doing the last minute operations. The boys are going to school next Monday and Tuesday and we leave for East London on Wednesday.'

Come Wednesday we were on our way. Up Wesley Street, past the familiar entrance to the hospital, a glance over the fence, through the trees, at the 'Viege house', out of Umtata on to the national road, across the Kei out of the Transkei and we were soon in East London with our friends the Lancasters. In the cool of the evening, relaxed at last in the comfort of their home, no longer in the employment of the State Health Department, I shared my profound sense of relief with Avril and our hosts. The next day we'd have a few last minute formalities to attend to, take the car down to the docks and see it swung high into the air before being gently lowered into the hold of the mail ship we would be boarding ourselves the following day, receive and send a few greetings, see a reporter from the *Daily Dispatch* who wanted a story from us and have our last night in South Africa to look forward to. The last day in East London passed quickly by. The reporter came as arranged and Dick introduced her to me. She was pleasant and cheery, satisfied with what I gave her and took a few photographs. Next morning, the day we sailed, Dick and Norah were up early to take us to the docks to board and sail at noon. With a cup of tea in bed on the morning Dick brought us the

Daily Dispatch. 'British doctor quits Transkei after row!' Two familiar faces looked back at us as we read the headlines.

THE CENTRE FOR HIP SURGERY

The jubilant chatter and hugs of welcome reunion that greeted us on our arrival back in 'Morven' in our home country a week before Christmas 1972 were as transfixing as they were spontaneous. The nuclear family, even of today, embodies loyalty, devotion and responsibility which spring naturally from belonging to a unique unit, having a 'home' of its own, being identified by a name of its own. It brings with it commitment, duty and faithfulness, at their best the bedrock of fulfilment, a purpose in life, but also, sometimes, a fear of entrapment which can stifle uninhibited love. Ours was never ever anything else than a unique family unit. We're 'The Nicols', exclusive of any other Nicolls or Nichols. Nicol spelt with a double 'l' or an 'h' or an 's' is quite foreign to us. In our many moves from home to home, from our Dornoch days to Umtata, apart from my Primary Fellowship course in Edinburgh, we'd had a home of our own which gave us belonging, ensured togetherness. The harsh reality of having no family home of our own for an indefinite period of time dawned on us like a bolt of lightning from outer space. The prospect of separation and isolation at a time when crucial decisions had to be made with very little opportunity for adequate discussion took their toll on both Avril and me probably more than we realised.

But the excitement of Christmas in 'Morven' filled our moments. The boys thrilled to it. They'd been fixed up to start school after the holidays and immediately dismissed the prospects from their minds. The girls revelled in being spoilt by their doting grandparents. The homely security of 'Morven' was at the same time comforting and alarming because of the glaring contrast between the home we gladly adopted and the home of our own we didn't have. All too quickly the coming round of the last day of another year saw me being seen off at the station in Dunblane bound for the Centre for Hip Surgery in Wrightington.

Along with two other new Registrars I was shown round the Centre and met John Charnley briefly. His dedication to the work of the Centre for Hip Surgery, which he had initiated, was infectious. His fanatical enthusiasm for every minute detail of Low Friction Arthroplasty of the hip, which he had made his exclusive field, was electrifying. From the moment his new apprentices met him they were converted. The whole ethos of the Hip Centre became part of us. We would no longer talk about Artificial Hip Joints or even Total Hip Replacements but Low Friction Arthroplasty (LFA) and we would never again think of doing the operation in any other way we were instructed, nor in any other environment than a Sterile Enclosure to which we soon adapted. My conversion to the man and his Low Friction Arthroplasty was complete, as complete as the first disciples who followed another JC, Jesus Christ.

Then I was in Dunblane for a weekend. The boys had settled well in school. Jim's teacher had reserved a seat near a radiator for him on his first day. 'The new boy from South Africa,' she thought, 'would be feeling the cold, and need to keep warm.' Katie in her pushchair required constant supervision. Ailsa, restless in the confines of 'Morven', needed regular walks out along the riverside and to the park. Avril was coping, but just. Subdued tensions were not far from the surface. She felt isolated in the protective homeliness of

81

'Morven'. She was glad to see me back but felt she had nothing much to share. The answer to an application for a Consultant post in Orthopaedics in the Borders came through the door. We opened the letter. 'Thank you' it read, but I was not even short-listed. Our mood swings were at the same time comforting and perplexing. My approach to work, the responsibilities of the kind of life that lay ahead of me, the combination of professional satisfaction and family commitment, would colour my destiny throughout my life, from one profession to another, in full time and part time work, in retirement, in times of fulfilment and in times of isolation from the world around me.

When I was next in Dunblane we decided on a change of plan. We'd have to do something radical about our predicament. Six months of separation, each of us in our own worlds trying to plan for another together would be too much to endure. In my spare time in Wrightington I'd look around for a small house to rent with a view to moving at the Easter holidays and was lucky enough to find a minute two bed-roomed, furnished house with a box room in Appley Bridge not far from the Hip Centre as the school term in Dunblane was coming to an end. It would be cramped and basic but home, 'our home', all together again. Morale improved at the very thought of it.

On the way to Dunblane, with final arrangements for the move completed, I called into the kennels outside Edinburgh. Cindy's six months quarantine had come to an end. Constrained and a bit on edge, she sat in the front seat of the car beside me glancing at me from time to time for reassurance. It was teatime when we drove through the gates of 'Morven' to the back door. I led her out of the car, in through the back door to the morning room in a strange house. She hesitated for a minute. 'Excuse me!'s forgotten, the boys and Ailsa were down from the table and around Cindy as soon as they saw her. Avril wasn't far behind with Katie in her arms. The family was re-united, Granny and Grandad looking on approvingly. Later at night we decided to be firm. 'Cindy is used to kennel life now', we all agreed, 'and it will be a good chance to train her anew.' She'd sleep downstairs in a basket, like any other well-trained dog, when we went off to bed at night. Baths over and 'Good Nights' said, the boys ran up to bed, but Cindy was there before them, sound asleep on one of the beds, as she did in Umtata before she left six months before. So much for the dog basket.

With the Easter holidays came our move to Appley Bridge in rural Lancashire, not far from Wrightington and the Hip Centre. Everyone was prepared for what to expect – a small semidetached house in a side street, off the canal, in a small village. We were soon past the few shops and the coal yard at the end of our street. A gang of children stood by curiously, watching. We off-loaded and I went next door to our friendly neighbour, a small, almost dwarf-like, lady in a small house like ours, for the keys. The lady's six-foot son gave us a hand in and left to feed his pet owl with raw meat and fresh mice in his back yard next to ours. The exhibition distracted us from the vacant builder's yard behind, rutted, muddy in the rain, dry and dusty in the sun, an ideal play-ground but not so good for drying washing. Downstairs, the through and through sitting room-cum-dining room was soon filled with our possessions. Round the unlit coal fire and the black and white TV we took stock of the day before supper in the cramped kitchen at the back. And then to bed, up the narrow stairway for quick washes in the attic bathroom and into the holiday-style bunk bedrooms I'd crammed too many beds into, tired and soon fast asleep, together at last as a family unit in our own home.

A new pattern to our routine emerged. After a week or two before the holidays were over exploring new haunts, roaming the disused builder's yard and nearby canal brought new friend's dirty faces to the back door attracted by their new Scottish playmates and their feathered bird of prey, especially at feeding time. The boys had more pals to go to school with than they'd had for a long time. Avril would drop David and John off at their school when it started, Jim off at the bus stop for his bus to his, and me at the Hip Centre, before returning home with the girls, leaving Cindy in charge of the house.

In one respect life had suddenly changed for the better for us. The boys were soon staunch members of the Boys Brigade. They'd gather in the coal yard on Sunday mornings to march with the Company, drums drumming and bugles blowing, to the Methodist Chapel, their parents and sisters waving cheerily from among groups of admiring parents along the street side. In the church we'd all crowd in, the boys with the officers and other ranks, Avril and me with Ailsa and Kate between us in the front seat, our diminutive neighbour showing us where to sit, on the other side of me. The rousing hymn, 'Will your anchor hold in the storms of life?' announced and the chorus played through on the organ, the congregation rose to sing. It came naturally for me to lift, first Katie, then Ailsa, and stand them on the pew, then do the same with our diminutive neighbour. A frantic tug on my sleeve from Avril saved the humiliating embarrassment just in time.

Then, out of the blue, came a job in Halifax. My friend the Senior Orthopaedic Consultant had had a heart attack and was retiring. Events moved quickly on. By the end of May I was on my way to the Yorkshire Regional Health Authority headquarters in Harrogate for an interview for the vacant post, Consultant Surgeon in Accident and Emergency and

Orthopaedics. In a strange way I was composed and assured, confident and calm, not overly sure but more than just hopeful. This time I was the one of four to be offered the post. 'I expect,' said the Chairman of the Board, 'it'll be on a Maximum Part-time basis you'll be wanting the contract, Nine-elevenths of the Full-time salary?' 'Yes,' I replied hesitatingly, and left. A poster, 'Congratulations! Well done, Daddy!' greeted me on my return to Appley Bridge. Exhaustion and relief overwhelmed us all. Our fate was assured. I'd start on 1st July 1973. Halifax would be 'our home', where we all belonged, for almost twenty years.

ACT FIVE

'And then the justice,
In fair round belly with good capon lined,
With eyes severe and beard of formal cut,
Full of wise saws and modern instances;
And so he plays his part.'

HALIFAX and the spin-offs from it cover the longest period of our lives together as a family in any one place. It accounts for a period of stability, of belonging in a home and a place where we could all, in our own ways, grow in our own rights, develop our own individual characteristics, grow together as a family unit but at the same time grow apart, away, to encompass a wider world beyond ourselves. These were in many ways our formative years. Schooldays came and went for the children, infants one moment, teenagers wrestling with life the next, and adolescents on the threshold of adulthood all too soon. Relationships, security, insecurity, achievements, failures, feelings of satisfaction and also of inadequacy, confidence one minute, uncertainty the next, all played their part on the road to maturity. Though home-building, establishing and maintaining a place of our own, guiding and encouraging the family was always our first priority, neither Avril nor I was to be immune from the ups and downs of life in Halifax. My professional life was to all but take me over, though I always thought I had it under control. Avril's was more easily defined. What all but took her over were her family and her home. In our different ways we tended to isolate ourselves from the wider society around us. We became church-orientated almost to a fault. As time passed it excluded us from other aspects of life. And all through our time in Halifax the past was to impinge on the present. In a defining period of our lives Halifax was not to be compartmentalised. No one part of any of our lives can.

A search of the local papers and a run or two through to see any houses on the market brought no immediate prospects till a large semi-detached Victorian house, one of six, on Skircoat Green Road, not far from our previous home on Green Park turned up. 'It would be a good house for you', the seller told us and how right he was. With a 100% mortgage for the asking price of £17,500 the purchase was sealed. The house named 'Wheatstone' would be 'our home' for almost twenty years.

Schools were to be fixed up. John would go to All Saints Primary School on Dudwell Lane where Jim and David had gone before him. He was easily enrolled. It was more of a problem with his brothers. Combing the neighbourhood of the Royal Halifax Infirmary and Skircoat Green which we knew of old, the Crossley & Porter Grammar School, later to unite with Heath Grammar to form the Crossley Heath Grammar School, seemed ideal. There were still a few places unfilled for the coming year but they were for pupils who had passed the Eleven-Plus for entry from Primary Schools, or equivalent examinations for more senior classes. Dave would have to take the Eleven-Plus exam and Jim a 'Twelve-Plus' exam specially arranged in the Department of Education. The mental trauma of organising a new job and setting up a new home was nothing compared with that of our two students. On the day, they went along for the exams, composed, almost too casual, but passed 'nae bother'.

Like a new boy at school on his first day I faced my first day at the Royal Halifax Infirmary as Consultant Orthopaedic Surgeon with an element of apprehension but overwhelmed by far by the thrill of expectation, the quiet confidence of achievement, of an ambition realised. I met my secretary and she told me what my timetable for the week would probably be, about my colleagues John Gill and Ken Oyston, and how we could all work equitably together. I would inherit all my predecessor's patients including his waiting list for surgery and all patients under my care would carry the same distinctive rich golden-orange sticker with my name in bold capitals, 'Mr W.J.NICOL', on their case notes. Confronted with your name displayed on notes and operation lists, at clinics and on patients' beds has two effects. Your ego is inflated, but, at the same time, it's brought home to you that the 'buck stops here'. The glory is yours, but so are the headaches.

Looking around town I opted for rented rooms at 'Kent House' with a Dental friend and a General Surgery colleague in a down town, unimpressive, area on Bull Close Lane not far from the newly designed Halifax Building Society Headquarters straddling the town centre. My name on a name plate was screwed on to the wall on the roadside outside Kent House alongside the Dentist and the General Surgeon, appointment cards were printed, name headed bills and receipts ordered and an accountant engaged to keep track of the Private Practice Account. The general pattern of my work was set out. The details would fall into place.

The degree of expectation which arrived with me in Halifax, was overwhelming. A few doctors and nurses in the Infirmary remembered me vaguely from earlier years. More knew about me from the word about any new consultant, which gets around, even before they take up their appointment. Many of the General Practitioners up and down the Calder Valley had heard about my credentials. My experience in the Transkei might have interested some of them but my strongest card was coming from the Centre for Hip Surgery in Wrightington. Whatever else I might bring, I would have behind me the name, 'Charnley', synonymous with hip replacement surgery.

I was carried along with the initial flush of enthusiasm. Talks to GPs, nurses and physiotherapists, lectures in the Post-graduate Centre to medical and allied staff from many disciplines, were well received. Arrangements were made for my junior colleagues, as well as theatre and ward staff, to visit Wrightington and familiarise themselves with the environment of the Hip Centre. The staff there took ours to their hearts and Charnley himself acknowledged our mutual interest.

The stage was set to start the operations but the most important prop was still not there. The Royal Halifax Infirmary management authority had happily met most of the financial demands of its new Consultant Orthopaedic Surgeon furnishing him with the instruments required to perform his choice of operation for hip replacement surgery with its increasingly costly prostheses but its generosity ended there. My request for a Sterile Enclosure costing around £12,000 was out of the question – perhaps later on. The expense of the latest sterile environment was, of course, understandable in an innovative centre like the Centre for Hip Surgery where it had been perfected, but judged to be unnecessary in a peripheral hospital like Halifax. Most hospitals managed to carry out hip replacements in their ordinary theatres without an Enclosure. In fact, there was only one in the Yorkshire Region, the University Teaching Hospital, St James's, in Leeds. 'Make a start on the many patients you have on your waiting list for hip replacements, and make the best of what you've got, like your colleagues' I was told. The temptation never really crossed my mind. I knew what I wanted for my patients and myself but wondered how it could be acquired.

In life we're often faced with apparently insurmountable barriers. Direct confrontation is sometimes justified, but usually traumatising. A devious change of tact, a calm but persistent alternative, can sometimes wear objections down and bring capitulation. I had the statistics of wound infection following surgery at my finger-tips and took mental stock of the Yorkshire breweries in and around Halifax, especially the home of Pennine Bitter. I visited a few of them and confirmed the high level of sterility in which their beer was brewed. It had to be so. Otherwise, if a batch of new brew was contaminated by the least trace of bacteria, it would multiply so rapidly that the whole batch would be ruined. Thousands of pounds of good beer would have to be destroyed. Sterility in an efficient brewery is, therefore, as near perfect as can be, like that in a Sterile Enclosure. I made three slides and set off with a projector on a lecture tour of anyone who was interested. I covered groups of hospital workers, all kinds of clubs, church organisations, Women's groups, Youth groups, Old People's groups, Round Tables, Rotarians, Town Councillors on hospital boards, and social and political leaders who could get things done. I showed my first slide, a little man with twisted hips, high, on his own, on one pan of scales heavily weighed down by a batch of Pennine Bitter overflowing its pan and explained that the sterility in our breweries far outweighed our operating theatres. The financial priority lay with the breweries. Then the second slide, after proclaiming the unquestionable advantages of surgery in a Sterile Enclosure, a pan on the scales weighed down by a crowd of dancing figures after successful operations, and the other pan high and almost empty, with only one can of beer on it, financial priorities with a patient bias. Then the third slide with a group of smiling, dancing figures each with a can of beer in their hand, and the scales evenly balanced with a batch of beer on the other side. A balanced approach was needed – money for beer and money for Hip Replacement Surgery (LFAs) in a Sterile Enclosure in Halifax.

Our Hospital Management Board was inundated with questions, letters and phone calls. It got the message. An Enclosure was installed six months after my appointment, to keep me quiet, and my experience with joint replacement surgery started. Halifax was the second centre in the Yorkshire Region to acquire the facility. It was, I think, justified, as patients were to come from far and near for operations in it and surgeons were to come to see it in use, and some to use it themselves. Patients and surgeons alike were to reap its benefits.

The boys soon settled into school life in Halifax, each in his own way. Jim, the pioneer, took his work seriously fitting into the lifestyle of his peers. It wasn't cool to be too bright. His problem, as the school years passed, was indifference. David, though he worked hard and did well, never really felt at home at school. His sensitivity led to his being a scapegoat in his early years till exasperation boiled over one day and he lashed out at a ring-leader bully subduing him once and for all and gaining his classmates' respect. John was always methodical in his work, on top of it, a good pupil destined to be a credit to his school. He did well at All Saints' and was more than a credit to his brothers' name when he moved to Crossley-Porter. Outside school all three made their mark on the Boys Brigade which gave them an outlet in developing relationships with boys from different backgrounds, pride in themselves and their Company, disciplined respect for their officers and their cause, 'Sure and

Steadfast', an opportunity to play the bugle, drum the drum or sound the cymbals in the band, attend regular Church parades and celebrations in many parts of Halifax, and take as keen a part as they wished in football, hiking, camping, swimming and the annual pantomime. In time, they were each to win all the prestigious Company prizes. No sooner would one return his award for a year than another would win it and bring it home. Our mantelpiece was seldom clear for very long.

In our first year back in Halifax, before Ailsa started school, she and Katie revelled in the security of their new home. Avril was always there to attend to their every need, to share moments of anxiety and moments of hilarity, to bond with them in the mix of domestic activity, and Cindy a contented good-natured companion.

They grew proud of their brothers, waving them off to school in the morning, greeting them on their return, squabbling and playing with them according to their moods and the opportunity. But all too soon the pre-school days would be over. The business of school would start. For Avril, the cycle of standing with a child on its first day at school waiting for the line of new pupils to go in which started with Jim in 1968 would start again with Ailsa in 1974 and end only with Kate in 1976. In fourteen years all five of our children would have attended Primary School at All Saints' in Halifax.

The freshly painted blue notice board outside the massive church building opposite the Royal Halifax Infirmary which was rapidly becoming a second home to me proclaimed to anyone who read it:- 'Heath United Reformed Church', and in brackets to explain itself, 'Former Congregationalist.' The United Reformed Church came into existence in 1972 with the union of most of the churches in the Congregational Church in

England and Wales and most of their counterparts in the Presbyterian Church of England. It was, from the start, the blend of Congregationalism and Presbyterianism which attracted us to the new Church. It was then only a year old, different, unknown, nonconformist. Avril and I spent several hours questioning and re-questioning the poor minister of Heath URC. He was tireless, patient, as persistent with his explanations as we were with our inquisition. It seemed the natural spiritual home for us. We were soon part of it.

Within a year or so of our return to Halifax our new life had all but taken us over. My work and Avril's reintroduction to Family Planning, which she could contain in the domesticity of our family, took on an enjoyable routine, fulfilling but increasingly exacting. The family had found a niche for itself. Cindy, faithful and good-natured as ever, could lie on the hot tar road at the back of our house asleep until a passing car might rouse her, at peace with herself and the world, a measure of which we all experienced. Granny and Grandad from 'Morven' would visit us now and again and we'd invade their peace in 'Morven' for short breaks whenever we could. Everyday life in 'Wheatstone', in Halifax, had almost completely possessed us, but not quite. Echoes from the past began to crop up, and not just of the ambulance drivers who wryly reminded me of my brush with them when I examined them for the St John's Ambulance Brigade a few years earlier and failed most candidates.

Carving a turkey on Christmas day in the Infirmary in Halifax was an unwritten part of my duties. I knew it and the patients and staff knew it and our family knew it. Five stockings opened before the sun was up, presents round the Christmas tree at home distributed and opened, a hasty breakfast, the turkey in the oven checked, its progress from before the day's excitement started guaranteed, and we were off to a short service at Heath, presents on display – all before crossing to the hospital and the ceremony of the turkey carving. In the early years the family willingly joined me doing the rounds on Christmas day but as the years passed and they grew older the novelty of their father carving the turkey on one of the wards, dressed sportingly in a well-padded over busty nurse's uniform, flaunting black stockings and suspenders, cavorting round the hospital spreading cheer before returning home for our own family Christmas dinner, left them with more than just their memories. Christmas carols round the wards on Christmas eve, often with a touching scene in the Children's ward, or a volley of oaths from a drunk with a head injury in Casualty drowning for a moment the mystic peace of 'Still the night; Holy the night!; Sleeps the world; hid from sight', left a more sobering lasting memory.

But on our first Christmas back in Halifax, word must have got round that I might read a Lesson at the Christmas Service on one of the wards on the Sunday before Christmas. Waiting my turn with the other readers I struck up a stilted conversation with a Staff Nurse only to learn that, Yes, she came from the West Indies, and Yes, it was from Guyana, and even more surprisingly, that, Yes, she came from Berbice and her married name was 'Cummings' of the same 'Miss Cummings' Kindergarten School' I first attended twenty-five years short of a century ago. Echoes of the distant past had started.

'Put me through to the Regional Transplant Officer,' I said to the switch-board operator late one night after careful consideration. I took my responsibilities in the A&E Department seriously, insisting that I be called in whenever a potentially fatal case was admitted in order to assess the viability of organs for transplantation. My patient was an elderly man with no dependent relatives, brain dead beyond all doubt but with viable kidneys suitable for transplant surgery. The formalities and practicalities were straightforward. I waited, wondering, for what seemed a long time, till the girl on the switchboard came back. 'You're through to Leeds,' she said and I could hear a chuckle at the other end, and then, as I explained who I was, 'It is you, Bill Nicol!' the voice said. We chatted animatedly for some time before we got round to the reason for my call. It was Ralph Kester, my General Surgical Senior Registrar colleague from my Dundee days. He was now the Consultant at St James' Hospital in Leeds in charge of the Transplant Service. A few hours later he was in Halifax with his Registrar and an icebox. The theatre had been prepared and the kidneys removed. As the first light of day broke through the darkness of a long night, we sat in our 'telly room' reminiscing over a dram. Ralph had at last found a niche for himself where his skills and academic excellence would be recognised in national surgical circles. He was soon a leading authority in the Teaching Unit at Leeds.

As he was leaving, a compatible recipient already selected and being prepared for a kidney transplant at St James', Ralph dropped the name of a friend of his who had qualified with him in Cape Town. 'Who?' I exclaimed, in disbelief. 'Yes, Don Luswazi!' he said again. My friend Don from Umtata was Ralph's friend too from their Cape Town days. Echoes of the past rang out and would reverberate through the years to come. We would all meet again before long, and in our back garden a year later, toast Don's success in the Glasgow Fellowship with 'I belong to Glasgow, dear old Glasgow toon'. The girl who got one of the kidneys in Leeds did well. She'll quite likely be a mother now. The other kidney went, as was the practice, to a hospital in the European Community where a successful transplant was performed.

Perhaps the strongest spur to our activities is necessity. Spreading our wings of involvement in life in Halifax, two principal restraints surfaced, cash and time. Without more funds our activities could not expand. Without more time, or the more disciplined use of it, priorities could be distorted and relationships suffer. The two, time and money, are inextricably related. As my private practice increased so did the income from it, but not commensurate with demands. I'd meet with my accountant at the end of every financial year. Usually each year was better than the year before. He was reassuring but had always to remind me that the taxman's demands had still to be accounted for in the year to come. No matter the heights of my achievements, the end result seemed much the same. Expenses invariably exceeded income. In our early years it was the installation of central heating that ran away with the money. Though the upheaval of rewiring the house as well, in winter, was badly timed the result was good. The penetrating cold of winter without central heating became a thing of the past overnight. The refurbished cloakroom downstairs and the new bathroom upstairs just happened. Increases in the mortgage and insurance cover took care of them, more or less. For more ambitious projects an extra source of income would be needed. Avril's return to Family Planning Clinics and, a little later, to Anaesthetics at the General Hospital and the Infirmary were a welcome addition to the overall finances while, at the same time re-establishing a professional identity for her.

Financial anxieties and the use of time crept into our lives. I prided myself on being able to take a broader view of things than Avril. I could look beyond the crisis of the moment to the broader side of the picture, no doubt with an element of naivety. Avril was always more cautious. The events of the day and where the money would come from to cope always dominated her thinking. When her parents came down to see us or we went to see them in 'Morven' the uncertainty of their future gave her concern. Grandad's health was deteriorating, his letters to the boys more prophetic, and gestures of generosity more meaningful. When he died of cancer of the lungs a few years later and she'd gone with her mother, her sister, Ailsa, and the minister from Dunblane to bury him in the family grave in Biggar a strand of security was buried with him. When her mother, after a year or so on her own in 'Morven', maintenance bills becoming an increasing liability, finally admitted that she, too, was failing, it was good that our children's last loved grandparent was able to come to us in Halifax to be looked after and cared for. In a remarkable way a remarkable Granny had the clarity of mind to put her affairs in order in 'Morven', pack her car methodically, and drive down to Halifax as if she was going on a holiday. The boys unpacked the car for her and showed her to the front upstairs room made ready for her. Children and adults alike, the boys, the girls, Avril, Leila, and I knew what lay ahead, but no one was afraid. Content and at peace, Bertie Mann, our Consultant Physician friend from across the road, looked after Granny. X-Rays confirmed the same as Grandad. They both smoked. When she died in the General Hospital, after a short Cremation Service in Halifax, we drove through to Dunblane with the family where we met up with Avril's sister, Ailsa, John and Mary, and the minister of Dunblane Cathedral, before journeying through to Biggar again, to lay Granny's ashes with Grandad's. With them, part of Avril which I was never able to resurrect, was gone as well.

From our first holiday in a borrowed caravan in Glencoe in our first year in Halifax we graduated to a trailer with a tent, camping in Wales the next year, and then to a mobile caravan parked and stored in a wooded caravan site in Grassington. In

North Wales, tent pitched, ours was the most organised family on the campsite. The kitchen tabletop served as a cover for the trailer that could be easily converted to a substantial camp table with more than adequate home-made legs. Each season and every holiday-time with the family left its memories. Flying kites with the boys on a windy Welsh beach, frolicking over a nearby hill with the girls like the Von Trapp family in 'The Sound of Music', and singing 'Puff the Magic Dragon' loud enough to wake the Loch Ness monster, are easily brought to mind, as are the barbecues, the saunas, and antique shops in the village of Grassington. But our next summer holiday, summer 1975, would be different. A new era lay ahead.

BAGHDAD

'Where are you going for your holidays?' asked Ailsa's teacher at All Saints School, and most of the class replied with familiar places. 'Baghdad,' murmured Ailsa in an undertone. 'Where?' asked her teacher again and got the same answer. Puzzled for a moment, her teacher then tumbled to where she thought her pupil was going. 'Ailsa's going on her holidays,' she explained to the class, 'to her Grandad'. Poor Ailsa didn't bother correcting her.

Cindy safely settled in the kennels; bags packed and labelled 'Baghdad Hotel', Baghdad, Iraq; passports checked, Avril's and mine each with the five children, Iraq Entrance Visas hardly dried; seven Iraqi Airways passenger tickets examined in detail over and over again; arms still aching from inoculations for typhoid and paratyphoid A and B, Tetanus and other things like Baghdad tummy but worst effects resolved; traveller's cheques and some loose Iraqi diners carefully counted and evaluated; letters of acceptance and welcome from my employer for the month, the President of Medical City Teaching Hospital, gone over again and placed with other documents in my satchel; a few neighbours informed, and it was late to bed with tales of Ali Baba and the Forty Thieves in our heads. Before dawn, around four a.m. next morning, each child primed, silent, sleeping but wide awake with expectation, Avril and I as spellbound as the other travellers, the packed car slid through the streets of Halifax, out on to the M62, and down the M1, the dancing shadows of the Sheffield kilns in the arc light of the steel works bringing us back to the reality of the occasion. The children asleep, or just about, I stifled a yawn. 'We'll soon be on the M4 on the way to Heathrow.' 'Should be there about 7,' said Avril, shifting in her seat.

Two months before I'd answered an advert in the back of the BMJ:- 'The Ministry of Health of Iraq Medical City Teaching Hospital invites applicants from Senior Consultants with appropriate qualifications. Those with teaching experience will be especially welcome.' A list of specialities followed, including Orthopaedics. 'Salary 7000 ID per calendar month (approximately £1000) negotiable, with tax concessions. Accommodation free, and travel free. Appointments 3 months to one year.' I wrote from curiosity more than anything else, sending my credentials and explaining that I couldn't come for even three months, but that I could for one, which I'd take as part of my annual leave. In less than a week a telegram arrived. 'Yes, please! When can you come? Next month, or the next. And will you be bringing your wife?' We hadn't thought of Avril going as well. Her airfare and accommodation would be included. It didn't take long for a quick calculation of airfares for the family and what my £1000 was likely to cover to be made. 'Sorry, unable to come next month,' was my reply, 'but can come the following month, in August 1975 and will bring

99

my wife and our five children aged 14, 13, 11, 6, and 4. Please include their tickets and charge the cost to me.' A few telegrams on, and phone calls to the Iraqi Embassy, and Airways, the final telegram dated 19th July 75, and our holiday had all but started.

Checking in at any airport can be an anxious time. Doing so at Terminal Three at Heathrow is often anything but smooth, but at the Iraqi desk, it was out of this world. Enveloped in a mass of humanity, pushing and shoving, chattering, shouting, laughing, arguing uncontrollably, words like *'imshi'* and *'macho* and meaningful expressions like *'Insh Alla!* and *'Sabach Alcare!'* which were soon to trip off our lips like native Iraqis filling the heavily heated and scented air around us, we jostled our way to a desk and checked in. The formalities of being frisked going through Passport Control and last minute shopping in Duty Free, though less traumatising, had been as exciting. Boarding passes in our hands, the Tannoy at last announced, 'Boarding Iraqi Airways Flight 044 for Baghdad.' The massive Jumbo Jet soon took to the air, smoothly and effortlessly. The clunk-clunk of the release of seat belts told everyone they were on the way.

With the setting of the sun we set down at Baghdad Airport. 'What would it be like?' The girls by the hand, the boys ahead we made our way down the stairs from the green and white monster that had brought us to Baghdad. On the tarmac below it was like standing in a hair dryer. The gentle breeze of the night was hot and dry. There would be no getting away from an unchanging day temperature of around 120 degrees Fahrenheit (approx 50 degrees Centigrade) anywhere outdoors in Baghdad till returning home four weeks later. A fellow passenger, a Cardiologist from Leeds, joined us and, crouched on the floor of the Arrivals Hall against a wall, our baggage reclaimed and stacked beside us, we waited for 'what next'. Before long we were in a pick-up, street lights and passing headlights, neon-lit poster billboards and illuminated characters illustrating many of the hot spots of Baghdad passing by on our way to 'Hotel Baghdad' in the centre of the city. Tired, half asleep, half awake, bemused by our new surroundings, the still hot dry air of the night fanning us soothingly, reminding us that we'd chosen the hottest time of the year to visit Baghdad, we reached our journey's end.

In the spacious lobby of the hotel we looked around before checking in at the Reception desk. Around midnight, everything was quiet. The cool air-conditioning was almost chilling. Ornate onyx ashtrays on ornate teak tables in the tile-floored lobby, luxurious lounging chairs in abundance announced that smoking was permitted, but a prominent notice at the entrance made it clear that a strict code of conduct was expected. In bold Arabic print with bolder English subtitles, which we could read, we got the message, 'No Consummation in the Lobby!' Neither sex nor alcohol was in our minds then. In no time we had checked in at the Reception desk and were all fast asleep in 'Hotel Baghdad'. Our experience in the land of the Arabian Nights had started.

Next morning, breakfast in the hotel dining room over, before going our different ways, Avril with the children to the British Club and me, with my new colleagues, to Medical City, we ventured down the lift to the mezzanine between the ground floor and the first floor, explored entrances to conference rooms, the casino, and the grand Presidential Suite reserved almost exclusively for the highest ranking government officials, before walking down the wide stairway to the lobby, friendly inquisitive eyes on us, and negotiated the revolving door entrance into the world outside. The sun was blazing bright, the temperature in the shade already over 90 degrees. Declining hooting red and white taxis eager for business, the girls in colourful cotton dresses, the boys in shorts and open neck, short sleeve shirts, Avril in a floral summer frock, me in light flannels, a blue shirt with neatly rolled up sleeves and tie, we made our way through the gathering morning crowd, along a small approach road, to busy Saadoon Street to turn and look back at our impressive Baghdad Hotel. Over the frontage, a bright red-lettered poster proclaimed something in Arabic, which meant 'One Arab Nation with Eternal Aim.' Cynics added to 'One Arab Nation with Eternal Aim', 'Along the Barrel of a Rifle.' Iraq has had a turbulent history for many years. Little did I know when I was graduating in Medicine at St Andrews in 1958, that at the same time, on July 14th , a new Republic was being proclaimed in Iraq, and that I would be in its capital, Baghdad, with my family seventeen years later. The blood of the execution of the King, King Faysal II, the Crown Prince and several others in the centre of Baghdad had hardly dried when the leader of the first Revolution in 1958, Brigadier Kassen, himself was executed in 1963. Then followed several military coups before a Baa'th Socialist Party with a Nationalist aim 'One Arab Nation' with close ties to the Soviet Union and deteriorating relations with our United Kingdom, was established with the Revolution of 1968, again in July. Al Baker, the leader of the Baa'th Party became President but power lay with the Army, and especially with the uncompromising Saddam Hussein who engineered the coup of 1968. From the roadside we'd soon become familiar with the cavalcades of dignitaries in limousines, outriders flanking them, lights flashing and sirens screeching, heavily armed security escorts more than just a presence, which were accepted as part of the city life. And closer still, we were to stand back in anonymity in the lobby of Baghdad Hotel while a procession made its way to the Presidential suite, the President, Al Baker in the forefront, but Saddam Hussein at his side. In our time in Baghdad overtures of friendship were being encouraged between our country and Iraq, but they were not to last long. Saddam Hussein was to succeed Al Baker as President, again in July, in 1979 and substantially suppress all opposition.

In the car on the way to Medical City with my Cardiologist friend from Leeds we were able to sit back and absorb the sights and sounds and smells of Baghdad. In the coffee houses and pavement cafes venerable gentlemen sucking at and puffing bubbling hookahs instilled a sense of calm in the otherwise chaos around. Others smoked their cigarettes while sipping their Turkish coffee, fingering their worry beads or studying the backgammon board in front of them. Glimpses down side streets revealed other worlds of wood-craft, metal-work, copper, silver and gold soukhs, silks and spices, professional signs attracting attention to travel agents, barbers, money exchangers, herbalists, homeopaths, chiropractors, dental practitioners and every kind of medical specialist. Name plates down one particular street with impressive qualifications like M.B., B.S., Specialist in Gynaecology, General Surgery, Bone Setting, Childhood Diseases, M.R.C.S., F.R.C.S., M.R.C.P., M.D. made Harley Street look tame in comparison. From ancient historic towering buildings invading many narrow streets shuttered windows, verandas displaying vocal owners, laundry, pets, cooking in progress, and air cooling boxes struggling valiantly to transform the stagnant heat of the city into bearable freshness for survival, a timeless age cried out to a passing twenty century.

Formal greetings and sincere words of welcome from the President of Medical City over numerous cups of thick black bitter Turkish coffee which I grew to like and found refreshing soon broke down any reserve there might have been. I warmed almost instantly to most of my new temporary Iraqi colleagues. A quick look round the Teaching Hospital, the Orthopaedic wards half empty, Clinics and Operating almost at a stand still confirmed what we were told. 'It's holidays. The students are on holiday for the summer, and most of the doctors are away, abroad in England or on the coast, in Kuwait or Saudi, to avoid the extreme heat in Baghdad.' We'd come at the height of the summer. There would be very little to do at Medical City, certainly no lectures to give and no students to teach. But the real reason for our presence was in Ibn Sina Hospital, the VIP Hospital in the Socialist Republic of Iraq which was, in effect, more private than most of the Private Hospitals at home. It would be there that the British Specialists would meet and treat the most wealthy or most influential government functionaries. Our names had gone out on TV with our specialities to attract patients with specific problems. British Medicine was in favour then but would decline a few years later when our countries fell out.

My first day's work was over and I could join my family. The heavy, iron gate slammed closed. The heat and noise and smells of Baghdad locked out, the welcome oasis of the British Club materialised like a mirage before my eyes. From a gently swinging hammock in an alcove of grape-vines at the side of the pool a figure sat up. A small body on a lie-low turned towards me. Hands in the swimming pool started waving. Avril and the family had spotted me. Shoes kicked off, tie removed, in the shade, on a pool-side chair, the events of the day unfolded. After I had left in the morning Avril had gathered her escorts around her, checked out of the hotel, hailed the first taxi she could attract, and was on her way to the British Club. I could at once live the taxi ride as if I was with them. From the girls I could all but feel the spray of the water cascading from the apex of the 'Ali Baba and the Forty Thieves' monument, each vessel overflowing into another, perpetually filled from the top by the handmaiden Morgiana who, you will remember from the stories of *The Thousand and One Nights,* had saved her master from being killed and robbed by the forty thieves hidden in the forty earthen jars by pouring boiling water on them. The traffic circling Morgiana and the forty thieves hidden in the forty jars hardly noticed her, but we did. From the boys the vivid description of their taxi ride to the Club confirmed mine to Medical City. Their accounts of the Iraqi taped music in the taxi and their friendly driver's non-stop broken English chatter along with the confusing blend of the sight of red London double-decker buses and the sights and sounds of mystical Baghdad, to say nothing of the incessant blaring of car horns, demanded that every detail be taken in. From Avril the massive blue domed mosque in the centre of Baghdad and the elaborate monument to commemorate the recent Revolutions of 1958 and 1968, the long bloody history of struggle through the years, etched in carvings about as gruesome as the blood on the streets at the time of critical beheadings, had made their mark on her, and she in turn on me. At last their taxi ride was over. In the Club they could relax, soak up the simple comforts of the pool, purchase appetising chips and fried eggs from the club house, or beans and toast, or salads and soft drinks like '7 Ups' and cokes, find new friends among other ex-patriots, talk of home and the heat, what was on at the open air film show in the relative cool of the evening, and exchange a fascinating blend of gossip and facts about how well we were all fitting into our new, transient life in Baghdad.

Back at the hotel for dinner and early bed, a surprise awaited us. The manager at the Reception desk greeted us like family friends. He had reorganised our accommodation arrangements to reduce the cost for our five children to virtually nil and was eager to tell what he had achieved.

Smiling, suppressed anticipation only partly concealed, he beckoned us over for a chat. 'It's been arranged,' he said. 'You and your wife and five children will be our guests. The hotel will be your home. Our pleasure!' We were all taken up in the lift to the second floor and shown to our room. Ceremoniously the door was unlocked, and we were ushered in. Along the long dividing wall between the room next door and ours were five beds, one double bed for Avril and me, four single beds, one each for the three boys and Ailsa, and a cot for Katie. With a window overlooking the drive to the hotel entrance, a balcony far too hot to sit out on except for the small hours of the night, and an en-suite bathroom, we had everything we needed. 'And you should not go to the dining room for meals', the accommodating manager continued. 'You should have breakfast and dinner in your room. Room Service! Like most of the other doctors with families. You'll want dinner for two in your room tonight?' he assumed as he left, 'In an hour?' 'Yes, please!' we said with one voice, hungry after our first long day in Baghdad. Room Service! –breakfast and dinner – was more than adequate but only one 'iron guts' (guess who??) in our family sampled the traditional 'sheep's brain' delicacy.

Clinics at Ibn Sina took on a regular pattern. Patients from far and near were booked in every morning and often in an afternoon. Through an interpreter, or relative who could speak some English, a history was taken. An examination followed and an assessment given. Seldom was there any need for urgent surgery or definitive treatment other than general advice. Invariably a plastic shopping bag, often with a 'Marks and Spencer's' name on it which raised no eyebrows, would be emptied on to the desk in front of me with all the medications prescribed over the course of an illness, from the UK, mostly Harley Street, the USA, many Eastern and most Western European countries, and neighbouring Arab countries. My medical upbringing made me resistant to adding to a bag of tablets merely to show that I had another name to add to an already overloaded list of cures. My approach of listening, discussing, reassuring and explaining why one course of action seemed most appropriate and another quite unnecessary was often refuted, but sometimes appreciated. Exploitation of vulnerable patients, often with more money than sense, by my own and allied professions made my blood boil. The worst of Harley Street and Private Medicine was exposed. My task was often to explain that my new patients could get as good treatment in Iraq as they could abroad, that half the tablets they had been given were unnecessary, that there was no need for a letter to the Ministry of Health advising that a patient and a family companion travel to the UK or USA for Physiotherapy or repeated X-Rays, and that popular mud baths in Bulgaria for most joint ailments, would be unlikely to improve things. But there were some patients with severe advanced disease, desperately in need of specialist treatment in centres of excellence. I had no hesitation in supporting their applications for urgent assessment and treatment out of the country if I was uncertain of local resources or skills. Specifically, the large number of grossly disabled patients, from infants to young children and people in their prime to people in advanced years, with hip joint disease, exceeded my expectation. Maybe word had got round that a Hip Surgeon was in the city. Many had had several operations with no clear-cut objective in sight, each compounding their overall problems. At an end stage, no further surgery could be of any help. Patient explanations, reconciling patient and family to the reality of their predicament, were always painful and time consuming, but gratifying in the end. Several, however, could be helped by Low Friction Arthroplasties, and would be seen again, this time in Halifax, on Princess Royal Ward before major surgery the following day. A growing number would feature in my series of *Less Common Indications for Low Friction Arthroplasty of the Hip Joint*

But when I joined the family at the British Club it was very often they who had more exciting news for me than I had for them. 'You'll never guess who turned up today!' they exclaimed, one day, in one voice. 'Two men from Halifax. Drivers of a great big Mackintosh toffee articulated container van from the factory behind the station in Halifax.' They'd driven day and night, more or less non-stop, down the A1, crossed the Channel (no 'Chunnel' then!) and raced across Europe to Iraq, ending up exhausted and dehydrated at the British Club in Baghdad two days earlier than they should have in order to have a few days in the sun before returning home. Grossly water and salt depleted, they'd made for the bar, downed a few pints of beer, and collapsed deeply comatose for several hours before coming round slowly to tell their tale. Intrigued by their new friends from Halifax, the boys couldn't help introducing themselves. 'How do you manage to find your way all that distance from Halifax to Baghdad?' they asked, and got the answer, 'It's simple, lad. Straight down the Motorway, across Europe on the autobahns to Ankara, and turn right at Ankara for Baghdad.' 'Do you know, by any chance, how the Dukes got on last week?' asked Jim, a keen follower of the Halifax Speedway Meetings. 'Of course!' replied one of the drivers, his blood sugar and electrolytes now in balance. He, too, was a fan of the Dukes. For the next half-hour they were both back in Halifax, the roar of the bikes in their ears, the smell of the dust in their nostrils, oblivious to the uniqueness of the Arabian nights of the moment.

All too soon our holiday was at an end. We'd said our Good-byes. Our affection for the friends we'd made and our fascination with the Arabian mysteries of magical Baghdad would endure the ups and downs of time, the destruction of warfare and the fanaticism of an Iraqi President who made a notorious name for himself in history. The day before we left was pay-day. Along with my Cardiologist friend from Leeds, I was taken to a small branch of the Rafidain Bank in a side street by an official from Medical City. A few signatures in a crowded lobby of the bank, waiting in silence trying to look as if we knew what was happening, and we were summoned to a guarded teller's grid. Papers exchanged, passports stamped, smiles and nods, and a wad of notes was thrust casually into our hands. "Check it," we were told, and fumbled through £1000 in £50 notes. I'd never had so much money in my hands before. Hotel bills paid, we took our leave. In Heathrow the air was cool and fresh in midsummer. On the flight home Katie wrote about it to her Granny. 'It was a big plane', she wrote, 'I was sick. And it was green and white.'

But apart from our general interest in other peoples, their cultures and mother customs, our family holidays in Baghdad in July 1975 and the following year were opportunities to earn some extra cash and the start of openings in other Middle Eastern countries which followed. By using part of my annual time off from my job in Halifax I could make enough to pay off the tax man from time to time, finance holidays abroad for the family and subsidise a continuous series of home improvements to 'Wheatstone', 'our home', 'our house', the place where we all belonged. A kitchen extension, a new double garage, two additional bedrooms and a bathroom in the attic, rewiring and central heating, and a new stairway to the attic would all, in time, be made possible. To a fault, if that's possible, I was always open with my accountant, declaring every dinar and riyal I made. In all, during our seventeen years in Halifax I would be away from home, somewhere in the Middle East, for a total period of almost a year. The opportunities were there to be taken, the advantages there to be seen, the disadvantages less obvious, hidden, never articulated, but no less real. This letter from Avril at home, in 'our home' in 'Wheatstone' in Halifax to me on my own in Baghdad, in retrospect gave more than hints of our inner feelings:-

'Friday night,' she wrote, *'was the BB P. and F. night, and a most triumphant event. The whole thing went with a great swing and the boys collected all their hard earned badges. John got the 'Best Recruit' shield and David the medal for attendance, uniform etc. and to crown it all Jimmy got the highest honour – the Lyon Trophy for loyalty to the Company.*

I do wish you'd been there to share his glory. He was so overcome and we all felt very proud. It is a silver plated figure of a discus-thrower-type of Olympic man and holds pride of place in the window alcove, with John's shield. The big wig who was there to present the prizes had said to Jim when he went up for his badges, 'You're well on the way to the President's Badge.' When he went up for his trophy he said there was no doubt about it. I was so glad for Jim. The Ackroyds congratulated me later, and also Mr Jagger and Mr Hoyle. I felt great. I wish you'd been there. The girls enjoyed the do and we saw John with his drum for the first time. On Thursday evening I took David to the Woodside Baths to take his swimming test. It was most arduous – he was the only one – swimming clothed and treading water for three minutes. He said he was exhausted, but he passed. Mr J told me that he'd done extremely well. Good old Dave.'

Out of the blue, one day, a letter arrived from the Vatican, or at least from Rome. The 'Vatican City' franked envelope confirmed it and a week later a phone call confirmed its contents. 'Doctor,' said a distant voice from the past, 'it's Sister Oranna. How are you, and Mrs Nicol, and the children?'

Before I could answer, without any excitement in her measured tones, which was in my immediate response, she started into the business at hand. She'd moved from Umtata soon after we'd left and spent a few weeks in the former Rhodesia before being transferred to a nursing home in Rome. The Mother Superior Matron of the home had been involved in a road accident a while ago and was left paralysed below the waist. From a wheelchair she'd managed to cope with her work till recently. Painful muscle spasms and cramps were making life intolerable for her. Watching her German-speaking Superior with a smattering of Italian but no English deteriorate, Sr Oranna thought back to our days at the Bedford Centre outside Umtata. Some of our Paraplegic patients with spinal tuberculosis which we operated on did well. Perhaps, even at this late date, surgery might be of help. At least an assessment with investigations might be worthwhile. Her patient, Sr Hemma, agreed. A letter from the Vatican, a phone call, and a week later the patient and her nurse flew into Leeds/Bradford Airport.

A Calderdale Area Health Authority ambulance was there to meet them. On the way along the corridor to Princess Royal Ward a little Filipino auxiliary nurse crossed herself. Our ward sister tossed her head. 'They've arrived!' she exclaimed. 'In that cubicle,' she pointed. Sr Oranna had already made herself known when I met them on the ward. She readily made herself available to our nursing staff to help with the heaviest nursing, advice on every detail of her patient, interpret for doctors, nurses, administrators and clerical staff in order to ensure that our patient, though she couldn't speak a word of English, understood and appreciated the implications of all that was said around her. Sr Oranna would escort her patient for X-Rays and other investigations, and to and from the operating theatre with her unique blend of authority and willing submission. She

111

would, in effect, work in our hospital supervising the care of her Mother Superior, but live at 'Wheatstone' with us.

Ours was, as you can imagine, like any family home, a centre towards its members gravitated, especially at meal times, and dispersed between times, often leaving in a hurry for some activity or project like an appointment or a meeting, buoyed up and in good mood, perhaps from some kind of achievement, or dismal and even dejected when things were not going well. We were all used to visits from grandparents and relatives and, occasionally, from friends, but never before by a nun, a nun with all her religious routines, the full flowing habit of a Nursing Sister and a Sister in ecclesiastical orders. We were all a little apprehensive. Our feelings were mixed; embarrassed at having a nun at such close quarters, but overjoyed at seeing an old friend with so many stories to share in again of special days in South Africa. As it turned out our fears were unfounded. Our guest noticed Cindy as soon as she walked in the back door. She made no fuss of the dog and Cindy made no fuss of her. They just knew each other like the old days in Umtata. The boys were a bit inhibited to start, but their curiosity soon got the better of them. They were soon chatting about incidents like the time they went to a Drakensberg Boys Choir concert in Umtata and one of the nuns recorded it all on a cassette recorder concealed in her all-enveloping apron unknown to the officials, and presented us with it as a farewell present when we left. At first they timed their departure for school carefully to avoid having to walk with Sr Oranna who left about the same time for the hospital, but after a few days they seemed not to be embarrassed by her with them. In fact, she soon got to know some of their friends who were intrigued by the stories she was happy to tell them on the way up the road. She reminded Ailsa about Foxy, the dog at Bedford, who became so attached to her and was photographed with her several times. Kate's memory of her is having her hair plaited so tightly that she felt she was being scalped. But being so afraid to move that she'd sit through anything without a word of complaint.

Avril and I enjoyed sitting in the kitchen with Sr Oranna reminiscing about our times in Bedford, especially the treble-layered, cross-cut sandwiches that the Sisters produced for us in the side room between operations. Once our good friend's spiritual needs had been met after we had shown her the way to the Roman Catholic Church on Skircoat Road and introduced her to the priest, and she could attend Mass whenever she could, we were free to talk religion as well as medicine and nursing without reserve. She and Sr Hemma were inundated with visitors from most churches around. As investigations progressed and a decision was made to carry out an exploratory operation at the site of spinal disruption, our patient's cubicle on Princess Royal Ward became a hive of activity with the two Sisters attracting more and more well-wishers. No-one, patient, nurse, attendant staff, doctor, priest, minister or cleaner would pass by without a word of encouragement or a cheery wave. The illuminated cross on the spire of the URC across the road, seen at night in the gap between the partly closed curtains through the clear glass of the upper panes of the otherwise frosted windows, seemed a natural focus.

Surgery was fixed for my Monday morning list. On the Sunday, prayers were said for Sr Hemma in many of the churches, the Nursing Home in Rome and in the Infirmary. At Mass in the little church which Sr Oranna had made her own, they must have been intense. In Sr Hemma's cubicle where she had become the focal point for many people in the hospital, prayers of many kinds were many and spontaneous. In our Heath URC they seemed to speak for everyone in the Church and especially to me. I never went in for much conscious prayer at the beginning of an operation. Any that there had ever been was implicit and unspoken. The next morning, in the changing room, I was unusually composed. Throughout the operation, as before and after, I was conscious of an ecumenical hot-line between heaven and earth. There was no miraculous cure. In fact, it was just what had been anticipated. The spinal cord had been completely severed at the time of injury. There was no question of any return of function. But surrounding constricting fibrous tissue was excised to decompress some remnants of nerve roots, and the end result was thought to have been well worthwhile. Muscle spasm and painful cramps subsided and were brought under control with antispasmodic therapy. When the two nuns returned to Rome a reception committee was at the airport to meet them. Their prayers of thanksgiving and gratitude were, for me, a lasting reminder that any specific surgery is set in a holistic background.

SAUDI ARABIA

On a ward round, one morning, my secretary called me to the phone. It was 'Hospital Corporation International'. Would I be available for a locum at the Specialist Hospital and Research Centre in Riyadh, Saudi Arabia as soon as possible, within two or three weeks at the latest. Sunk deeply in the soft leather seats in the waiting room of the Corporation's main office in London a week later I got chatting to another Orthopaedic Surgeon, from York, also being interviewed for a locum in the same hospital in Riyadh. They'd be glad to have us both, as soon as possible. There was no doubt about the urgency. Official contracts were quickly drawn up, every minute detail of employment conditions gone into in the thorough, meticulous American way of the employing agency. Two weeks later I was reclining in a lush, first class seat on a Saudia Airways Boeing 747 winging its way to a new experience in Riyadh at the heart of Saudi Arabia, munching a continuous supply of almond stuffed dates, sipping endless cups of Arabic coffee and non-alcoholic drinks between elaborate five-course meals in a flush of excitement amid perpetual reminders that I was welcome. The arrival and transfer to an accommodation village in the hospital grounds went like clockwork.

Refreshed after a few hours sleep, I walked through the entrance of the Hospital complex next door into the grounds of the King Faisal Specialist Hospital and Research Centre. The whole place was out of this world. Flower beds and lush green, regularly vacuumed lawns more than amply sprayed with water jets and fountains illuminated in every colour of the rainbow at night gushed heavenwards into the cloudless sky. The ceiling of the entrance hall was one massive crystal chandelier. The carpeted walls of all its long, wide, street-like corridors were, like the lawns on the outside, regularly vacuumed and sprayed with Arabic scent. The referral health-care facility, officially opened three years before, in1975, was every bit what it claimed in its glossy brochure.

After reporting to the Director of Medical Affairs I was taken on an orientation tour, given one set of standing orders after another, checked through security, passed through Personnel where I gave, among other details, permission for my remains to be disposed of as requested in the event of my death, and finally taken to the Operating Room where I was given a white coat and met Bill, one of two Orthopaedists. By this time I was beginning to get used to the highly efficient, American-orientated, organisation of the hospital. But what I was not prepared for was the reception I got from Bill, my colleague with whom I was to work or replace.

When he was introduced to 'Dr Nicol from England' he was taken aback. He knew nothing about my coming. With a hostile air, he turned and walked out. I followed, bewildered. Along one of the long corridors to the entrance hall, and out the automatic, electrically controlled front door, to the solitude of the open air, in the blazing sunshine of the morning, but out of earshot of any observers we strode. At last Bill broke the awkward silence. An explanation broke through his pensive mood. 'Oh Yes!' he said, 'I think I see.' He'd been at work at a routine clinic three weeks before and had asked one of his patients to wait a minute till he'd finished seeing another. The girl, who happened to be a Princess, went to her brother, who went to one of the Princes, who went to another, etc. etc. who went to the King, who said, in his wisdom, 'The doctor was busy. He must have had too much work to do. How many Orthopaedists are there at the hospital?' 'Two, your Majesty!' he was informed. 'Get two more,' he demanded, and the phone rang during my ward round in Halifax. The urgency in the voice of the caller from 'Hospital Corporation International' was accounted for. 'If you're surprised to see me here,' I told Bill, 'there's another Orthopod coming next week, Brian from York!'

I found life at the 'King Faisal Specialist Hospital and Research Centre' stimulating and challenging, but, at the same time, perplexing and frightening. The enthusiasm for excellence in all aspects of medicine and nursing care was overwhelming. It rekindled in me the vibrant attention to detail that the Hip Centre in Wrightington had instilled in me. I was glad I had my experience with Low Friction Arthroplasty of the Hip and surgery in a Sterile Enclosure behind me. My lecture on the subject in a superb auditorium was well received. Some of the cases I saw shed light on the general culture of the Kingdom of Saudi Arabia far beyond their medical significance. Amputation was clearly indicated on purely clinical examination supported by radiological and bacteriological investigations when a poor man from the desert was brought to see me with a fungating cancer of his leg. The first obstacle in getting on with the job was convincing my litigation-minded American specialist colleagues that procrastinating with over-elaborate, unnecessary investigations was not in our patient's interests. My course of action finally accepted, hospitalisation for amputation well above the malignant lesion agreed to, albeit with some reluctance from my medical colleagues but not from most of the nurses and certainly not from my patient or his relatives, the second obstacle reared its head. Insurmountable, it looked to me! 'He has no money,' my interpreter informed me, 'and he can't pay for the treatment he needs in hospital.' My pleas for the man's cause were cut short. 'No money to pay for the treatment you want for him?' asked the hospital administrator at Reception more as a statement of confirmation than a question. 'No problem!' My patient's relatives were sent to a government department not far away with a copy of recommendation. An official listened passively to the man's predicament, then lightened up, and said, 'No problem! How much will it cost?' When told he put his hand in his pocket, beneath his robe, and pulled out a wad of notes. 'There you are, take it,' he said. That kind of health care is a bit different from our National Health Service. Reflection of one aspect of life in Saudi is encouraging if not unreservedly reassuring but bewildering.

But there were other facets of life at the 'King Faisal Specialist and Research Centre' which I found decidedly frightening when I was first there in 1978. They mirrored the mood of Saudi then and as I write now, forty years on, have no reason to detect any material change today. Stories of religious sensitivity abounded, even more so than the taboo on alcohol. Tales of floggings for drinking contraband alcoholic drinks like whisky or gin or home-made commonly drunk "Sidiki" and the experiences of unsuspecting Western nurses and secretaries accused of seducing poor, upright but vulnerable, innocent Saudi gentlemen, were never far from everyone's mind. From behind the ample leaves of the financial section of an English local Saudi newspaper, in the library one Saturday morning, scanning the exchange rates to determine the value of the riyals I'd be taking home with me, my face still smarting from over exposure to the Arabian sunrays at the pool-side on the weekend day off, Friday, the day before, a short, inconspicuous article caught my eye. 'Execution After Prayers on Friday.' While I had been sipping my soda, soaking up the sun, trying to decide which curry to choose for lunch, a Saudi girl, caught in adultery, was being stoned to death in the square down town. Judgement had been made. The penalty had been carried out. The next time I met a mullah (Religious leader overseeing Islamic observance) at prayer time in town I jumped at his command, prompted by a big stick, to get inside, off the streets, before the 'Call to Prayer'.

As the years have passed, and now as I write many years in the aftermath of the horrors of destruction of the World Trade Centre in New York and the Pentagon on 11th September, 2001, the relationship between the USA and the Kingdom of Saudi Arabia remains perplexing. I'm still unsure which of the two partners is exploiting the other more. My first encounter with Saudi Arabia was never to be matched again. I'd be back again in Riyadh at the Military Hospital, at the KFSHRC, at the Guard's Hospital in Jeddah, in Dammam, and in Sharjah in the United Arab Emirates on several occasions, as well as once more to Baghdad. Each visit holds its own memories but none made such a profound impression on me as the 'King Faisal Specialist Hospital and Research Centre' on my first visit to the Kingdom of Saudi Arabia.

YORKSHIRE'S THREE PEAKS

'You could come along and take some photos,' I was told. Carlton Boys Brigade was going to do Yorkshire's Three Peaks, Whernside, Pen-y-Ghent and Ingleborough, each well over 2000 ft. high. Well clad for the cold mountain air, good boots for the rocky hill sides and rocky shale slopes, backpacks as light as possible with only essential things like waterproofs, a drink and a few snacks, the boys would set out from Ingleton around 8 a.m., walk to the foot of one of the peaks, climb up it and over it, walk to the next and do the same, completing the Three Peaks and returning to the starting point in Ingleton within twelve hours to collect their authenticated certificates of achievement. At strategic points between the peaks parents and supporters would have feeding points and rest stations prepared. There would be quite a lot of backup and ferrying around to support the actual walkers. My job was to take some photos, just a few with a small camera, but as the date for the Three Peaks approached my role had grown. From a few snaps to some coloured and some black and white, from with my own camera to with some of the boys' as well, the enterprise was extended to include a comprehensive record of the momentous occasion with my heavy-duty cinecamera as well. Avril would meet and drive me to and from the foot of one mountain after another.

On the day, the sky was overcast, a drizzle in the air. On the way home at night each boy proudly clutched his Three

Peaks certificate. There was none for me, but my sense of achievement was no less than that of the boys. Weighed down with photographic equipment getting heavier at every step, snapping boys round every turn, setting off up a peak to be at the top before them and take them coming up through the mist and rain, scrambling down ahead of them while they admired the view from the top to take them coming down, racing from the foot of one peak to the foot of another, and being at rest and food stops between times to record the climbers' every mixed moment, sometimes over talkative, sometimes morose, tired out and weary, inexhaustible at other times are images as clear to me now as the day we did the Three Peaks. It was one of the last projects the boys did together in Halifax before they started leaving home.

It's easy, if we're not careful, to get caught up in the immediacy of the moment in the pattern of our everyday lives, to be perceptive of what's uppermost in our minds and miss out on more subtle nuances crying out for attention but going unheard. My life in our 'boys' family, and amidst the essentially 'mans' professional world around me was a bit like that. I was aware of the 'girls' in our family who played as essential a role as the 'boys' but was, looking back, less conscious of their needs than I should have been. It was only when 'the girls' time at All Saints came to an end, and later when the 'boys' had left home and the 'girls' came into their own that the full realisation that our family was now no longer predominantly a 'boys' family dawned on me. And with it came Avril's increasing assertion of her control over our family affairs. What she had perhaps wanted for us all but hadn't quite achieved in the past, she insisted, in her own way, she would get in the future. With my pragmatic assertions our world had become my world. With the new-found feminism which she found in the changing world we were living through, as well as her determination to 'do what was best for both girls', Avril retired to some extent into herself, like a mother hen with her chicks. Though we didn't realise it, or chose not to realise it, we were being threatened with becoming isolated from each other even though our loyalty to each other never faltered. Our love was assured, but less often demonstrated. In my travels abroad to the Middle East on my own I longed to be home again, to be with Avril again, to rekindle a spark that was always there but in danger of lying dormant. At home again, sleepless nights of frustration tormented me. Avril's propensity for escaping into the world of a good book at bed time became, for me, an obsession which I was to find more and more exclusive, relieved only when I embarked on an Open University course which kept me up reading into the small hours of the night as well.

Towards the end of their Primary School days the girls were moved to 'Rishworth', a Church of England Private School up the Calder Valley on the way to the M62 just beyond Rippenden. The decision for their move was questionable, dominated unwittingly by my assumption that their best interests lay in them both facing the move together rather than one on her own. For Ailsa All Saints' school-days were probably her happiest. Frustrations surrounded her at Rishworth and in her last year at school back in Halifax. In contrast, Kate's school days were mostly happy days. At All Saints' Katie was Ailsa's little sister who soon developed an identity of her own making friends readily and progressing easily through the school, a keen, bright pupil. When she started at Rishworth with Ailsa I was blind to the friendships she had formed at All Saints' which she would sorely miss in her new school. But it was really only when she passed an entrance examination for a place in the same Crossley-Heath-Grammar School her brothers had attended in their time that school days became happy days again. The girls' passing days through Primary and Secondary schools were, therefore, mixed in their individual ways but always supported from their home environment.

But our home in 'Wheatstone' didn't just revolve round Avril and me and our activities and interests, nor the 'boys' or the 'girls'. Family pets also played their part. Cindy, our Maltese poodle from South Africa, who'd traversed the Atlantic and endured six months quarantine before rejoining the family first in Dunblane, then in Appley Bridge, moved with us to 'Wheatstone'. She was always part of the family and part of the home, faithfully placid, running on the moors her mischievous eyes bright and alert, ragged coat blowing in the wind. A reliable favourite of everyone, tolerant of our own family pets but no others, like a Shetland pony at the fire side in the winter, a panting mound of wool on the hot tar roads in the summer, Cindy's life was good for a while until she began to fade away. Subdued for months, her kidney function began to deteriorate. Weak and soulful, just wanting to hide away beneath a bush in the garden on her own, the time came for us to consult our friend the vet next door. Everyone at school, and me at work, the task of taking her for her final trip fell to Avril. With heavy heart she ruffled Cindy's woolly head. Her eyes closed. Peacefully she was gone. At tea-time we all knew. Even our black and white cat, 'Whiskey', knew her friend had left. Always rather detached from the family scene, he wandered off soon after and never returned though we thought we saw him in the distance from time to time. Cindy's successor, a highly-strung Welsh Springer Spaniel, 'Meggie', was quite unique though equally loveable and memorable.

BANGLADESH – A RETURN TO AVRIL'S ROOTS

With getting on for ten years' experience of Low Friction Arthroplasty of the Hip for routine cases of osteoarthritis and an accumulating series of less common indications behind me I was ready, at the drop of a hat, to lecture on or demonstrate my speciality. I had kept detailed records up-to-date as I followed through all my hip and knee arthroplasties personally, analysing the statistics regularly. Most of my lectures and previews to learned bodies calling for papers included the sentence, 'One man's experience of Low Friction Arthroplasty of the hip joint in a peripheral hospital over a period of...' and I upgraded the time span as time passed. So in March 1982, when the 'First National Conference of the Bangladesh Orthopaedic Society' circulated requests in small print in an obscure corner of the Journal of Bone and Joint Surgery I was at once interested. My offer was received with open arms. In fact, I was only one of two Orthopaedic Surgeons from the UK to submit a paper, other guest speakers from foreign countries coming from India and Pakistan. Our visit was to be the first time we would be away from our family as Avril was especially keen to accompany me to Bangladesh and take in Delhi and Agra in India as well. We were not disappointed. Echoes of the very distant past were to mingle with the present in a mixed world of the day which held a fascination for each of us beyond our dearest dreams.

From between the clouds the mosaic of green and brown, more flooded paddy fields and expanses of brilliant blue sea than islets of land that was Bangladesh appeared beneath us as the 'British Air' Dacca flight descended for its final approach. It seemed at one time that there was at least as much chance of landing in the sea as on the land but the touch down was uneventful. The warm night air a welcome change from the artificial air-conditioning of the aircraft, Dacca airport was much better than we had imagined, efficient, well ordered, with welcoming, well-mannered staff. In no time we had made contact with someone from the hospital in Dacca and were on our way to the Intercontinental Hotel. Checked in and escorted to an ample upper floor en suite room, it wasn't long before we were fast asleep in a comfortable bed after the long flight. A doctor would call for us the next morning to take us to the conference.

We both slept like logs. Waking with the dawn of another day, I threw open the curtains. The sprawl of Dacca stretched out before us, smells rising from the warming street beneath. Level with our bedroom window, directly in front of it, the top of the National Broadcasting Building towered over the city below. From a parapet surmounting the building, in front of the aerial, it looked as if someone was looking in on us. 'It looks as if someone is looking at us from the top of the building over there,' I remarked to Avril, still half asleep. 'In fact, there are two or three figures, crouching with sticks or something, pointing at us with guns!' They were. In the night there had been a coup. A new General was in control now. Yesterday's Government had gone. The strategic centres were occupied by the military. The Broadcasting Centre was, naturally, a key point.

Our host was a little late in calling for us but was welcoming and reassuring when we met. 'Sorry for the trouble in the night,' he said, and explained what had happened. It wouldn't affect us much, apart from the curfew, which would restrict movements after dark. And, of course, some of the formalities of the opening ceremony at the conference would have to be changed. The Minister for Health who was to have addressed the gathering was no longer the Minister for Health.

In fact, all the Ministers had gone. What his contribution might have been we never knew, but what we came to experience, the friends we were to meet, the insights we were to be part of, the feelings of national pride still heavy with grief from wounds not yet healed which we were to share in more than compensated for the inconvenience of a disturbed land still trying to come to terms with being no longer the East part of a divided Pakistan but a new, independent, Bengali nation of Bangladesh of only a few years standing.

'The First National Conference of the Bangladesh Orthopaedic Society' was inaugurated with ceremony and poignancy. With the foreign dignitaries and guests, we were all welcomed. In a strange way Avril and I felt as if we belonged in the unique setting amid a largely alien gathering. We stood proudly with our new friends in remembrance of the sixty-four doctors who had been martyred during the liberation movement which culminated in the independence of Bangladesh on March 26, 1971. Then followed a reading from the Koran by one of the doctors and a gesture to the motto of the Orthopaedic Society emblazoned on a banner behind the podium. Written in Bengali, we didn't know what it meant, but nodded dutifully with everyone else. It was only later when we found out what it meant that its full significance struck us – 'Expect great things from God. Attempt great things for God.' These are the words of William Carey, the Baptist, shoemaker, missionary, who left England with his family the year after the formation of the Baptist Missionary Society (the first foreign missionary society) in 1792 and dedicated his life to work as an independent missionary in many parts of India, but mostly in Bengal (now Bangladesh) translating the Bible into several dialects. Primarily devoted to the spread of the Christian Gospel, Carey's love of the Indian people and his respect for their many and varied religious convictions endeared him to the people of his day and posterity. In a predominantly Muslim gathering, in a land far removed from England, in another age of the post-modernism of recent times, in another language, his words 'Expect great things from God. Attempt great things for God', have transcended time, language, professional claim on them, and religious understanding – like the Word of God itself.

My paper went down quite well. It was the first of a long day. All the speakers were briefed on sticking strictly to time. Warning green, then red lights, reinforced with buzzers, would prevent over-running. I rushed through my presentation just in time but as the day progressed less and less attention was paid to the lights and buzzers. Restrictions on timing were relaxed. I was up to most of the questions which came my way and used them as further talking points to emphasise my theme. But one caught me out completely. 'You'll know,' said one bright questioner, 'that in this part of the world, like the whole of the Indian subcontinent, the Middle and Far East, as well as China, most people squat at toilet. How will your Low Friction Arthroplasty for the hip joint stand up to this?' 'It won't,' I confessed. Dislocation of the artificial joint would certainly be a strong possibility under these conditions. My paper was, of course, incongruous with life outside the Western orientated society of the times, a humbling thought.

During daylight hours the streets of Dacca and the neighbouring countryside were as busy as ever. At night, with the curfew, the place was dead outside but hyperactive inside. We were able, however, to see around the 'Rehabilitation Institute and Hospital for the Disabled', admire the live adaptation of a Music and Drama Performance for Bangladesh TV, and empathise with very earnest young doctor friends we'd come to know on a pilgrimage to a memorial monument to the fallen martyrs of the War of Liberation. Having studied the map carefully long before coming to the Bangladesh conference we had, of course, planned a week in India after the Dacca visit taking in the Taj Mahal and other sites, but also a more personal visit down memory lane to what had been the tea growing area in Sylhet in former Assam. What we wanted to do was to capture the atmosphere of the tea gardens of old and enquired hopefully about where best to go and how to get there. 'Chittagong, by air,' our new friends told us emphatically. 'It's in the south-east on the border of the hill tracts with Burma. We'll arrange it for you and put you up at the Country Club.' Most of the Bangladeshi doctors were Army Officers having spent several years on full-time active service or were on active service then. We'd leave most of our luggage at the International Hotel in Dacca, take hand baggage only on the flight to Chittagong, and return for a night back in Dacca before flying on to Delhi.

From a cursory glance at a map, Dacca is no more than 200 miles north-east of Calcutta, not much more than 200 miles south-east of Assam, the tea gardens of India of old with Sylhet at its centre. Though Dacca of the new Bangladesh we were in was a completely new experience for Avril and me, in spite of the restrictions of Martial Law coinciding with our arrival, an air of *déjà vu* hung over the streets of Dacca and the countryside of Bangladesh. Jute mills burnt down in riots in the early sixties reminded us of the headlines in the *Dundee Courier* when we were in Dundee in 1961 and the mill workers there were being laid off work because there was no raw jute from East Pakistan before Bangladesh was Bangladesh. But it wasn't this that we could feel in our bones. Our associations went back much further, to Avril's Grandma and Grandpa Mackintosh. From a job as gardener on an estate near Forres in Morayshire, Scotland, her paternal grandfather set sail for the

Tea Gardens of Assam. In no time he was established in the trade in Sylhet and sent home for the girl to be his bride. Her Grandma set sail for Calcutta immediately. Married at St Andrew's Presbyterian Church there on her arrival, the couple set off up country to a life 'in tea'. Vivid accounts of the kind of life her grandmother lived stuck in Avril's mind. Children were sent home to school not long after they were out of nappies. The isolated life, especially for women, the days of the Raj, of men folk shooting fowl and Bengal tigers, playing polo and carousing in the club house were ingrained in her being and spilled over into mine. The conference over, the advice and generous help from our new friends gladly accepted, a memorable trip back in history was about to unfold.

The Biman Bangladesh Airlines twelve-seat, single prop aircraft swept low over the lagoon at the mouth of the river Chittagong is on. A nod from a uniformed Army doctor accompanying us and an armed escort was authorised. From the airfield and through the busy town it wended its way to the gates of the Chittagong Club. At the door of our chalet we waved 'Good-bye' to our escort and turned inside. Cane furniture, no running water but sparsely-shaded electric lights, meshed doors and windows to exclude unwanted insects and, of course, a heavy mosquito net smothering a straw mattress, and a central fan struggling to rotate fast enough to obliterate the images of its blades set the scene for us. It must have been much the same in Avril's grandparent's time. A respected, ageing, Anglo-Indian chalet attendant was over-helpful. Effusive to a fault, he soon learnt the reason for our visit. 'The good old days of the Raj were golden days,' he confided. 'Not like today,' he added in muffled tones. The Club House would be open in the evening. 'Pop in and settle the account, and have a drink!'

The sun setting rapidly over Chittagong, freshened up with a cold water wash in a floral painted porcelain basin in a freely standing teak frame, we couldn't hide our eagerness to visit the Clubhouse. A short stroll up the wooded driveway and we'd be there. In the fading light the headlights of a few gently purring, high performance, not inexpensive cars pierced the shadows on the way to the Clubhouse. On a veranda at the entrance, a smartly dressed steward was there to welcome us. 'Come in. You're welcome, Madam and Sir, Doctors.' The seats in the grounds around the tennis courts and distant polo field were empty. You'd think that our fore-bearers had just left. The hallway to the reception desk where we settled our account was lined with glass-fronted cabinets containing silver trophies and photographs from bygone days. Engraved shields and cups immortalised past champions. Proud members of polo teams and tennis stars stood out from the many photos which included teams through the years, annual club membership photos outside the Clubhouse and pheasant, partridge and other exotic fowl shoots, none, however, matching the magnificence of the ultimate prize of them all, the Bengal Tiger. It was the tiger which spoke to each of us most forcibly of Grandpa and Grandma Mackintosh, as if they were alive and kicking then as still today.

The ghosts of Avril's grandparents behind us, a day or two on the 75-mile stretch of silvery-golden sand beach at Cox's Bazaar overlooking the Bay of Bengal, a glimpse only of some of the treasures of India through the windows of Taj Express and it was time to move on. In the Charles de Gaul Airport, Paris, on a Sunday morning, our India and Bangladesh experience still fresh in our minds, we began to focus on home again. It would be good to be on the connecting flight to Heathrow soon and back with the family in 'Wheatstone'. The headlines on an English Sunday paper caught our attention. We eyed each other quizzically. 'Task Force sails for Falklands', it read. The Falklands War was under way. The reality of the day had, at a glance, overtaken the nostalgia of our very recent yesterday.

GHANA – A RETURN TO MY ROOTS

The Ghanaian experience had been planned for some time. Letters from Accra and my sister, Mary, and her husband, John Wilson when he was minister of the Ridge Church there hinted at an unusual life in an interesting part of the world, well worth a visit. But the single greatest attraction for me was my boyhood roots in British Guiana and its association with the shame of the Atlantic Slave Trade. I had always been fascinated by the concepts of plate tectonics, continental drift and palaeontology. I poured over maps of the world at different geological times. I pinpointed the coast of Guyana and the coast of Ghana, and traced them back, in my mind's eye, long before continental drift, to one point in a common land mass. I felt with the slaves transported for 300 years or more from the west coast of Africa to the New World, and especially the West Indies. Men and women, boys and girls, torn from their home environments to an unknown life miles across an endless sea touched my sensitivity, but, I wondered, if the time lapse of shifting land masses and the lifespan of mortal man could be seen through infinitely distant eyes... perhaps then, the slaves from the coast of places like Ghana had only stepped a step or two westward to their new homes in places like Guyana. Of course, Guyana and Ghana had been more than near neighbours in past aeons.

In this way the seeds of the Ghana trip germinated. It would be an experience of a lifetime but would have to be, partly, a working holiday for me. The air fares for four adults and two children would be prohibitive. To spend four weeks in Ghana to do justice to the experience I'd use up all but a week of my annual leave. Time passed and the summer months were approaching. We couldn't possibly afford a Ghana trip. We'd have to accept the disappointment and postpone Ghana for another year at least, but providence or something else played a hand. Out of the blue came another request for four weeks in the 'King Faisal Hospital and Research Centre'. The dates coincided with the proposed Ghana trip and a compromise was reached. I'd fly to Ghana with Avril and the family. They'd all stay for four weeks and come home on their own. After less than two weeks I'd leave for Riyadh for four weeks there to earn the funds to cover the Ghana trip. And that's what we did.

Our Ghana contacts had put us in the picture. Ghana was a poor country. Life was austere. Coups were commonplace. Crime was high. Best take travellers cheques in sterling or dollars, no cash, or very little, and, by law, no Ghanaian cedes, only the prescribed cede vouchers, eight cedes to the pound officially but eighty to the pound on the black market. There would be very little to be bought in the shops as anything that appeared in them was almost immediately bought up by street vendors and especially mammies who controlled the economy. Cases packed with practical commodities like three bottles of whisky, six bibles, soap, packets of pre-cooked foods, sweets and six missing scrabble counters which we were asked to take with us, our enthusiasm soaring high, off we set. The arrival gate at Accra was pandemonium. Somehow we gathered our luggage and ourselves together and gravitated to the exit point. From a seat on high at a desk towering over everyone the Customs Officer gave us hell. He assumed that it was his job to do so to everyone coming into the country and did it well. We took it all in good part, patiently answering all the questions we were asked and giving no back-handers to anyone. In time the official gave in and waved us through. In the sea of smiling, shouting, scowling, screeching, crying, laughing faces we saw John Wilson and immediately gave him the thumbs up. Thumbs up from all of us to all our new friends! We'd made it through the customs system and would soon be in one another's arms. But it was stony faces we were met with. A thumbs up gesture, given smilingly or menacingly in Ghana, is the same as our two fingers 'up yours'. We'd failed our first lesson on observing the finer points of sensitive customs.

More attentive to detail, we kept our eyes on all our possessions, even when they were in our hands. Pickpockets and con men were all around. Off-loaded and inside Mary and John's house, we breathed a sigh of relief, sat back and tried to take in our new surroundings. Everyone was talking at the same time. It was an open house. Friends called round to see us eyeing us curiously and advising us how to conduct ourselves, among them a persistent Ghanaian policeman just passing and dropping in to see that everything was all right and what he might get from us. We soon got the meaning of a 'dash', a tip expected from almost everyone for everything and anything, to be resisted if at all possible at all costs.

In the next few days we began to get the feel of life in and around Accra and Ghana in general. Our initial intimidating introduction began to recede. The fear of crimes of violence, accidents on the roads, robbery and being left in an alien land with absolutely no hope of help became less of an obsession though no less a reality. What I could not get over was the uncanny feeling I had about almost every aspect of life in Ghana which I could relate to my schooldays in British Guiana. The colour of the earth itself, like the symbolic colours of Ghana in the 'kente' I was later privileged to be presented with, the burnt earth brown and orange, the green of the plant life, vegetables and fruit in the market, and the blue of the raging Atlantic surf all spoke of the oneness in the origin of both Guiana and Ghana. The minerals were the same, bauxite exploited through the power released by the Akosombo dam harnessing the waters of the mighty Volta almost identical to the potential in the raw materials of the aluminium refinement in Guiana, and the gold and diamonds of both countries. Through his 'baroni', 'white man's eyes the clinically experienced white Orthopaedic Surgeon with a clear perception of everything around him saw in the Ghana which was getting to him images of an imaginative little 'white boy' at school at Queen's College, BG.

I'd been struck by the inhumanity of the Atlantic Slave Trade and knew about and admired the writer of 'Amazing Grace', John Newton, but had only one side of the picture from personal experience in British Guiana. Could the missing other side become personal to me in only a few days in the Ghana of today? Hardly likely. My time there was rapidly coming to an end. It would be off to Saudi for me with the family extending their holiday in Ghana for another two weeks. A day's outing to Cape Coast would be all I could fit in before saying my farewells.

And so it was that we drove off one-day westward along the coast past Lagon University campus to Cape Coast. It is said that 'The most uninformed traveller arriving in Cape Coast senses a historical past lurking in these broad streets with their many handsome stone houses.' What this more informed traveller sensed was indeed a profound foreboding from the past in the dirty, still crowded, cobbled streets and murky, unkempt, ancient European-style buildings that formed the background to the glaring poverty of the busy fishing town of today. Even from a distance the thunder of distant breakers from the Atlantic Ocean lashing the coastal belt imposed itself on one's consciousness. It was at Cape Coast that the first navigators from across the sea made contact with the Gold Coast and started the infamous trading in human lives and other commodities with the Fanti population. Soon the powerful maritime nations like France, Portugal, England, Holland and even Sweden started rivalling one another for trading rights and trading posts. Slavery trade castles heavily fortified for the protection of their personnel and the security of their valuable human goods against attack from other traders and occasional slaves escaping back into the trading market sprung up like mushrooms on a warm summer's morning. Elmina Castle west of Cape Coast is probably one of the best preserved. The town still shows traces of 15th Century Portuguese architecture and Cape Coast Castle those of succeeding masters – Portuguese, French and finally British – responsible for the erection of the present stronghold in 1662.

It was on the battlements of Cape Coast Castle Fort, the quietly deceptive rollers lapping the shore, in the heat of a Ghanaian midday looking out to sea, that the British Guiana side of the slave trade surfaced in my mind for only a fleeting second before being snuffed out by the reality of the moment. We explored the battlements further. Two graves were set in the scorching forecourt cobbles, those of Governor Maclean and his poetess wife Leatitia Landon. Hundreds of others, white traders, soldiers, sailors, fortune hunters must have left behind similar legacies of long weary days and years of service in a distant, foreign, disease-ridden land. We went below through wide dark passageways to the basement of the fort. In the vaulted cellars, with remnants of last-minute messages still etched in the limestone walls, not much imagination was needed to smell the stench of tortured bodies, to hear the mourning and sobbing, the high pitched screams of demented folk, tethered, pent up, buried already from life above being herded onto the beach and into open long boats to ride the surf to the waiting trans-Atlantic slave ships. In a moment I had a conjoined picture of both sides of the Atlantic before me at the same time as if I straddled the continents.

THE OPEN UNIVERSITY

From an Information sheet dated 1984 I learned something about the University with, by far, 'the greatest number of students in the British Isles'. On account of my previous academic record I was exempt three credits each demanding a year's study. That left three credits for me to get to qualify for the Ordinary Degree of Bachelor of Arts. A full foundation course in the first year was mandatory and I elected to do it in the Sciences. My background was Science and a lot of the work in Subjects like Physics and Chemistry as well as Biology would, I reasoned, be familiar to me. It would be a good way back to systematic study. How wrong I was! The scope of the course was much broader than I bargained for. Each subject had moved on since my time at school and in Medicine. Each was much more precise. Details and cross-references could not be avoided. The subjects I thought I'd have very little difficulty with, like the Physiology of the heart and even basic metabolism, were seen from a much wider perspective than my narrow medical viewpoint. The Earth Sciences were new to me and the ones I found most stimulating. Plate Tectonics, Geological Time and the Changing Earth in an infinite solar system fascinated me. An in-depth study of Cellular Structure, Physiological Regulation, Natural Selection and Chromosomal DNA, stretched me to almost breaking point but held my attention more than Meiosis and Mitosis.

Towards the end of the first year of the OU, after a Summer School in Stirling sifting sand on a Geological field project in a quarry not far from Dunblane put a different light on the Forth Valley Flood Plain, I gathered my experiences of Low Friction Arthroplasty of the Hip together for a Joint Meeting of the Royal College of Surgeons of Edinburgh and the Chapter of Surgeons, Academy of Medicine in Singapore. The paper was accepted. Singapore in '84 was on the agenda.

As my professional work was reaching a peak so also were the academic spin-offs. Lectures, Papers, and experiences were soon to follow in rapid succession. And as the Open University unfolded as well, so did much more. Horizons were to extend beyond the 'Basic Sciences' to 'Third World Studies', 'Man's Religious Quest', 'Theology' and the Ministry to 'African Studies' and visits to many places like Ghana, new parts of South Africa and the Western Seaboard of the United States of America, which we were all able to share in and which brought Avril and me closer and ever more so as the years passed. Our family home in 'Wheatstone', in Halifax, was passing imperceptibly from a predominantly boys to a predominantly girls to an indeterminate centre where we all belonged to the mothering nest from which we'd sooner or later fly to fresh 'homes' on fresh horizons.

But less day dreaming. Back to my task in hand. I threw myself wholeheartedly into 'Man's Religious Quest' in the second year with the Open University. I enjoyed reading up and delving into the material for regular Tutor Marked Assignments. Every unit of the course was as fascinating as another. I was able to empathise with my tutor who quickly grasped my style and soon had me weighed up. In some ways, when we met at occasional tutorials or at visits to Sikh or

Buddhist temples or a Mosque, she didn't fit into my perception of her. When I wrote an essay, I opened my heart and soul to my tutor on its subject matter, as if I was there, in it, myself. When she replied, by post, it was as if she had been there too. In one essay I was a philosopher searching for the meaning of life; in another a poor low-cast Hindu thirsting for a drink of water, scrounging for a crumb, longing desperately for liberation from the endless cycle of destiny; in yet another, a Buddhist on the Noble Path, or a Sikh in tune with the voice of his Guru or a devout, uncompromising follower of Islam; and in another again, a rebel revolutionary with way-out radical beliefs or scandalous secular opinions. When it came to the unit on 'The Christian Way' I gave it a miss.

In my third year I chose a course on 'Third World Studies'. From my experiences at different times of my life in British Guiana as a boy, in Malaya in the Army as a young man and in South Africa with Avril and our family on two occasions in the Transkei I reasoned that I'd have personal insight to bring to such a subject and, at the same time, I looked to the course to bring me up-to-date with the Third World as well as putting into context my past experiences. I was not to be disappointed. To begin with I found the terminology forbidding. It took me ages to get round terms like GDP (Gross Domestic Product), populist, conceptualisation, sustainable and non-sustainable development, subsistence levels, modernisation, multinational conglomerate, equalisation of income distribution, structural development and structural differentiation, but once I did, I began to use the same language myself. I could trot out expressions like 'technological improvements' and 'intermediate technology' with the best of them and write confidently in an essay that 'agriculture may be commercialised without any concomitant industrialisation'.

My travelogue of personal experiences came to life. I thumbed through the 'Third World Atlas' over and over. 'The Green Revolution in India' caught my imagination more than anything. Marrying our brief encounter with Bangladesh and India in 1982 with the case study and our impressions of dire deprivation in the Transkei in past years, I had no hesitation in choosing the topic for a project on Small Scale Intermediate Technology – 'The impact of the India Mark II Hand Operated Deep Well Pump on Rural Life in Bangladesh.' In the summer months I gathered together all the data on the subject which I had at my disposal. A two-week package holiday with Avril and the girls in Minorca didn't shake my resolve to complete the project for the Summer School a few weeks later. Stretched out in the tropical sun on the golden sands, the girls (Avril, Ailsa and Kate) acquired healthy tans as the holiday progressed. It was one of the best for us all. I pored over my papers in the chalet, white skinned, un-tanned, unhealthy but satisfied. The project on the Hand Operated Deep Well was completed as we flew out of Minorca and its commendation marked the end of my Open University studies. At the graduation ceremony in Leeds I think I felt as thrilled at the thought of Avril and our two daughters, Ailsa and Kate, supporting me from the gallery among other wives and husbands, soul mates and contemporaries, children, grandchildren, as I was in St Andrews in 1958 when my parents, among other parents and even grandparents, were there to clap their offspring with their lives ahead of them.

NOT INDIGESTION BUT A REVELATION

In the humdrum routine of our slowly moving lives, or the hectic hassle of life running away from us, there are times when, suddenly, everything seems frozen in time and space for a defining moment which can be a critical turning point. One such defining moment for us, more a moment of revelation than realisation dictated by more than an element of predestination was the night after our eldest son, Jim's, wedding to Anne in Sheffield on 19th July, 1986. The occasion had everyone in its spell. The service in the family Methodist Church in the city, the reception in St Andrew's Hotel, the dancing and the 'Good Nights' over, it was off to bed in the hotel where the reception was held. Soon sound asleep, unconscious memories of our own wedding night must have contributed to the mutual harmony, our unquestioned affection for the young ones, our tested love for each other through the years. Before the dawn chorus in the trees overlooking our bedroom had heralded in the next new day I was wide awake. It wasn't indigestion or still the rhythm of the dancing of the night before. It was a revelation. My mind was clear. The doubts of days and years before had gone. The way forward was as certain as it was predestined. I sat bolt upright in bed, Avril awake at the same time. 'I've had a revelation,' I said. 'We'll be leaving Halifax in a year or two. I'm going in for the Ministry.' It wasn't an easy option leaving a world of Medicine which was inbred in us, escaping from the rat race which was catching up on us, or even an escape from the pressures and imprisonment in a world of the familiar. It was a change of direction, a setting out on a new way, a fresh start in another direction, on a life of service in the Ministry. Like Paul on the road to Damascus, it was a clear enough revelation to me but it included, also, Avril by my side, not as a useful appendage, or even a loyal lover, but as part of a joint resurrection, a twinned new birth not of our making. And strangest of all, my revelation didn't seem ridiculous. The family accepted it for what it was. Soon everyone knew what lay ahead. And it came to pass.

'Wheatstone', 'our home', 'our house' in Halifax was our family home from which the family was beginning to fly but, at the same time, the familiar nest to which each member loved to return. It was a haven for us all. To replace it would be difficult. A smaller house more suited to our needs would be the sensible thing to look for. One easily kept, for a retired couple, in a country setting, like many of our contemporaries, would be ideal, the obvious choice, but that was the last thing in our minds. Our vision was of a home like 'Wheatstone', a rambling house with plenty room for our extending family, with ideally a drive of its own to satisfy my long-felt dream and an ample walled garden to satisfy Avril's, not too far north and not too far south to be too far away from any one of our family not living abroad. We viewed a few properties in Perthshire, around Edinburgh and Dundee, on the Borders from the east coast to the west and recalled some of the attractive houses we were familiar with in Yorkshire and Northumberland. None turned us on. Their glossy brochures did nothing for us. We were getting nowhere fast until one morning the 'Particulars of Sale of Kelso Manse' came through the door. We liked what we saw, the big old house and the walled garden in the shade of Kelso Abbey. A minute through the back gate was the cobble-stoned town square. Across the drive skirting three sides of the house, from the front door facing south stretched the golden wheat in the glebe beyond which the salmon-filled Tweed flowed with the hills beyond. A cross on the summit of the well-kept war memorial just over the Old Bridge into Kelso peeked over the wall at the fruit trees surrounding the lawn and the well-stocked border beds in the garden. We read the details of the 180 year-old manse and chuckled, but were not put off.

'The subjects of sale or any part thereof and the buildings erected or to be erected thereon shall never be occupied or

*used or be permitted by the purchaser or his successors to be
occupied or used as a meeting house, meeting place or
institution for any religious denomination or for religious
purposes or for betting, gambling or gaming or for the sale or
keeping for sale of alcoholic liquor……*

*'The word 'Manse' shall cease to be used as the name or
part of the name of the subjects for sale.'*

A few weeks later we cleared a patch in the overgrown
grass in the unkempt walled garden and sat on a rug with a
flask of tea and a sandwich, the Abbey silhouetted against the
sunny summer's sky and knew that it was for us. The garden
alone was enough for Avril. Neither of us had had much of a
look at the house which needed a lot to make it habitable but
from my experience with alterations to 'Wheatstone' I was sure
that we could turn the manse into a comfortable family home.
With mixed feelings, we put in an offer which matched the
address of the Church of Scotland at 121 George Street, in
Edinburgh and went off on holiday to one of the Greek Islands
with the two girls till just after the closing date for offers.
Perhaps we were taking on too much? Did we really want it?
'It's yours,' our solicitor told us on our return, and we never
regretted buying it.

PARACHUTE JUMP

My 58th birthday, my last in Halifax, was different, sharing a
cake with a girl on her 18th birthday in a cold, windswept field
at the Doncaster Parachute Club. No more than an hour before
I found myself upside down pointing backwards in mid air still
counting in my mind 1001, 1002, 1003 only to be gently jerked
to my senses. Looking upwards, the canopy, open, spread like
an all protecting dome, was at once a comfort and a

reassurance. I had done the prescribed training, jumping from a platform, landing one way and another, falling to the right and falling to the left, and knew what to do if the parachute didn't open or got caught up in the undercarriage of the aircraft I'd vacated. With a mixed group of fearless friends, including the Hospital Administrator and Personnel Manager, I had enrolled for the jump to raise funds for a new scanner for our hospital. Most of my colleagues were duly impressed and supportive, some dubious, others openly critical of me attempting such a feat at my age. Avril, who was in the last category, took me along when the day came for the big event and, like me, would have been glad to get it over and done with, but conditions were unsuitable for the kind of individual parachuting most of us preferred. Only one of our party came down from twice the height that we would be falling accompanied by an instructor. The rest of us would have to 'come back next week and hope the weather is better'.

Next week, on 26th November 1988, though my pride was bruised, I was relieved to find that I would be issued with one of the biggest parachutes, 'Because,' I was told, 'of your age and weight, to give you a more gentle descent.' Photographed for posterity, my supporting team looking on with their own thoughts, the time was rapidly approaching. Sitting, with the others on one of six chairs in an open field, composed or resigned, we waited our turn. Small planes circled overhead dropping specks which opened out with their 'chutes and drifted to the ground. When our time came we were on our feet walking towards the 'plane, reassuring glances at one another, still composed. But into the fragile aircraft and all composure vanished. The pilot in the front throttled up; the instructor at the back checked his six parachutists, three on each side, crouched, squashed between one another's knees, facing backwards, each parachute securely anchored to the roof of the 'plane by a cord to pull the 'chute open at the start of the fall. Even before we started the cold winter wind gusting past an open door on either side of the aircraft took the warm glow from my flushed cheeks. We were off. As the 'plane gathered speed, bouncing its cargo up and down, shaking our already trembling frames all the more till it took to the air, circling the airfield, the instructor put his head out of one of the open doors to show us how we'd look with the rushing wind pinning back every mobile fleshy feature of our faces. It was terrifying. 'Altitude two thousand five hundred feet!' the pilot announced. One by one the instructor counted us out. By the time it came to my turn I was glad to get out.

Drifting down, a silent, tranquil pattern of the countryside beneath, it was heaven. But not for long. It wouldn't be long before the landing. A comforting voice in the ear-phone announced, 'You're doing well, Bill, but pull on the right side of the 'chute.' Then, 'Pull the right side!' Then, 'The Right side!' Then, 'You're over the fence, outside the airfield, but don't worry!' I tried to concentrate on landing. 'The Landing Position' – okay, I thought, and got into it in good time, but landing to the right or left, backwards or forwards? I had no idea. I was falling, I felt, straight down. When I hit the ground I felt as if I was going through it. Then, lying on the grass on one side, I could wriggle on to my back, move my feet, my knees, my legs. The recovery truck was at my side. 'Gather your parachute in, and get in yourself,' I could hear someone saying. Inside, some of the terrified faces I'd left behind in the aircraft were now smiling, like mine. I think we must all have been laughing into ourselves as well. The birthday cake with a cup of tea was welcome, everyone agreed. My 18-year-old parachuting friend was cheery and talkative. I tried to look the same but couldn't. The strain of the morning had left me overcome with relief, and silent, some might say for once.

Certificates presented, we were told we'd all done well. 'There were only two who missed the field,' said the organiser, with a knowing look at me, 'and only one who landed on the cross you should all have landed on.' It was, of course, the birthday girl, unlike the birthday boy, who landed on the cross.

In the remaining days of our time in Halifax, with the increased tempo of life closing in on us all, word started getting round that we were leaving. My motivation was acknowledged if not fully understood, but what of Avril. What kind of wife would stick to such a fickle husband? These thoughts had crossed my mind as well before and I had confided with Avril in some of the analogues which might be applied to her. 'A Doormat' didn't go down well. 'Devoted Ruth' refusing to abandon her mother, Naomi, when she was returning home to her roots in Bethlehem had profoundly religious connotations, but was not one Avril felt she could identify with. In no way did she doubt the sincerity of Ruth's words of reassurance, 'Where you go I will go, and where you lodge I will lodge; your people shall be my people, and your God my God.' (Ruth 1: 16), but they smacked, she felt, too much of spiritual duty. Strangely, the analogy to a pelican didn't upset her as much as I thought it might. In fact the likeness grew on her as it grew on me. She warmed to it, and as she did I developed the theme of self-sacrifice which was to be the inspiration for several sermons in years to come based on the motto of our Halifax nurses, on their badges and the carving at the entrance of The Royal Halifax Infirmary, 'Herself Unmindful of Herself'. The sacrificial nature of the mother bird feeding her offspring with her very life-blood by allowing them to peck her breast until it bled and drink the blood spoke more of Avril than many other analogies. She approved of the pelican.

From the day I started work at the Infirmary in Halifax on 1st July 1973 as Consultant Orthopaedic Surgeon until the day I retired on the last day of September1989 my name was synonymous with the hip joint, and more specifically Low Friction Arthroplasty of the joint. It was the field of Orthopaedics which I had come to make my own. It was the one speciality that excited me more than any other and the one in which expertise was the greatest. When the British Orthopaedic Association decided to set up the Wishbone Appeal to support various urgently needed research projects in the UK and to start it off by organising 'The Great Hip Walk' nationally on 4th June 1989 it was a most appropriate privilege for me to end my career in Orthopaedics by organising the Hip Walk in Halifax.

On the day of the mile long Walk, each participant the recipient of an artificial hip joint, walkers and sponsors gathered along with supporters and organisers in the DIY forecourt a mile from the Town Hall in the centre of Halifax. You might have thought it was the start of the London Marathon. The whole town, as well as far-flung neighbouring centres, was behind the project. Traffic Police, marshals, and the Ambulance Brigade conspicuous in their efficiency, our hospital staff running here and there, checking papers, encouraging, calming worried relatives, laughing, singing along with one another, were all eager to show what a new hip joint meant to so many. It was a touching time for me, humble and proud, anxious that everything would go well but in no doubt of the confidence and the capabilities of all our walkers. As the Walk got going it was a tonic to run up and down the stream of walkers cheering, reassuring one minute, assisting the very old and very frail the next, supporting the supporters whenever required, always encouraging. 'You'll be glad when it's over!' said one well-wisher. 'It must be a nightmare being responsible for all these walkers. Something could happen to any of them anytime, and you'll be responsible.' The thought hadn't occurred to me. The confidence of surgeon and patients was never in question. The Walk ended without incident. Climbing the steps of the Town Hall, everyone was overwhelmed by the sense of achievement. Speeches from the Mayor and other Civic dignitaries, 'Thank you!'s all round, personally from me to the walkers, colleagues, all our hospital staff, especially my secretary, and the day was over. A cheque for £7,593.54 was forwarded to the Wishbone Appeal.

TRANSITION OR METAMORPHOSIS

Moving house is seldom just a matter of packing up and leaving one house and unpacking in another. Leaving and arriving usually span intermediate periods of time. They follow each other strictly chronologically but its never as simple as one life in one place one day and another in another the next. Moving from Halifax to Kelso was no exception. It was complicated by my starting the new life of a student again, this time at Mansfield College in Oxford, before we had left the familiarity of our home in 'Wheatstone' and before we had claimed the house we'd bought in Kelso as our own by moving into it. For two months Avril was living one life keeping our family home in Halifax on an even keel, part of the time on her own without me, and part of the time with me compounding her bewilderment with my anecdotes from Oxford, while projecting her thoughts on our new home in Kelso which we would never totally occupy for over half a decade of one building, garden and home readjustment and 'settling in' project after another.

As for me at this critical time, my life was being dominated more and more by my Mansfield connection. I had checked into the Oxford scene along with all the other 'freshers' in a house that had been purchased by the URC for some of its Ordinands and dedicated for their use. In no time I was familiar with the Common Room my fellow students frequented, the library fewer of them were ever even seen in except when examinations were imminent, and the College Chapel which we all attended at least each morning for prayers and frequently for more formal traditional or evangelical services as well, of course, as Sermon Classes. From Tuesday to Friday I was a devout Ordinand. Come the end of the week my student image was over. Already packed and the car checked for petrol, a hasty wave to my house-mates, found me weaving my way through the rush hour traffic towards Banbury and the M1 North, off the slip-road to the M62 and well on the way to Halifax, but soon to be further north to Kelso.

In the course of my training at Mansfield College I was to become more understanding of human nature, to look with more compassion on things I didn't agree with and accept and forgive errors of social graces without anger. What I found was that when I was staying in Oxford I lived in one mind set, and when in Kelso, in another. When I was in Oxford I spoke of things ecclesiastical, in Kelso of things like the frustration of the constant noise of hammering, the clouds of dust in the rubble of building, the mud and wind and cold of the building site outside the house invading every corner of the interior, weary long days and weary long nights, problems with supplies, questions of expense. Avril was soon almost totally taken over by the work around her. When we met she had nothing much else to talk about. My feeble talk of student life in Oxford did nothing to dispel her feelings of despair. The only consolation for both of us was that the non-stop pressures of our lives was driving us on and better days would come in our new 'home', 'our house' in Kelso. 'What about 'Abbey Royd'? How about 'Abbey Royd' for a name for the house?' asked Avril, one day, 'It's next to the Abbey, really part of it. There are so many names with 'Abbey' in them, 'Abbey Row', 'Abbey view', 'Abbey Way', and even, no doubt, 'Abbey Road' after the Beetles, but this is 'our home', our bit, our patch or clearing.' 'Royd' is a common name in Yorkshire. Its meaning is a clearing or yard, my patch, 'our home'. 'There couldn't be a better name,' I happily agreed. The 'Old Manse' had gone. 'Abbey Royd' had arrived.

As the momentous task of transforming 'Abbey Royd' into a home to replace our former, now receding, home in 'Wheatstone' in Halifax into our new home in Kelso continued unrelentingly alongside my spiritual renaissance the process of metamorphosis was unfolding. In the dust and digging of building reconstruction and the germination of latent aspirations which was not far removed from rebirth destiny seemed to have a hand. On one of the first Sundays of Advent, back in Kelso with Avril, there was little chance of the building programme being sufficiently advanced for the planned break through of the extension into the house proper by Christmas but, surprisingly, we were not particularly concerned. We had other things on our minds. An introduction to a church in Newcastle upon Tyne in the Northern Province had been arranged and I was invited to come and meet some of the people, see the building, have a look round the neighbourhood of Heaton, conduct a service, and see how things went. The service, we thought, went well, Avril's Readings being well received, the one from Isaiah about a vision for the future (Isaiah 2: 1-5) giving me an appropriate lead into an apt sermon. The following day we met the elders formally. Full and frank opinions on the way ahead for the church, which had been vacant for two years, were aired. Aspirant minister and expectant parishioners were open and to the point. Their strengths and shortcomings, their wishes and their fears, were expressed and accepted. The match seemed right but one or two important people were on holiday. Could I come back again after Christmas and let them hear me preach? 'Well, all right,' I agreed with some reluctance.

On Sunday 4th February I was back at Heaton to preach again, this time with Kate as my reader. At the Church Meeting a few days later just over 70% of the congregation voted in favour of calling me to be their minister. I had seldom exceeded this percentage in any examination and was delighted. Back at Mansfield my fellow Ordinands were keen to hear the news. 'How did it go, Bill?' they asked and I told them. 'Too bad!' they said and pointed out that for every seven in favour of me three were against. 'Don't touch it with a barge pole,' most of my discerning friends concluded, but naïve and 'knowing better', I was deaf to their advice. I accepted the 'Call' without hesitation and the formalities were set in motion. On Saturday 7th July 1990 I would be ordained to the ministry of the United Reformed Church and inducted to the Pastorate of Heaton in Newcastle upon Tyne.

Then, suddenly as it seemed, one Friday afternoon it was the end of Trinity, and the end of student days at Mansfield. The Ordinands met in the Upper Common Room with their tutors and representatives of the URC. Nice things were said. Words of inspiration still ringing in our ears, farewells and good wishes over, three of us were presented with Leaving Certificates. Mine said, 'This is to certify that William J Nicol has completed the Ordination Course at Mansfield College to the satisfaction of the Authorities and is hereby commended by them to the Churches.' I read it and left.

GALLERY

In Canada with
my father, my
brother, Douglas
and sister, Mary,
in the early 30s.

In Hull for our
wedding in 1960

Composite of pictures of early days:

Early Days (clockwise from top left)
1. My parents on their wedding day
2. Me
3. My parents at West Wemyss
4. My father in his study in Berbice
5. Me and my granddad
6. Two of the schools I attended

With Avril on our wedding day

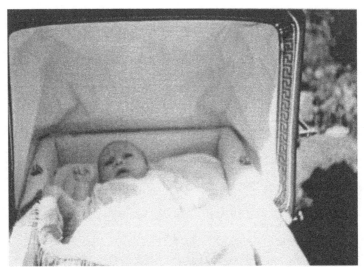

Jim, the first of our five children and seven grandchildren

Avril with our young family

At home in Abbey Royd

Avril in the walled garden in winter

Avril and the Author

Cup of tea in the garden
Avril and Ailsa, her sister

Sulenkama Mission Hospital: Main entrance and OPD

Avril with Jim and David (top) and John's christening
in the chapel (bottom)

Ward round at Bedford Orthopaedic Centre

Kate in front of "our home" in the "*Viege House*"

"Wheatstone" – "our home" in Halifax

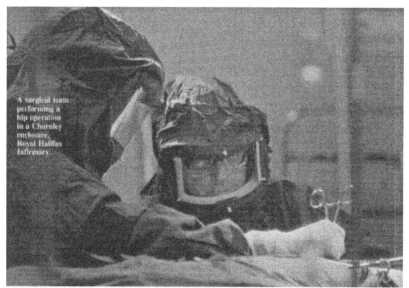

A surgical team performing a hip operation in a Charnley enclosure, Royal Halifax Infirmary.

Me in the sterile enclosure

Me and the inspiration of my life, Avril
outside McEwan Hall for the MSc in African Studies

Me in various modes – thinking, running and jumping!

At the Baghdad Hotel:
"One Arab Nation With Eternal Aim"

At Home!

On the back of a Sri Lankan Elephant

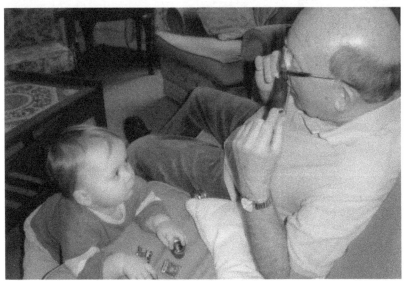

Music to the ears!

Heaton United Reformed Church before the fire
(Inserts – Right: After the fire. Left: A new transient logo, like me!)

The logo shows the cross and the fish which are standard signs of our URC. The burning bush, with flames, retains our heritage in Presbyterianism and will remind us, in the future, of the flames which could not destroy our 'Church'. The words 'Consumed together by the Spirit' are a gesture of union by consummation with other members of Heaton Churches Together.

Jan Hus monument, Prague

Avril and Meggie at "*Pinehurst*"

Avril and me with Jim and Kate at Laura's baptism
at Second Avenue Chapel

Refurbished Trinity Church, Ashington, like a table, looking
outward through transparent doors to the world outside

Round the baptismal font where I christened our second grandson, William, in Sheffield in Avril's last few weeks

Avril and me at the first Presbyterian Church in Kelso, Washington, with Mount St Helens in the background

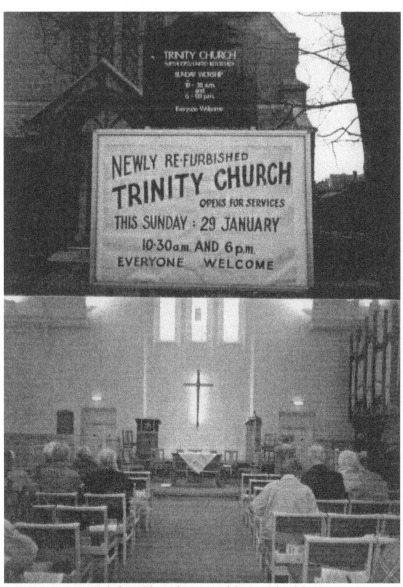

Trinity Church – outside and inside

The Fifth
Biblical Bike Ride for
The Nazareth Hospital

over
Jordan

from the Sea of Galilee to the Red Sea

2-10 November 1996

"The Experience of a Lifetime"

CYCLE THROUGH THE BIBLE from the Sea of Galilee, following the Jordan Rift Valley all the way to the Red Sea, taking in Nazareth, crossing into Jordan to visit Petra and Karak, and finishing in Aqaba.

THE FIFTH BIBLICAL BIKE RIDE for the Nazareth Hospital takes place from 2-10 November 1996

* 250 miles of changing scenery and history, from the Old and New Testament.
* challenge, adventure, friendship and fun, all in a good cause

TO SHARE IN THE BIKE RIDE EXPERIENCE, you should
be fit and healthy, and at least 18 years old

Biblical Bike Ride over Jordan, 1996 – The route, and me
with David in training in the walled garden at Abbey Royd

170

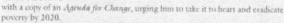

An ecumenical group of 12 Christians walked 670 miles from Iona to London in October on a "Pilgrimage Against Poverty", which culminated in a meeting with the Chancellor of the Exchequer, Gordon Brown.

Angered by "the scandal of the degree of poverty in our country" the walkers presented Mr Brown with a copy of an *Agenda for Change*, urging him to take it to heart and eradicate poverty by 2020.

The group was joined throughout the journey south by others committed to the cause, and hospitality was provided by churches of all denominations. Arriving in London, the campaigners held a rally in Trafalgar Square and took part in a service in the church there, St Martin-in-the-Fields. At a meeting with Church and political figures, the level of poverty in Britain was described as "heresy" and "blasphemy".

LIFE & WORK JANUARY 2000.

A pilgrim in front of the house in Glasgow where he was born long before the concept of *"our home"* ever entered his head

"Up, up and away…"

… But not as high as the Pulpit with me in it in the Dutch Reformed Church in Port Galle shortly after it celebrated its 350th Anniversary

Graduation photograph of Margaret

Her house all her life in Buckhaven

Graduation photograph of the Author – Me.

Red-tiled-roofed house. Watercolour painting by the Author in his schooldays in West Wemyss, Fife.

Margaret and the Author on Remembrance Sunday, 2007

A statue in memory of Alexander Selkirk,
a distant relative of Margaret, on the site of
the cottage in which Selkirk was born, in Largo, Fife.

The Balmoral

Welcome on Board

At Dinner on board *The Balmoral*

At dinner on board *The Balmoral*

Margaret on board *The Balmoral*

Brandenburg Gate, Berlin

Berlin Wall

Checkpoint Charlie, Berlin

Margaret and the Author standing in front of *The Aurora*, from which the sound of a single canon shot proclaimed the start of The Great October Revolution of 1917.

On Hadrian's Wall

The Angels of the North!

Margaret at home in "Grandad's Deluxe Apartment"

Buying a carpet in Istanbul

Margaret at the Turkish Memorial at Anzac Cove.

Margaret and me in Gallipoli

Personal pictures from our Pilgrimage in Turkey

The kind of scene from the battle site

The Author – me – in a Pulpit in Ancient Pergamon associated with Asklepios, the God of Health and Life

Margaret, the sole congregation, inspired and illumined like the Greeks, Persians and Romans before her with eyes looking east and west at the same time.

On top of Snowdon!

Margaret

The Author

Margaret and me on the way up Snowdon

Celebrations after the climb!

Margaret at Heather's first birthday

Christmas time at home with Avril

Me with the two loves of my life, Avril and Margaret, to whom this book is dedicated

Enjoying an Anniversary "Mud Sludge": Mt St Helens

Just down from Snowdon

ACT SIX

ORDAINED to the MINISTRY of the UNITED REFORMED CHURCH

'The sixth age shifts
Into the lean and slippered pantaloon,
With spectacles on nose and pouch on side,
His youthful hose well saved a world too wide
For his shrunk shank.'

IT WAS SATURDAY 7th July 1990. We awoke in the manse at 3 Crompton Road, Newcastle upon Tyne, which was to be our home for the next three years. The day before, 'Abbey Royd' was bursting at the seams, our extended family mingling freely with longstanding friends who Avril and I had made through the years. Today was on all their minds. When the phone rang to let us know that it was ready our good friend Ralph Ackroyd echoed my relief. 'And not before time!' he said, impatiently. The congregation at Heaton had generously offered to present me with a cassock at my ordination and asked me to purchase one to my liking, but I chose a Geneva Preaching Gown in preference. I could see myself wearing a gown but not a cassock and ordered one from a well-known robe maker in Edinburgh. Though assured that it would be ready in good time, 'in good time' was 'just in time'. A quick dash to collect it before closing time saw us back in Kelso to gather a few things together and leave for Newcastle. The night there was quiet and balmy. Ralph and Phyllis Ackroyd were soon asleep and up like clockwork the next day. In our new surroundings, the enormity of the next day before us, all the preparation completed, there was little more for Avril and me to say. At one in our own thoughts it was a while before we were asleep. Suddenly, in what seemed to be the twinkling of an eye, it was Saturday 7th July 1990.

Self-conscious in my familiar charcoal grey suit and wearing a dog collar for the first time, but strangely composed, with an unassuming yet assuredly supportive Ralph at my side, the walk from Crompton Road to the church was an opportunity for quiet reflection. In the anterooms off a corridor at the back of the church, people were beginning to arrive. Someone from the Newcastle District Council was there to meet us and show us to where it would meet officially to initiate the business of the day. 'It's along there to the right,' I heard a voice say and caught a glimpse of Jim, our eldest son, making a beeline to the toilets with our only grandson, Andrew. I knew that the family had arrived. The meeting of the District Council duly constituted, formalities, introductions and words of welcome were soon completed. The Leaving Certificate which I'd been reminded over and over to remember to bring with me, was scrutinised. Background organ music rising and falling to my heartbeat reminded us that the church was filling up. It would soon be time to file in, but not before some comforting words from a stranger to me. 'You won't know me,' said an elderly, dignified clergyman with a hint of an Aberdeen accent, 'but I knew your father in British Guiana. When he was in Berbice I was the minister at St Andrews Church in Georgetown. We met occasionally at Presbytery. He would have been proud of you today.' My father's former friend and colleague, who later moved south from the Church of Scotland to the Presbyterian Church in England before its union with the Congregationalists to form the URC would soon, become, also, one of mine.

In no time the congregation was Called to Worship and we were on our feet for the first hymn:-

'Christ is made the sure foundation,
Christ the head and corner stone...'

The prayer of Adoration and Confession, and the Statement of Purpose followed by Bible Readings and another hymn that followed must have meant something to me at the time, but I have no recollection of them today. It was only when, as it appeared on the printed Order of Service, 'Rev. R.L. Ackroyd, MA (Former Minister of Heath URC, Halifax, now retired', appeared in the pulpit to deliver the 'Ordination Charge to Minister Elect and Congregation' that lasting memories of the moment were engraved on my heart. Then followed the hymn I'd chosen as most personal to me at the time and which I plan having sung at my funeral:-

'Make me a captive, Lord,
And then I shall be free;
Force me to render up my sword
And I shall conqueror be.
I sink in life's alarms
When by myself I stand;
Imprison me within thine arms,
And strong shall be my hand.'
(Hymn 505, 'Rejoice and Sing',
George Matheson, 1842-1906)

Several important people then said several important things which I heard but didn't really listen to until I'd made my Statement based on 'Make me a captive, Lord, and then I shall be free'. With that off my chest all that remained was the Act itself.

Kneeling at the top of the steps to the chancel for the Prayer of Ordination and Induction, my unsupported feet were shaking like a leaf. The congregation behind me which had been invited to stand, couldn't, I felt sure, fail to notice the soles of my shoes vibrating to the words of the Moderator beaming reassuringly down at me. At ease with my attire but aware of my clerical collar restricting my neck movements, the moment had come. 'And now,' I heard the words clearly, 'we thank you especially for calling William Nicol to serve you as a minister in your Church.' According to the usual practice selected members of the District Council and representatives of the Church who had gathered round the Moderator laid their hands on the Ordinand's head. It was like a weight driving my head through my neck. 'Fill your servant, William Nicol, with your Holy Spirit, as in your name we ordain him to be a Minister in your Church.' The Act of Ordination was over. Induction to the Pastorate of Heaton United Reformed Church followed and the Benediction brought the Service to an end, but not before hands were shaken in the traditional manner known as the Right Hand of Fellowship.

In the first few weeks at Heaton life started taking on a new routine for us. Minor repairs, painting and papering here and there as well as grass cutting and tidying in the garden, and the addition of a few extra essential sticks of furniture to the already well-furnished manse made moving in and settling in easy. Our dog, Meggie, accustomed herself to the house quicker than expected. A short walk from Crompton Road, along Heaton Road past St Theresa's Church, took us on an evening walk through Armstrong Park which led to Jesmond Dene frequented by joggers and other dog walkers where Meggie could bound around till she tired and we set off back home.

Having only one Sunday Service at 10.45 a.m. each week was good for me at the start of my days in the ministry as I could spend a day or two preparing a sermon for it, and carefully research hymns, readings and prayers to go with the theme. Challenging and at the same time satisfying, I relished the discipline. Surprisingly, there was seldom any difficulty finding an appropriate theme for any week or suitable Bible readings because either dates like Christmas or Easter on the church calendar or topical issues arising from current items of news or local anxieties dictated the specific need of the day. Only occasionally did I find I needed to resort to a lectionary for guidance in structuring a service. As I started getting the URC Prayer Handbook, and using it, I found it most helpful. Invariably, however, the resources for most services I've ever conducted have come from my own personal experiences of life, the needs of the people I try to serve and, of course, the inspiration of Scripture and prayer. In Sermons and Services in general I have always seen my role as minister as an arbitrator relating my fellow worshippers to the world around them, the wider world of time and space and other people, and another dimension that is Spiritual and of God. When I've come to the end of a Sermon or a Service I've always tried to ask myself, 'What good has it been?' If it has revealed, even for a brief moment, a clearer image of a loving God measured with the yardstick of Jesus, I reckon it's done some good. I sleep well at night. Though unaware of it at the time the sermons I was to preach at Heaton were to serve me well in the future.

But there was another advantage of a One Service Sunday to be shared with Avril with as much eager anticipation as me. Home for lunch by twelve noon after the service at Heaton, it wouldn't take long to secure Meggie in the back of the car and be up the road on the way to Kelso to arrive in good time to get the place heated up in the winter or do some gardening in the better weather before settling down for the evening in our non-working surroundings and taking in 'Songs of Praise'. I considered Monday to be my day off and Avril made sure the day was free from any of her growing number of Family Planning Clinics. With mixed feelings we'd be back in Heaton late on Monday night to start our working week the next day. At my desk in the spacious back bedroom which was my study, suitable books on the ample shelves, I'd gaze out, in pensive mood, through the well double-glazed windows over the allotments at the back of Crompton Road and Jesmond Dene beyond to the lights of Newcastle in the distance at night or the haze of traffic on a sunny day in search of inspiration and was seldom disappointed.

In the long summer days of July and August when most of the church activities were at a low and organisations suspended because of the holidays I took the opportunity of making introductory visits to most of our members accompanied by their District Elder to show me round and introduce me. It was good to hear their stories and share some of mine with them. Soon word got round about the new minister and his wife. Visiting and Sunday services were going well. At the door of our Heaton Road Church after a service, looking as I thought like a minister, used now to the dog collar, a grey clerical shirt matching my grey suit, the Geneva Preaching Gown which I had become quite at home in fluttering in the breeze or wrapped round me to shelter me from the rain, my thoughts still lingered on the sermon. Shaking hands, and smiles and nods and words of assurance took on a familiar pattern at the door of the church: 'Good morning! Nice day...' (or 'Rainy day!') 'Thank you! Thank you very much for a wonderful sermon. Most helpful! The best I've heard for a long time!' (or even 'Ever heard!'). I always fell for it until reality cut in.

'Yes,' I thought to myself, 'it was pretty good. Perhaps I missed my true vocation. I should have been at the preaching long ago.' Then, releasing the warm grip on my receptive hand, my admirer would place their hand on a hip or a knee and add, 'What should I do about this, Mr Nicol?', and launch into the gory details. It was only a free private consultation they were after, after all. My ego was immediately deflated. I was reduced to size. Perhaps the sermon wasn't quite so good. Humility is probably a more appropriate attribute than arrogance in a minister.

Many surprises and several searching questions lay ahead of me. 'It must be a big change for you in the ministry now? A big difference from Orthopaedic Surgery?', I found I was being asked so often that I was asking myself the same question in my sleep. 'What's the difference between Medicine and the Ministry?' And then, of course, why? 'What made you go into the Ministry? Why did you do it?'

I knew, of course, that the big difference between Medicine and the Ministry would be remuneration. We had long reconciled ourselves to that. Popular opinion had lost no time in making it clear to us that the change would be from one of relative affluence of an Orthopaedic Consultant to the austerity of Ministry. In my former days I had become used to grateful patients or inspired junior doctors coming along at Christmas time to present me with a bottle of the finest malt whisky any Scottish doctor would appreciate. We were never short of a few bottles in the house. All that, we realised, would change. But after a few hands had been shaken at the door of the church and word got round about the new minister, our doorbell rang one day. It was a lady from the church whom we had begun to get to know, with a plastic bag with a long heavy object in it. 'Just a little something to welcome you to Heaton,' she announced handing the gift over. 'Come in,' I said, my mind running away with myself. 'A bottle of whisky!' I thought, and opened the bag. A cucumber! 'From the allotments,' our benefactor explained, 'over the fence. If you ever want a lettuce or a cucumber, just let me know.' We knew then. 'What's the difference between Medicine and the Ministry?' The difference between a bottle of whisky and a cucumber.

What changed, then, you may ask, perceptive reader, when I retired from Orthopaedics and embarked on a life in the Ministry, when I moved with my wife, Avril, from 'our home' in Halifax to a new home, still to become 'our home', 'Abbey Royd', in Kelso, at a time of life aptly described by the bard, William Shakespeare, as passing from the 'stage' of 'the justice' into 'the sixth age of lean and slippered pantaloon, with spectacles on nose and pouch on side'? Not much. I'm still just trying to help people along the road of life. I'm still the carpenter I've always been as an Orthopaedic Surgeon but am now, also, a carpenter trying his best to follow the carpenter of Nazareth.

In the first few holiday months after my Induction to Heaton URC I began to get to know the people in the church, and they me. In church on Sunday, as I became familiar with the building and the needs of the congregation my efforts to conform to the usual style of service were acknowledged. I was well received. The happy honeymoon period was a learning period. In their homes on visits and on casual encounters in the streets I began to pick up on the things that made my flock tick. Carpet bowls was a top priority where much of the social life of the church was centred, but it never really turned me on, and excited Avril even less. In general the life of the church was ticking over as it had for years. It met the needs of the people in the community in which they lived. Only rarely, at first, could I detect a hint of disquiet. The way the country at large was going, and especially in the North-East, was occasionally betrayed by expressions of disgust. The mugging of one of our oldest members almost on her doorstep, not far from the church, was met with the righteous rage of indignation you might have expected. Another 'ram-raid' on a local Post Office already partly protected by firmly secured concrete bollards was a new phenomenon to me, but one I'd soon become acquainted with through Avril's direct involvement at the Health Centre on the Meadowell estate. Crashing a stolen car into a shop window, loading it up with whatever could be stolen, and making off in the same car at high speed, often in broad daylight, all in a minute or two before the police could be alerted, was the in, 'ram-raid' way for a quick robbery. I must have appeared naive in the extreme to my reticent friends conditioned to the rising rate of violence on the streets.

But most of the conversation in church circles was about the new minister. What most people liked about me was that I was a good-natured, down-to-earth, respected and responsible, experienced, professional man with a good string of letters after my name which would go well with the name of the church, Heaton United Reformed Church. At my age, retired from the Medical profession with a limited number of years ahead of him in the Ministry, their minister and his likeable wife would most likely be with them until he retired for the second time. In the main, from my easy conversation, the people were reassured, but not entirely. Hints of a break from waning traditions, different priorities, questioning established outlooks, and even an open interest in politico-social life on the streets, and poverty, deprivation, injustice and inequality aroused visible suspicions.

The first 'Minister's Letter' which I wrote in the church magazine, *The Messenger,* in September 1990 included a copy of the Statement which I made at the Service of Ordination and Induction and concluded with these words:-

'In the Ordination Charge given by Revd R L Ackroyd to you the congregation elect and me the Minister elect, we were charged, as a pilgrim people, to 'get up and walk' so that Christ's love and healing may, through us, help to transform the world. You were specifically charged to get up and walk into the world, into society, into the Church and into yourselves. I was specifically charged to offer to all who will receive it, not a hip replacement, but the hope for a new beginning.

What faces us now is to respond to these charges together. I will share in what is routine to you for a short time, then invite you to share in what I would wish for a short time, then we'll embark on what we all feel is our collective response to what God wills us to do—how He wills us to take up our beds and walk.

In these exciting times, it is my prayer that we all grow in faith together and share it with others.

Peace be with you.

Revd. William J. Nicol.'

By our first Christmas at Heaton the honeymoon period was coming to an end. Both Avril and I warmed to the people from the start and this remained unchanged. But cracks were beginning to show. My constant talk of change and proposals for outreach, moving in line with our United Reformed Church, moving from the still dominant Presbyterian outlook of the past, adopting the new URC hymnbook, *Rejoice and Sing,* to supplement or replace the Third Edition of the *Church Hymnary*, was wearing thin. When I started taking some of the services without using my gown or wearing a clerical collar, some of the congregation were not impressed. Traditions die hard, they say, and they did. Talk of social justice, human rights and poverty was met by embarrassment. Reference to Avril's work as a Family Planning doctor in one of the most deprived areas of Newcastle where grumbling disquiet was about to erupt into seething violence provoked an ominous silence of disapproval. Political bias was never far from the surface.

'Go slow, Bill,' said my loyal Church Secretary one night, 'Don't push us so far so fast. Please don't try to change us,' she begged, and colleagues and friends echoed her advice. The consensus was something like this:- 'For the first five years just keep things going; then introduce a few alternatives for a while, gradually; only then can you expect things to change.' As I could see, the advice was sound, except for the timing. I had no time to wait and no time to waste.

Normal activity in the church moved on apace. New members were admitted, new elders ordained, seasonal highlights like Harvest Thanksgiving and Remembrance Day observed, and the Baptism of our first grand-daughter celebrated. Exchange preaching visits to sister churches in London and less far flung places like small country churches between Newcastle and Kelso each widened the spectrum of our United Reformed Church for me. But the incompatibility of Minister and the hard core of members of his local church remained an issue.

The uncanny foreboding which pervaded my relationship with a congregation with whom I had so much in common but was never quite on the same wavelength did not, however, extend to the wider work of the church. In fact, as if to compensate, I found that I was throwing myself with renewed zeal into every other channel of my work. The idea of a Decade of Evangelism excited me. Membership of Heaton Churches Together introduced me to our five ecumenical brother and sister churches on Heaton Road. Regular meetings with clergy from all the churches stimulated my interest in them. Lenten meetings took on a new meaning. Sharing in services together was both a privilege and a broadening experience. The churches in the Northern Province came to life for me as I got to know some of their problems through their ministers whom I met at Council and Provincial level, and especially at meetings for what was commonly known as Potty Training (Post-Ordination Training sessions) which started being held 'in the comfort and congenial home of Bill and Avril at Abbey Royd, Kelso'. The new ministers and their families enjoyed a weekend in Kelso as much as we enjoyed having them. A cherry tree grown from a sapling and a 'Rambling Rector' rosebush in the walled garden today are lasting tokens of appreciation. When a vacancy arose for a World Church Correspondent in the Northern Province to co-ordinate the work of the church and its partners abroad, a well-travelled person with an interest in foreign parts like me seemed the natural choice. It was in this way, then, that outside interests came to hold our attention more than our home base at Heaton, and to sustain us in our moments of anxiety.

At The General Assembly of the United Reformed Church in Torquay almost a year after my Ordination, I thrilled to the magnitude of the event. Presented along with other new clergy and announcing to the gathering that I would be re-visiting South Africa with my wife for a holiday and be meeting friends from the Reformed Presbyterian Church there I offered to tell them about the Assembly here. 'Please do,' replied the Moderator. 'Take official greetings from the Assembly to the

Churches in South Africa!' and I did. When I returned home from Torquay and related the experience of my first Assembly I was glad I was a minister of the United Reformed Church. The Church at Heaton shared in their minister's good fortune accepting the news of our proposed short visit to South Africa in good spirits. This time it would be back to Umtata, at the Bedford Orthopaedic Centre, at the invitation of the American-based African Medical Mission through my present successor. We were on a high and the church was on a high. The church sanctuary had been redecorated. All the organisations were ticking over. It even looked as if 'Rejoice and Sing' might be adopted after all.

With the dawn of 22nd July 1991 we were off, on our way back to South Africa, the Bedford Orthopaedic Centre, outside Umtata in the Transkei. Our minds raced backwards to the Transkei we had known and forwards to what we might find. Back in Umtata after only a brief visit in 1987 we were warmly welcomed to 'our home' in the Convent Farm at Bedford Orthopaedic Centre. A substantial chalet had been made ready for us in the compound of the hospital grounds behind the kitchens, between the church and the grave-yard where the earliest enthusiasts had died like flies in their missionary zeal. Chris McConnachie, the Orthopaedic Surgeon in charge, welcomed me as the 'Pioneer Orthopaedist' who started the speciality and Avril as my able 'Anaesthesiologist' who would be keen to help out in the operating room. The terminology was different. 'Pioneer' aged me instantly. 'Orthopaedist' transported me to the King Faisal Specialist Hospital and Research Centre in Riyadh with its dominating American presence. 'Anaesthesiologist' was as unreal to Avril as 'Orthopaedist' was to me and she was anything but keen to start giving anaesthetics again after being out of it for several years. Family Planning was now her speciality, the field she was at home in. Away from medicine for almost two years, I too had reservations about what on call emergencies and cold clinics in unfamiliar surroundings involved, especially when a multinational preponderance of short term volunteer doctors recruited mainly from the States and several non-English speaking European countries competed openly to assert their national expertise on an unsuspecting pool of patients.

Fresh from my church in the North East of England I'd still the novelty of my church work and my recent student days in Oxford in me but soon settled into a routine. I'd do occasional ward rounds and assist with some more interesting operations but my main function would be lecturing to nurses and undergraduate doctors from Umtata University. I enjoyed the formal lectures, but, even more so, the tutorials round the bedside. Most clinical work dated me and after a few sessions looking round the operating room Avril opted out of routine lists and her Family Planning skills were not called upon. Towards the end of our time it was clear that our place in the Medical world of the day had passed us by. We had our time when we were on top of our subjects in conditions familiar to us. Chris reassured me that my contribution to the African Medical Mission's Orthopaedic Programme was well received but I had my reservations.

But domestic and social life on the Bedford Convent Farm was not without its drama. Sunday with the Zionists was one that I described at length in an article in our church magazine when we returned home. An American Mennonite couple had told us about them and offered to take us to a service the following week. We didn't need to be asked twice. I started the article with an introduction:-

'They're one of many African Independent Churches. They're bible-based. They claim the power and the gifts of New Testament times. They're strong on prophecy, revelation and healing. Healing is often combined with pre-Christian practices and culture. Some mix Christian and traditional practices, but many have grown away from witchcraft, charms and fetish, and tobacco and alcohol and gambling. They want to be part of the World Church. Several have joined the World Council of Churches. Some are afraid of being taken over, and want to retain their own peculiarities. Most of the mainstream churches – Protestant, Roman Catholic and the Orthodox Church – are suspicious of churches like the Zionists. They don't know what to make of them'.

An accurate description of an experience which made an equally non-forgettable impression on both Avril and me then followed:-

'Encouraged by our friend's account, we had no hesitation accepting an offer to go along with our American Mennonite friends to share in a service with a Zionist Church in the Transkei a week later. We drove along a national tar road for about half an hour and then along a dirt road. The dirt road faded out and we drove between huts and groups of huts to a more impressive kraal, one with a dry closet facing out on to a parched mealie field. We met the leader of the Zionist church – the widow of the former bishop who was, herself, the leading prophetess. People began to gather – one lady had walked for three hours with her year old baby on her back and would walk back home after the four-hour service. Our hostess left us for a while and then emerged wearing a bright blue cloak surmounted with a white cross on her back and head-gear. The lady with the baby put on her green gown and other women similar uniforms. A horn was sounded outside the hut next door

as a 'call to worship'. We were shown into the church hut. It was dimly lit with a small table with two candles on it at one end. The worshippers stood or squatted around the circular wall and sang quietly to the beat of a drum. We took our seats behind the small table. Most of the leaders collected palm branches on long sticks and danced in a circle.

The service started. All the formalities were there – welcome praise to God, thanksgiving, Bible readings in Xhosa, a formal sermon and several testimonies; a children's story from a picture book about Joseph – the 20-odd children in their bright uniforms sat pop-eyed and speechless – creeds, the Lord's Prayer, the Ten Commandments each punctuated by praise and hallelujahs, and singing and dancing which became louder and faster and shriller as the drum beat changed tempo and the petrol can maracas rhythm rose to a climax with the healing session. Anyone with a problem, anxiety, mental or physical illness, or a sin to confess, came to the centre of the circle. The leader danced round, nimble-toed, faster and faster, sweating, singing, and screeching feverishly. The prophetess or one of her assistants would listen intently to each needy soul, embrace, lay on hands, shake, extol, exorcise, counsel, pray with them and then listen to the prayer of response – all done in a frenzy, but a frenzy of sincerity – until everyone had been dealt with. The dust died down, the horn blowing subsided and the closing formalities of hand shaking, blessings on us all to be taken back to our friends and churches in distant lands, sincere concern and best wishes to be taken back to our congregation at Heaton whose church had gone up in flames, washing of hands, singing, prayers and the final benediction. As we drove off, four hours later, thankful for the dry closet, we were thankful, also, for the privilege of sharing the worship of God in an uninhibited, different, sincere way with people who read the Scriptures, pray, sing, give testimonies, heal, help the needy and praise God in very similar, yet different ways from *ours – differences dictated by their traditions and cultures and social demands.'*

Between the ceremonial unveiling of a plaque to mark the opening of a new theatre suite at the Bedford Orthopaedic Centre and visitors filing into the crowded reception hall I was called to the phone. 'Don't worry!' said a faint voice consciously controlled, 'There's no need to come home right away. Continue your holiday as planned, but there's been a fire. The church has been badly damaged.' The Church Secretary was informing me the day after our church at home, Heaton URC, had gone up in flames. A workman had been checking the roof of the large Victorian building and was using a blowtorch to seal off the roof after replacing a faulty slate. A clump of bird's feathers in the eaves had caught fire and a gust of wind fanned the flames. What part of the building not damaged by the fire was saturated by the copious jets of water used by the fire engines promptly on the scene, clouds of smoke and raging flames billowing into the Newcastle upon Tyne skyline. Reassured that there was nothing we could do by returning home at once, 'Everything is in hand', our natural impulse to get back as soon as we could receded and our time in South Africa continued as planned.

In the short time we'd been back in South Africa, at Bedford in Umtata, the uncertainties of life 'on the edge' were, at the same time, stimulating and satisfying, challenging and exhilarating, but they had come to an end for us. With our farewell goodbyes went the realisation that our time of useful work with the Xhosa People in the Transkei, first in Sulenkama in a Mission Hospital, then in Umtata at the Bedford Orthopaedic Centre initiating the Orthopaedic Service, and finally teaching doctors and nurses in a changed and changing environment, had come to an end. Any further involvement in the country would be in another role in different circumstances.

Always at the back of our minds since the day we heard about the fire at Heaton, the instant we lifted off from South Africa at Johannesburg the gutted building that was our church and the people who were our people came flooding to the forefront. By the time we touched down and were back home we were fully focused, at one with our church community. The embers of the badly damaged Church in Heaton had subsided but the flames of Meadowell still flickered.

A look at the church we'd known, bedecked with scaffolding, enormous sheets of tarpaulin flapping in the breeze trying their best to cover over huge holes in the damaged roof, and the notice board in front of the undamaged hall alongside it viewed from the front and side street boldly proclaiming that *Heaton United Reformed Church is Not Burnt Out* spelt the inevitable, the demise of familiar Victorian landmark and the birth of a new Heaton Church from the hall. Like a phoenix from the ashes around it the hall would be transformed to the *Heaton United Reformed Church of today.* When we spoke to the people we all knew in the heart of our hearts the same thing. No official, final, decision had, of course, been made by then, and would take time to come to, but we all knew. The task before me was clear. My first priority was to stand alongside the people, to share in their profound sorrow, to enter their minds, to try to identify with the heritage gone up in flames, to attempt to inspire trust, to strengthen faith in the ever-present Spirit of God. In the weeks to come, I thought, I'd have my work as a counsellor cut out. But not so. In a very short time, almost before the embers stopped smoking, a fixed pattern of response emerged. The people knew what they wanted and were resolved.

My second priority was also clear, to carry the people on, into the changing world around them, to face the challenges of the reality of life enveloping them in which setting our home in order was not by any means the only or most important issue in life. This would be a much more formidable task. All around us circumstances were changing almost every day, in our community of Heaton, the wider community of Newcastle and the North-East, and especially in Meadowell. The very fabric of life in our own country, in South Africa, and Europe East and West, was crying out for radical political and social readjustment. There would be little time to take stock of either the most minute or most expansive tapestry of our lives. On the one hand our local activities would take us over. We'd do no more than attend to our own affairs. On the other hand far-reaching demands would crowd in on us. Each of us in our own particular work and in the things in which we shared in the church and our family was to be caught up in unexpected challenges we'd have to face up to over the coming years. Though many and varied, nothing would occur in isolation.

In reflective mood one day soon after our return home after the fire I wandered through the damaged, damp, dust-covered, mutilated carcass which was the vaulted building, our church. On impulse I checked that no one was around and made my way to the steps to the pulpit. Cautiously climbing the dusty stairs I was there, before me an empty derelict. There was no sermon, but where my notes might have been was something familiar. The bread-board I'd carefully positioned to be just right for me from which I could stand confidently at and deliver a sermon. Warped and roughened from drying out after water damage, charred at the edges, I knew where to find it at home in *Abbey Royd* for a few years but can no longer trace it. Later in the sepulchral church with Avril and the Moderator of the General Assembly of the United Reformed Church on a short visit we stood together, each with our own thoughts, and shared a prayer for our fellowship at Heaton, the past and the future, and ended by commending our church, us and our church buildings, to the care of God to do the best for us.

At home in 'our home', rapidly becoming 'our treasured home' in *Abbey Royd* for a few days over the Christmas 1991 and New Year 1992 break we draped a few tinsels over the pictures on the walls and over the grandfather clocks in the drawing room, switched on the sometimes intermittently flashing lights on the artificial Christmas tree, the familiar well worn angel perched precariously on it's top, and sat back, secure in the tranquillity of Kelso, away briefly from the pressures of Heaton. I checked Avril's clock gifted to her grandfather Loch on his retirement for devoted service as a teacher. Home-made, skilfully fashioned, wooden wedges were carefully readjusted, a *tap tap* with a hammer or a kick with the back of my shoe, to balance the delicate pendulum, to make sure it swung evenly and smoothly. With nimble fingers and confident knowledge of where the key was kept it was becoming a habit for Avril to locate it from a recess at the back of the clock-face, wind it up, and replace the key for another year. On the stroke of midnight on the last day of another December, the clock would strike in unison with Big Ben on the telly next to it. Looking back and looking forward, the single thing that seemed to dominate our lives was the fire that ravished our church.

But the fire in our church was not the only fire in 1991. There were no literal fires outside our front door at 3 Crompton Road but there was fire smouldering in the hearts and minds of many of the vandals who stalked the streets at night. Unguarded shouts of derision, threatening outbursts followed by a piercing scream or feeble whimper, the crash of broken glass, an expletive or two and footsteps running away, the sounds of fermenting violence on our doorsteps and not far off on Heaton Road often broke the silence of the night. In Heaton, as in most places in the North-East, we seemed to be in the eye of a storm of remorselessness, with Avril at her clinics at the epicentre. We soon gave up replacing her car radios. Twice within a month, once outside our own front door and once outside the clinic in Meadowell, the story was the same. 'Would you describe the incident for us?' the police would ask, presenting her with a claim form. 'Someone suspicious near the car, the sound of broken glass or a screwdriver being forced into the lock on the driver's door, the shadow of someone in the driving seat, nimble fingers disconnecting the wires at the back of the radio set, the slam of a door, a figure disappearing, laughing, something with wires dangling from it in his hand.' 'Fill in the form and send it to your insurer.' We knew the procedure, which would be repeated several times in the years to come. 'This is your crime number. We're getting more and more these days. Best take a portable radio with you if you want a radio. It's not worth bothering about a set in your car.' It was good advice. And hubcaps were two a penny – best don't bother about them either!

We were not around when our church went up in flames on Thursday, August 1st 1991, but we were when the Meadowell Health Centre was set ablaze. Feelings had been running high on the estate for some time. Opposition to the frustrations of social exclusion, deprivation partly self-perpetuated but mainly politically induced, a strong Mrs Thatcher in conflict with despairing and desperate trade unions could no longer be controlled. Hostility gave way to violence reported in the local press, TV and our Northern Province as 'the recent Tyneside riots' centred around the Community Centre on the Meadowell

Estate. Staff at the neighbouring Health Centre were vulnerable. Cars were being vandalised within sight of the clinic receptionist. The culprits were mainly children, innocent, naïve maybe but nevertheless threatening and abusive.

When fighting in the streets and lawlessness escalated 'increasing violence on the Meadowell Estate' was reportedly reclassified as 'Tyneside Riots'. A Police presence and the Emergency Services in the mayhem of Meadowell featured on the local TV nightly. Then the night of the fire. The Health Centre was ablaze, acrid smoke billowing into the night sky, figures, men, women and children running amok, shouts of frenzied abuse mingling with the crackling of the flames. A sad picture of anarchy but at its worst a note of sanity! Many of the women from the clinic, girls and mothers who had come to own the Service as their own, were as much outraged at its violation as the firebrands themselves hell-bent on destruction. In solidarity they ran to the burning Health Centre, confronted the arsonists, too late to avert the conflagration but not to assert their authority and minimise looting. Among the remains of the burnt-out clinic were Avril's notes, charred beyond recognition. Watching the scenes on the TV with Avril on the night of the fire I could only feel objectively what she took to her heart, her subjective oneness with her patients striking a chord the depths of which I could not fathom. Patients and Family Planning doctor alike started the clinic anew with a blank piece of paper for a case sheet when the clinic reopened.

Looking back, I'm sure the Easter words of encouragement in my *Minister's Letter* in the April *Messenger* in 1992 marked a major turning point in our time at Heaton. The letter was, therefore, as much for the minister and his wife as the people in the church.

'A few weeks ago,' it started, *'we planted a bean during one of our services. It was planted in a jar, wedged between a blotting paper roll and the glass side of the jar so that you could see it and watch what happens over the coming few weeks. We put some water in the bottom of the jar and we hope it will be absorbed by the blotting paper up to the bean; and we left the top open to let in* the air. *This is an old experiment to show how, with water and air and nourishment from the seed, something will happen – a new plant will grow, new life will emerge.*

All kinds of event are crowding in on us in all aspects of our lives, not least in our church lives in Heaton. The fire, the sadness of the loss of our church building and the plans for a new building, disappointment and satisfaction, opportunities grasped and those lost, hopes for survival and visions of a new approach have come and gone. But let's not be despondent. By letting go of ourselves, dying and rising to life in Jesus, our church – the people, not the building – can give hope to those on our doorsteps and world-wide. Like the bean, our trust is in the seed that dies as it nourishes new life. Like the bean, new life and growth extends upwards and outwards into the fresh air. Like the bean new life is rooted in soil that satisfies the thirst for life.

May your beans sprout! May your trees blossom! May your flowers bloom to bring brightness and colour and beauty and fragrance this springtime! Happy Easter!'

Back in Newcastle after a momentous two-week holiday in Prague the impasse of our situation came flooding in on us. Far from dispelling our dis-ease the holiday had, if anything, compounded it. Before the fire I had had most of my proposals for renewal rejected. After the fire this had not changed but any question of moving on, making a new start, with better prospects of fulfilment for me, were shelved in favour of hanging in with the people. The world around us, however, was crying out for attention. The language of peace and justice, and racial, sexual, traditional and social acceptance demanded its translation into action. In her work Avril was engaged in action. In mine, through the wider church aligning itself with the issues on our door- steps and world-wide, I found myself devoting more and more of my energies in the same direction. But in our local church in Heaton, which seemed to stride through life indifferent to the crying needs around it, I felt as if I was surplus to requirements. The every detail of the fire and its consequences dominated its life. As time passed the frustrations of waiting, and waiting, and waiting, waiting for every step of the seemingly endless number of decisions to be made, gathered momentum. Whatever the ultimate wishes of the people it seemed the District Council disapproved. Exasperation festered. Hostility almost broke out. Battle lines were drawn and I was caught in the crossfire. In attempting to understand opposing minds like a true arbitrator I found myself being ostracised by the power core of our fellowship. There seemed so much to be done outside our church, so little for me inside. Our holiday did nothing to console me. In fact, identifying myself with Jan Hus, the martyr to the cause of church reform and Czech nationalism burnt at the stake in 1415 and my other reforming heroes, Patrick Hamilton burnt at the stake in St Andrews in 1528 and Thomas Cranmer commemorated at the Martyr's Memorial in Oxford for his death at the stake in 1556, only strengthened my resolve to fulfil my destiny. My time, and with me Avril's, in Newcastle could not continue much longer.

In not too long a time a vacancy for a minister at a Local Ecumenical Partnership in Ashington came up and I jumped at the possible offer of a call which came my way and was gladly accepted.

Prompted by the stimulating insights of many friends we'd made during our time in Heaton moving on brought with it a sense of liberation to embark on whatever lay ahead for us unfettered and uninhibited. My letter in the May *Messenger* was only to commend the words of Fred Kaan's hymn which would come to take on a particular significance for us.

The church is like a table,
a table that is round.
It has no sides or corners,
no first or last, no honours;
here people are in one-ness
and love together bound.

The church is like a table
set in an open house;
no protocol for seating,
a symbol of inviting,
of sharing, drinking, eating;
an end to 'them' and 'us'.

The church is like a table,
a table for a feast
to celebrate the healing
of all excluded feeling,
(while Christ is serving, kneeling,
a towel round his waist).

The church is like a table,
where every head is crowned.
As guests of God created,
all are to each related;

the whole world is awaited
to make the circle round.
Fred Kaan (1929-)

TRINITY CHURCH, ASHINGTON
A LOCAL ECUMENICAL PARTNERSHIP

The Service of Induction to the Pastorate of Trinity Church, Ashington, was not unfamiliar. Only three years earlier it had been accompanied by Ordination at Heaton. In the big red brick building in the city centre on Station Road I felt, with Avril, strangely at home in the family of our new Methodist and URC friends. When the time came for me to deliver my Statement as I had at the start of my Ministry only three years earlier in Newcastle I was, as then, in a strange way, focused almost solely from beyond myself on the most minute details of life around me, my family and friends, and my new companions in pilgrimage in our new community of Ashington.

'There's a thermometer outside this building,' I concluded, 'and a target to aim at to start our building programme. I'm happy to play my part in this aspect of our work. But it's not our primary task. Our first concern is the job of the Church, the people in any way connected to it, to witness to the Kingdom of God in all aspects of our lives; to break down barriers of denominational and social and traditional and cultural differences, and see in life around us, the love of God revealed in Jesus Christ.
I see my task as your minister to enable and empower us all to respond to the Holy Spirit – to respond each in our own way, free from pretensions. It's important that we be ourselves. I'll be myself and I hope you'll all be the same. I'll wear what I

217

think appropriate – maybe a collar and a gown – maybe not. I'll continue as minister of the United Reformed Church, as I've been nurtured, but I'll function also, with unreserved enthusiasm, as a 'Recognised and Regarded' Minister of the Methodist Church. My role will be to grow with all of you as the Holy Spirit of a loving God dictates. I'm not here to swing the pendulum towards the URC –to counteract a swing to the Methodists another time. My only hope and prayer is that our ecumenical, free, reformed church here in Ashington might grow as part of the Church Universal into a fellowship where every brother and sister in Christ, and all God's created children, may find a home.

With God's grace, let his will be done.'

On the way home from church after the Induction I had time to think as I walked. It was the biggest of several buildings that the people had chosen for their new church. Formerly the Presbyterian Church in Ashington known as St George's it became St George's URC when the United Reformed Church became an entity in the early 70s, and in recent years Trinity Church (Methodist and URC) with the formation of the Local Ecumenical Partnership with several Methodist churches in town. Most St George's members were still Presbyterian in outlook even well after they had become part of the URC. Relating to Methodists was at best questionable, at worst viewed with suspicion. Statistically there were more Methodist than URC members and many still looked back to the good old days as independent Methodist congregations and wondered what the future held for them. In the meantime the Methodists consolidated round what had become a focal point for them at the Second Avenue Methodist Church where all services would be held until the refurbished Trinity Church was up and running.

I had visited Ashington only a few weeks before, along with Avril. It had the same effect on both of us. Depression hung heavily over the town centre. It looked and felt run down. A thriving mining town, the biggest mining village in Europe in better years, devaluation, depression, unemployment and redundancy had sapped endurance. The shops stocked only cheaper goods. Charity shops abounded. Betting shops and gaming machines provided transient hope. Paradoxically, on the outskirts of the town relatively affluent homes, executive houses with a good car in the drive were spreading into surrounding green fields. Commuters lived well outside the town looking to supermarkets in neighbouring bigger towns like Blyth and the malls and metros of Newcastle and Gateshead for their shopping. The town was dying while the periphery was growing into itself and away. Setting off across the green grass of a playing field not far from our new home in the 'Methodist Manse' a day or two after our arrival in Ashington I was struck by the same sombre feeling of dereliction I was familiar with in my boyhood days in the coal mining village of West Wemyss in Fife. The setting was the same – fertile pastures for the healing of wounds of lost people being side-stepped, reconciling differing outlooks, encouraging, supporting, inspiring gifted though often down-trodden folk to reach beyond themselves to a hope which could become a certainty if nurtured and given the opportunity for self expression. Along Wansbeck Road to *Pinehurst* and there was Avril at the door with a cheery smile on her face and Meggie at her feet, the smell of a good casserole, the laughter of some of the children in the air. A knowing look from Avril confirmed that Ashington was the place for us.

From my first service in the Second Avenue Church the day after my induction I warmed to the small compact Methodist church and the people. I felt at home in the church, even secure, in the sanctuary with a familiar communion table, lectern and pulpit, an impressive pipe organ, plain cross on the pale blue wall and an enclosing communion rail which seemed naturally part of the mahogany furniture. It wouldn't be long before I'd dispense the Sacraments of bread and wine to thirsty souls at the communion rail like any good Methodist minister as if I had done it all my days. I thrilled to the task of merging the two traditions into one, retaining individuality but at the same time growing into a wider ecumenical fellowship. A short prayer from a Steward in the vestry before going into the church was helpful. No one was slow to take up the request to do a reading or lead a prayer. A Presbyterian, URC, reserve was offset by a Methodist confidence in getting involved. And the Methodists brought every hymn to life. Good, well-rehearsed male and female voices harmonised as I'd never known before.

Though I saw to it that I was in my own church for most of the morning services and all services of any particular note, my Sundays were not restricted to Ashington alone. I'd take my turn with services in all the churches and chapels in our Circuit. Soon I began to look forward to returning to the small congregations as well as the people in the bigger Methodist churches and another LEP like ours. And the routine of helping to make out the Plan for the month ahead under the supervision of our able and helpful Northeast Northumberland Circuit Superintendent, at first a mystery, eventually began to make sense to me. A notable feature of Wesley's Methodism, the Plan ensures that every church or chapel is covered, receiving regular ministry from an Ordained Minister or recognised Lay Preacher at Sunday morning or evening services. Though reluctant to recognise the value of the arrangement our URC, and now in harder times the Church of Scotland as well, frequently resorts to a similar plan in today's world.

In time, when the work on our new Trinity Church was finished and we moved, the centre of our church community would be in the town centre, but in our first almost two years the central focus for our work would be the Second Avenue Church. It was there that I sowed the seeds of union in the roots of our ecumenical partnership. It was there that I'd attempt to marry the value of and need for the well-tried Methodist hymn book, *Hymns and Psalms* and the newer *Rejoice and Sing* book of the URC, the first in the church's history giving it an identity it had never had before. I think the people smiled, or shuddered, whenever I stood before them, a Methodist hymn book in one hand and *Rejoice and Sing* in the other, expounding the differences between and the similarities in the two. Many hymns were naturally common to both books, some favourites in only one, an education to us all and an opportunity to introduce peace, justice and social issues including care of the environment to the life of our community.

Within a few months of Communion services every month at Second Avenue and between times at some of the other churches in the circuit I adapted myself to the idea of people coming forward to receive the elements. 'On alternate months you could have a URC 'sit in your seat and be served' style service for the benefit of the Presbyterians', I was told, 'and at other times the Methodist way to satisfy them.' It was tempting to comply, but my mind raced ahead. 'Oh No!' I replied, 'Communion is special for all of us, and it should include us all, even children.' At the start of the Communion part of the service, which is essentially identical in all denominations, it was common practice to escort the children from the church for an instructional time with their Sunday-School teachers. I wrestled with the problem for a while. Sleepless hours at night saw me trying to sort out a logistic nightmare. The whole

Sacrament might end in chaos. But a better way than alternative standard rituals must be possible, I kept telling myself, and another way did evolve in our LEP at Trinity Church in Ashington, rooted in a pattern initiated in our Second Avenue Church.

On the Sunday of the first experimental, all-inclusive Communion at the now familiar chapel on Second Avenue, I was apprehensive but strangely composed and confident. Avril felt much the same, and we were both reassured by the united response from the people. Without exception they had all given the proposals thought. Some strongly in favour, others with no convictions either way but willing to go along, and a substantial body of opinion passionately opposed to non-members and children being involved, they'd all openly discussed their feelings and were prepared, when it came to the test, to give it a fair trial. Unlike our previous encounters in our former church, widely differing views in the church in Ashington were not a stumbling block to progress. They were consumed by oneness, which included their imaginative minister and his loyal wife.

During the first verse of the Communion hymn, *'Lord Jesus Christ, you have come to us, you are one with us, Mary's son'*, (Ref. Number 373, 'Living Lord' in *Rejoice and Sing'* and *617 in Hymns and Psalms.)* the Sunday School Superintendent left the church to return with the children in the later verses. 'Now that the children are with us,' I started from behind the Communion Table, an Elder and a Steward on either side of me, the elements uncovered, 'our Church family is complete' – and started with a welcome call and invitation. After the variously named Eucharistic Prayer, Great Prayer of Thanksgiving or just The Thanksgiving including reference to the Narrative of the Institution if not read separately, came the distribution of the elements.

The Bread broken and the Cup of the New Covenant demonstrated, the celebrant and those behind the Communion Table having taken of 'The body of Christ, given for you' and 'The blood of Christ, shed for you' came the distribution of the bread and the wine to the people. I explained, 'Those who wish to come forward and receive the bread and the wine do so as you wish. Those who wish to be served in their seats remain seated; the bread and the wine will be brought to you. The children will come forward and receive the elements if they, their families or their teachers wish; if not they will receive a blessing and return with the others from the Communion rail.' I took a deep breath, a reassuring glance from Avril catching my eye, could all but hear the silent prayer for the practicalities enlisted, and waited.

As if a miracle, everything went like clockwork. The Methodists came forward to the Communion rail as they wanted to, received the bread and wine and returned to their seats after a dismissal blessing. The still Presbyterian-orientated URC members remained seated and were served in their seats as they wanted. No one seemed offended by the children. One grandmother said later how pleased her ten-year-old granddaughter was at dinner after the service, telling the rest of the family about taking bread and the wine with granny. Most people had to admit that the reverence and dignity of the traditional Communion had been retained and a broader, more inclusive meaning introduced. With Fred Kaan's hymn still ringing in our ears, the service was over. We were on our way home to meet the 'challenge of tomorrow's day'.

Commitments in connection with funerals, weddings and the building programme, which were gathering momentum, restricted our visits to *Abbey Royd*. Less often than every second week, we patiently looked forward to each visit more and more. The animated chat with some of our friends outside the church at the end of an evening service in Ashington must have betrayed our anticipation. Home to pack up, collect Meggie and head north to Kelso, we could hardly wait. To arrive even late at night was well worth the effort. To wake the next morning in a Kelso environment was a tonic. Though I very often arranged details of funerals on the phone with a persistent but understanding undertaker, we could almost always be assured of a day away on Monday, in another world, Avril in the garden, no clinics to distract the tranquillity of her concentration. Back to Ashington on Tuesday morning in time for Avril's clinic in the afternoon, I was at once into the pastoral cares of my vocation.

Then, on a Tuesday morning in a week we had not been to Kelso the phone rang. It was not another funeral or anything to do with the church. 'It's the Police in Kelso,' I heard the voice at the other end say, slowly and deliberately. Alerted at once, my suspicions were confirmed. 'Are you Mr Nicol, the owner of *Abbey Royd*?' 'Yes, Yes!' 'I've got some bad news for you. Your house has been burgled. We're here just now, investigating the robbery. There's been a lot taken. Almost every room has been ransacked. We're taking photographs and fingerprints. You'd better come as soon as you can.' What could I say but, 'Of course. I'll be there in an hour or two.' From the tone of the conversation and the look on my face, Avril knew. We held each other, stifling our trembling. I'd have to be on my way. Avril would soon be on her way to the waiting patients at her clinic. Conditioned to her priorities, she'd give her undivided attention to their every care. She might phone me in Kelso, or see me when I was back, after the clinic.

It all seemed so unreal. I wandered through the hall. The strong front door, bolts and locks intact, swung half open, the beading where it had been secured ripped off, shredded, when the door was rammed from, perhaps, the back of a sturdy van at the bottom of the steps. Remnants of pipes and buttresses strewn around, cast to one side, spoke of a professional hand. The fragile inner door was propped against the wall its lower panelled half kicked in, the woodwork on either side brushed aside with ease by heavy-handed intruders just walking in as though there were no barriers to their entry. A Policewoman emerged from one of the rooms, a camera in one hand and fingerprint-dusting brush in the other. An Inspector would be along in a minute and they'd both go through the house with me taking notes. More rational then, I'd hear what they had to say, but, alone in the unreal world around me, aware of their presence but unaware of what was being said, I picked my way through the debris which littered every room in the house.

With Avril with me later, in Kelso after her clinic in Ashington, together we went through 'our home', the house in Kelso that had been burgled, the *Abbey Royd* which suddenly with the robbery felt 'not ours'. But the thought of disowning 'our home', even our desecrated house, was never anything more than a transient reaction. In the silence of the midsummer night in *Abbey Royd* we surveyed the scene again. Almost dead emotionally, exhausted, sapped of any remaining energy, there was not much Avril had to say to me or me to her. What we were both sure of was that, violated though our home had been, it was still 'our home'. Deprived of our treasured memories snatched from our homestead we'd have to reclaim it for ourselves. Avril replaced what she could of her belongings in our bedroom on her dressing table. We cleared the bed for sleeping in our dishevelled bedroom, had a cup of tea, and got into our bed in our desecrated *Abbey Royd*. The shadows in trees around closed in on the house. The doors secured, the shutters closed, the light out, it was time for sleep to drown the depths of despond. At one and yet each isolated on our own, Avril nestled in. Coorying down, she sobbed herself to sleep. A lump in my throat, I wasn't long behind.

Next day at the crack of dawn we set to methodically, unhurried but determined to complete our task as quickly as we could, tidying up. Avril insisted on cleaning every square inch with any evidence of an intruder's presence meticulously, replacing our smallest possession in its rightful place huge gaps accentuating the absence of many treasures. The Police were back to interview us both, procuring a more comprehensive list of missing items from Avril than me the day before. In the drawing room she gave her own description of the grandfather clock in the far-away corner of the room describing where she'd placed its key and on the ruffled carpet, all but hidden by the leg of an easy chair, there it was. 'Look!' she exclaimed, picking it up and grasping it to herself. It must have fallen off when the clock was being moved. Never again would she wind the clock at Christmas time with its key, but neither would anyone else either. We gave the key to the Police in case they found the clock and would be able to identify it but were told the chances of recovery were next to nothing.

As at Heaton three years earlier, with the burglary behind us, by autumn 1993 we had settled into Ashington. A pattern of familiarity with our church, the people, the services and ever increasing activities in the community as well as a day in Kelso whenever we could, was not unlike Heaton. But Ashington was much busier, and it differed also in another crucial manner. We warmed to a people who were more responsive, open to the challenge of life around them and in need of encouragement, more than the self-sufficient, dogged independence of our former friends. Avril was soon established in Family Planning clinics in Northumberland in addition to her North Tyneside commitments. As in Heaton soon after our arrival when Rebecca was Christened, this time it was Laura who was centre stage. Photographs in the Second Avenue church and in Kelso with the family the following day tell a similar story.

Hardly before we knew where we were, a year was over in Ashington. Life was moving on apace. A new church magazine entitled *Witness* with the *t* twice the size of the other letters to emphasise the cross, declaring that it was the magazine of Trinity Church, Methodist/United Reformed Church, Ashington, and displaying the logos of the Methodist Church on one bottom corner and the United Reformed Church on the other had been introduced by Christmas 1993. Our disparate peoples found an identity in it. Through its pages they could keep abreast of comings and goings most uppermost in everyone's mind, especially our rebuilding programme.

By June 1994 I was able to share something of the tempo of life I was experiencing through the pages of *Witness*. May seemed like one race after another, running round and round in circles with so much to do by tighter and tighter deadlines, in greater detail and in wider fields than ever. The pressure was on to get started on the physical building of our new church and, at the same time, restructure ourselves to share and give our gifts, to move with the times, to reach out to those in need and accept help and advice and criticism ourselves. At Pentecost on Sunday morning 1994 a baby was baptised, two new elders ordained, six new members admitted to the fellowship, new Stewards and Councillors recognised, the

227

Lord's Supper celebrated and our life in Christ renewed. By June Trinity Church was 'bursting out all over'. With the summer holidays school and college days were coming to an end. I was elected to the Board of Governors of our Middle School in Ashington and would be an integral part of its life for the next two years. Perhaps it was the thought of further education that prompted me to follow up an advert in the *New Internationalist* about an MSc course at the Centre of African Studies in Edinburgh at a time when I thought I had some spare time. I enrolled for the full-time one-year course as a part-time student for two years starting in October 1994.

In the second term of the first year I broke with the more regular routine of my contemporary postgraduate fellow students to attend *The Centre for the Study of Christianity in the Non-Western World*, part of the *Faculty of Divinity at New College*. With new classmates from theological backgrounds in mostly Africa, Asia, and the Pacific, each bringing a fresh, challenging perspective to the often-heated debates, I thrilled to the whole concept of Non-Western Christianity. Empathising with my tutor, Kwame Bediako, from the start I read his book *Theology and Identity* from cover to cover and used much of its content for a marked essay entitled, *'A Critical Evaluation of the Factors that Shaped African Christian Theology in the 20th Century'*, at the end of the module. Like many of my better sermons which started and ended with a text, the essay started and ended with a quotation:-

'Umntu Ngumntu Ngbantu,' I started, *'A person's a person because of people.' This Xhosa expression is echoed in many other languages among many other peoples in Africa and underscores the importance attached to relationships between an individual and all those with whom he or she comes in contact. All the factors which shape African Christian*

Theology, in one way or another, impinge on relationships of people to other people, and their God in whose image they are made.' And I ended with the conclusion, *'Umntu Ngumntu Ngbantu' – A person's a person because of people. The factors outlined above that have shaped African Christian Theology in the 20th. Century are all, in some way, concerned with Relationships – of people with people, and their God,'*

The essay went down well. It was well presented. Avril had typed it out meticulously but at no small cost. Recovering at last from six weeks enforced bed rest with an acute disc lesion (slipped disc), she had forced herself to complete my work, typing in pain, supine but twisted to strike the key board, to meet the dead line for my rush back to Edinburgh to hand it in for assessment.

But my essay wasn't the only thing being prepared for assessment. Work on our town centre church was gathering momentum. Would it be completed by April 1995 for the Service of Dedication? Broken stained glass windows were repaired and a celebrated local artist was commissioned to fashion a flock of birds in flight representing our gathered congregation in the three-in-one lead latticed window towering from floor to the roof overlooking the chancel, a focal point on entering the building. With a central cross partly illuminated and the flock of birds fluttering in suggestive motion with the passing of every racing cloud in an otherwise clear sky when the sun shone through into the church, it was hoped that the one-step-raised sanctuary enfolded in the circle of chairs around it would be light and roomy. On it the moveable pulpit, lectern and a selection of choice chairs, but most of all the circular Communion Table which I had longed for since our days at Heath Church in Halifax and was so touched by when the congregation willingly agreed to have installed, would be readily seen by everyone in the congregation seated around on their new Presbyterian blue communion-glass and hymn-book-holding chairs. Far from providing a barrier, the discreet, detachable communion rail would enhance the occasion when in use at the Sacrament while allowing freer direct access when removed at other times. This was our dream.

Ironically, on the crest of a wave of satisfaction that the fruits of our labours in our LEP were about to ripen at the Rededication of our church on Saturday, 22nd April, 1995, any personal feelings of achievement I might have harboured were tempered by my concern for the one who had contributed most to bringing me to that point – Avril, my other, better half. I knew precisely the clinical diagnosis of her affliction, a clear cut lumbar disc lesion involving the first and second sacral nerve roots, and would, in my time as a Consultant Orthopaedic Surgeon, have been confident in her treatment – bed rest for a limited period of time and if no improvement, surgery. She and I, and her Medical advisers in Ashington, were all in agreement, but the ultimate decisions and the outcome would not be in my hands. I saw her suffer and longed to act more aggressively but conservative treatment brought slow improvement. At last she started mobilising, first round the bed, then in the house and on the stairs and on my arm in the street. Recovery was slow but steady and almost complete. Apart from minimal sensory deficit all symptoms and signs subsided and she was able, in time, to return to work.

But Avril was unable to share in my first services in our newly refurbished church or even to step through the glass front door and take even a few steps on the carpeted entrance lobby until the day of its Rededication the day before her birthday. On the day, in the silence of the Saturday morning, alone in the church, preparations well underway in the new kitchen for refreshments in the new all-purpose hall after the service, we walked through the church together in silence, each of us with our own thoughts, paused below the flock of birds in flight on the stained glass window and rested for a brief moment at the Round Communion Table, its significance recognised in a glance and a smile. On the way out we found a vacant spot at the entrance and Avril hung a framed cross-stitch tapestry she had been making to commemorate the day of Rededication on it. The presentation still hangs there today. She sat through the service in the afternoon but left before the refreshments. Next day the morning service was overmuch for her.

At the Service of Rededication the church was packed. My words of welcome included:-

'Who are we? you may ask. We are Trinity Church in Ashington, an LEP, a Local Ecumenical Partnership with our roots in the Methodist and the United Reformed traditions. We are first and foremost an LEP, sometimes referred to as a 'Leper'- Jesus had something to say about lepers. We are all Methodists who play our part in the South East Northumberland Circuit and in the wider Methodist Church and are responsible to the Methodist Church; but not only to the Methodist Church, for we belong also to the United Reformed Church, we play our part in the Nothumberland District Council and the wider United Reformed Church and are responsible to it. No wonder we're schizophrenic, but schizophrenic or not, we look upon ourselves as a pilgrim people, part of the People of God, who have arrived at this stage of our pilgrimage together, in our newly decorated 'Trinity Church'. We are trying to come to terms with our identity. In moving into this building which is to be re-dedicated as a resource for our LEP, which is us, we're

struggling, not to impose any preconceived ideas of what we are and who we are dictated by our past, but to put ourselves in the hands of God, be guided by and empowered by the Holy Spirit, and with the grace of the Lord Jesus Christ, be moulded into an Ecumenical Community Church where everyone and anyone can come, anytime, and feel at home.

So that's us. Look around you. What do you see?

People – some you know and some you don't.

A cross – symbol of our faith – the cross of the risen Christ.

A flock of birds in flight in a stained glass window – that's us, pilgrims on the move.

A Baptismal font – named by the Trinity.

An organ – music – singing.

A pulpit – preaching.

A Bible –Scriptures containing the Word of God.

A table – a circular table. The Church is like a table,
                          a table that is round

   God is here! Let's sing about it!'

And did we sing about it!

> *God is here! As we his people*
> *meet to offer praise and prayer,*
> *may we find in fuller measure*
> *what it is in Christ we share.*
> *Here, as in the world around us,*
> *all our varied skills and arts*
> *wait the coming of the Spirit*
> *into open minds and hearts.*
>
> *Here are symbols to remind us*
> *of our lifelong need of grace;*
> *here are table, font and pulpit;*
> *here the cross has central place.*

Here in honesty of preaching,
here in silence, as in speech,
here, in newness and in renewal,
God the Spirit comes to each.

Here our children find a welcome
in the Shepherd's flock and fold;
here as bread and wine are taken,
Christ sustains us, as of old;
here the servants of the Servant
seek in worship to explore
what it means in daily living
to believe and to adore.

Lord of all, of Church and Kingdom,
in an age of change and doubt,
keep us faithful to the gospel,
help us work your purpose out.
Here in this day's dedication,
all we have to give, receive:
we, who cannot live without you,
we adore you! We believe!
(Hymns and Psalms, No 653,
F. Pratt Green (1903-)

Pondering at my desk in the front room in *Pinehurst*, for something to write for my last letter to all my friends in the church in Ashington which had endeared itself to us, pen in hand, a blank page in a jotter before me, something on the back cover of one of our church magazines caught my eye. 'Over Jordan '96' – The Fifth Biblical Bike Ride for The Nazareth Hospital – November 1996'. I looked again and rang for an application pack. Forgetting my African Studies for a mad moment, I thought it might be something for me to do when I had time on my hands in Kelso. 'EMMS!' a cheerful voice replied. 'I'm interested in the Over Jordan Bike Ride in November but wonder what it involves. Would I be up to it?' I enquired. 'Are you fit?' I was asked. 'Not particularly just now, but I will be.' 'And have you done much cycling?' 'No, none at all, but I will have by November.' 'It sounds as if you'll do,' was the verdict. So it was that I enrolled for 'The Fifth Biblical Bike Ride for the Nazareth Hospital, Over Jordan 96', from the Sea of Galilee to the Red Sea, 2-10 November 1996, 'The Experience of a Lifetime.'

Leaving Ashington was like leaving a family get-together for a funeral, a wedding or an anniversary. The occasion had come to an end but there was no cut off as there had been at Heaton. At the farewell social on the Saturday before the last official services the next day, nice things were said confirming feelings from the heart. I was presented with a painting of Bamburgh castle which mirrored a similar work of Holy Island castle presented to Avril by her Family Planning friends, both reminders of our love of the open beauty of the Northumberland countryside. A handsome cheque was pressed in to my hand towards the purchase of a mountain bike for the Bike Ride Over Jordan. There would be no turning back now! And the flowers presented to Avril were not just the usual long-forgotten tokens of thanks, but given with genuine gratitude for her natural, unassuming interest in the cares and joys of all our friends in Ashington. Her well-known affinity for the refreshing smells, the vibrant life and ever-changing, sometimes mellow, sometimes vivid, colours of a garden were matched only by her love for her many admirers and theirs for her.

On the Sunday of my last official service in Ashington I used the sermon that I was to repeat, in substance, in three other churches at the end of special relationships touching my heart, as Avril's, as no other. Referring to a reading from 2 Samuel 23:8-12 about Shammah and chapter 18:6-15 about Absalom, (best from the Revised English Bible), I included an open assessment of my relationship with my partner in pilgrimage, my dear wife, Avril, and my congregation and us.

FAREWELL SERMON

'It's not often that I bring Avril into my sermons, so I'll start with her. She's been, in our family, like Shammah in the field of lentils. I've been like Absalom, always trying to do more and better, with my eye on a memorial. Let me explain. Avril's been quiet and unassuming, always there to support and inspire me, but never to share in the limelight. She's worked in her own right as a Family Planning doctor in the North-East of England and in Halifax in Yorkshire, as an Anaesthetist at Bridge of Earn and in Dundee, and with me in South Africa in the Transkei, but always put her family before herself. She's done the chores of feeding and washing, and being with our five children as they grew, and assumed the same role with our grandchildren. Like Shammah, she's struggled on in uninspiring places. And me, like Absalom, I've... Well, I'll leave you to judge.

What I'd like you to do, if you can, is to identify yourself with two of the characters we heard about in our readings from 2 Samuel – Shammah and Absalom.

From our first reading we heard that Shammah 'stood his ground in a field of lentils and saved it, and defeated the Philistines. So the Lord brought about a great victory.' The other two of David's heroes, his three best leaders, were Ishbosheth the Hachmonite and Eleazar. Ishbosheth killed 800 Philistines at one time with his spear, and Eleazar fought until his sword stuck to his hand; but Shammah stood in the middle of a field of lentils and defended it. What a contrast! What a comedown! The first two fought and were victorious; with the cheers and shouts of acclamation in their ears they were champions in the field of battle. Shammah won his victory standing, alone, in a field of lentils, cheered on only by a few farmers and peasants, womenfolk and children. The background to this story is that Israel was going through hard times. It was being attacked on all sides. The Philistines were running rings round them. The economy was in ruins and resources run down to almost nothing. The people were starving. Food was hard to come by, and a field of lentils was worth a fortune. The farmer and his family who owned the lentil field had watched the crop grow, and were about to harvest it, but the Philistines were also watching the crop mature, and were about to sweep down and steal it. There wasn't much at stake, just a few lentils and a poor farmer and his family, but it was for this Shammah fought. He stood in the field of lentils and defended it. There was no thrill in it, no glory.

Yet most battles for God, most victories for God, are won in fields of lentils. In a community like this, where someone is tempted to say, 'Yes' but says 'No'; in a family like any of ours, when someone is the first to break the silence after a quarrel; when a tired, worn-out mother rises at night to attend to a sick child, or a daughter to answer the demanding call of a cantankerous, demented parent; whenever and wherever men and women take a stand, and act for others, however small and insignificant the battle against pride and greed or selfishness or dishonesty might seem, a troop of Philistines is halted in its tracks. The growing menace of drugs and alcoholism especially in young people, the sordid abuse of children and the vulnerable casualties of society, degrading loss of respect for the elderly, the scandal of the growing number of marginalised under-classes on our doorsteps in this country and many others, including the wealthiest in the world, the rejection and exclusion of the outcasts of society on the basis of poverty, employment, education, race, and culture, sectarian bigotry fuelling violence and the hatred that boils over into terrorism – none of these will be halted by acts of Parliament, Prime Ministers or Presidents, elaborate campaigns or sensational demonstrations. They'll be controlled and reversed when more and more ordinary people like any of us put themselves out to help when help is needed, give where the need is greatest, love their neighbour and their enemies as themselves, in uninspiring fields of lentils, on their doorsteps and further afield. After this service, we'll all go our separate ways, each to our own fields of lentils which may seem uninspiring, difficult to defend, even not worth defending, but it's there that God has placed us, and it's there that we must make our stand and, like Shammah, fight for what God shows us to be right.

Now for Absalom and our second reading. Absalom set up a pillar for himself in the King's Vale for he said, 'I have no son to carry on my name.' The more we read the Bible and get under the skin of its many characters, the more we recognise, in them, ourselves, our hopes and fears, and dreams and longings, and, if you're anything like me, you'll know exactly how Absalom felt. He longed to be remembered, and so do I. And so do all of us, I suspect. The time comes when we all begin to ask ourselves questions like, 'What have I done in my life?' and 'Will anyone remember me?' and 'What, if they do, will they remember me for?' The nearest, I think, I ever came to having an obituary written about me was when we were on holiday in Xante, some years ago. We had hired bikes for the day and I was riding mine around the courtyard, among the washing on the lines, at the back of the self-catering flat we were staying in. Then, suddenly, I was on my back on the concrete yard. I'd been garrotted - well, not actually beheaded, but thrown off the back of the bike when my neck hit the wire washing line, and the back of my head crashed against the ground. Very much, but not quite as bad, as when Absalom was riding a mule, and it was passing beneath a great oak tree. His hair was caught in its boughs and he 'found himself in mid air, and the mule went on from under him.' Absalom was the third of David's 17 sons. He had made a name for himself twice in his life before he came to a dramatic end, tangled up in the branches of an oak tree. The first time he was involved in the rape of his sister, Tamar. It was his half brother, Amnon who actually raped Tamar and it was Absalom's duty to settle the outrage, but he couldn't face his responsibilities and did nothing for two long years. Then he invited all his brothers to a sheep-shearing party and, when they were all there, had Amnon murdered. But his father and many of his brothers were angry with him for the underhand way he had Amnon killed, and he fled to his father-in-law. Family tensions must have run high, and when Absalom next hit the head-lines he was organising a revolt against his father, King David, in an attempt to overthrow him and seize the throne. Absalom was a fine figure of a man, famous for his head of thick, golden hair. But he was all mixed up, discontented and ambitious. He wanted to make a name for himself but had done nothing much of any good to be remembered for. Then came his sudden death in the way we've heard about.

Though Absalom had been a very real threat to his life, David loved all his 17 sons, including Absalom, and when he heard that he was dead, he burst out, 'O! My son! My son, Absalom! Absalom, my son! If only I had died in your place, my son! Absalom, my son!'

After we're dead we live on, to some extent, in the hearts and minds of our children and the younger people who survive us. Most of us remember our parents, our aunts and uncles, *maybe even our grandparents or great-grandparents. Then memories are lost. So we try to make sure that we'll be remembered in the future. We solemnly erect gravestones, or raise memorials, or set up charity trusts. They do keep memories alive – for a while. The Taj Mahal, the Pyramids, the Sphinx – all magnificent monuments to posterity - but who knows much about the people these great monuments were erected for now? Very few, if anyone.*

> *'I met a traveller from an antique land*
> *who said, 'Two vast and trunkless legs of stone*
> *stand in the desert.'*
> *And on the pedestal these words appear*
> *'My name is Osymandius, King of Kings.*
> *Look on my works, ye mighty, and despair.'*
> *Nothing beside remains. Round the decay*
> *of that colossal wreck, boundless and bare*
> *the lone and level sands stretch far away.'*

Like Osymandius, Absalom raised his pillar in the hope that in it he would be remembered, but by the time 2 Samuel was written, the pillar had crumbled and decayed, though the place was called Absalom's Place, or Absalom's Monument for some time. Now everything has gone, and no-one even remembers where it was. And yet, and yet, even when very few people know or want to know the Bible in our own country Absalom is remembered. Not so long ago the popular novel, 'Absalom, Absalom' came out, and it was a hit, possibly even a best seller.

Why, then, is Absalom remembered after over 3000 years. By his pillar? – no, it's gone and its creation forgotten. By the battles he fought, much more dramatic than Shammah in the field of lentils? – No, they all ended in defeat and disgrace. For his good looks and his golden hair? – No, they were buried with his mangled remains. By his descendants? No, he had no sons.

Why, then, is Absalom remembered today? – Because of the heartbroken cry of the old father he despised and fought to overthrow. He's remembered for one reason, and one reason only, because David, his father, loved him with an understanding which embraced forgiveness and mercy, with the kind of love which made him mourn the victory that cost his son's life. At the time David cared nothing about crushing a rebellion in his country. The only question he asked about the battle was, 'Is the young man, Absalom, safe?' And when he heard the bitter truth there came from him the agonised cry that has echoed down the ages, a comfort to many a grieving heart today, 'O, my son! My son Absalom! Absalom, my son! If only I had died in your place, my son, Absalom, my son.'

We all long to be remembered, to know that our lives are worth something, and they are. Our value lies, not in what we make, nor in what we achieve, but in the affection we are held by the few people who love us in spite of our faults; the kind of affection each of us in this church is feeling now, the kind of affection you have shared with Avril and me in our time with you in Ashington and which we have grown to have for each of you. But, most of all, our value, our hope of being remembered, lies in the love of God for all of us, the love of God who 'So loved the world that he gave his only Son, that everyone who has faith in him may not die, but have eternal life.'

The Ashington chapter of our lives had all but come to an end. Loose ends started there would germinate to fruition in the first few months of our retirement in Kelso. Our priorities were, first, getting my dissertation completed in time for the closing date, then the Bike Ride over Jordan, and, last, integrating into the local church and social life. Would we warm to the comforting security of the latter or cringe from it?

Would we still be naturally drawn to the wider and more challenging visions presented through our URC connections with Northumberland in general and Crookham in particular, with new URC relationships in Scotland in general and Edinburgh and the Borders in particular, with our continuing interest in the World Church in general and South Africa in particular, or be content to withdraw to the parochial life around us?

The termination of my work at the Centre of African Studies came as suddenly as the impulse to embark on it two years earlier. The Dissertation, 'in partial fulfilment for the degree of Master of Science in African Studies, University of Edinburgh, 1996' entitled *The Work Culture and Identity of Migratory Labourers in Southern Africa* was finished and had been handed in.

BIKE RIDE OVER JORDAN

It's always more appealing to go for a 20-mile bike ride in the rain tomorrow. In the end it was desperation that forced me out. In my distinctive red helmet and yellow T-shirt I must have covered all the roads around Kelso within a radius of 30 miles. In the early weeks of late July and August, 1996 getting up at sunrise and setting off on, first, a 10-mile ride, then 20 miles, then 30, back for breakfast, attention to outstanding clerical spin-offs and, of course, my dissertation, came reasonably easy. Round rides over steep hills and even rough roads came well within my reach. But as I stretched myself to 50 miles and more in the later months as autumn changed to winter, the cold, dark mornings were less appealing. My most ambitious training ride was supposed to raise my confidence for the challenging route of the Bike Ride, 250 miles over five days ranging in height from 600 metres above in the Edom Mountains to 400 metres below sea level at the Red Sea.

On Sunday 2nd November, I set out for Heathrow uncertain of what lay ahead of me and apprehensive of what I'd taken on. The following day I was one of 100 others with similar mixed feelings fitting out our bikes on the shore of the Sea of Galilee so familiar to Jesus. After the first day's cycling through semitropical plantations of bananas, mangoes and peaches, and a night in a working kibbutz, I was reassured that I was as ready as most of us for the bike ride before us. I recognised the need for copious fluids laced with critical levels of essential salts, electrolytes, and other additives to replace both sensible and insensible fluid loss from perspiration, a range of vitamins, and an abundance of energy-promoting, glucose-providing carbohydrate. Then the going got tougher as we crossed into Jordan and headed south to end the day at the Dead Sea Rest House and indulge in the unique experience of reading a newspaper while floating on the salt-laden Dead Sea. The next day, against lashing rain and a fierce headwind, brought us to the foothills of Petra. Then followed a visit to the ancient city, a night in a Bedouin tent, and the final dash down the baking hot tar-macadam highway along part of the Great Rift Valley to the end of the Bike Ride at Aqaba on the Gulf of Aqaba.

No sooner was the Bike Ride '96 over than it was time for the Graduation Ceremony in McEwan Hall, in Edinburgh, on 7 December. Our younger daughter, Kate, went along with Avril to witness the Degree of Master of Science, African Studies, being conferred on six students in the Faculty of Sciences. One of them was me.

ACT SEVEN

'Last scene of all,
That ends this strange eventful history,
Is second childishness and mere oblivion,
Sans teeth, sans eyes, sans taste, sans everything.'

OUR JOURNEY INTO RETIREMENT beckoned. The 'last scene of all' would unfold naturally in the days left to come – or would they? They don't call me *Against the Grain* for nothing. Nor would my travelling companions accept the inevitable. We'd live every minute of every day in retirement as we've lived all our lives with or 'sans teeth, sans eyes, sans taste, sans everything'.

'Retirement brings with it a complex mix of satisfaction and completion, looking back and appraising, and forward with uncertainty, but also the conflict of an upsurge of restlessness because of a longing to settle into and relax in the comfort of a family home on the one hand and the compulsion to remain free to roam at will when and where the heart dictates.' These were my words when I first put pen to paper to start my autobiography in December 1996. Going to press in August 2006, the intervening years had brought with them fulfilment on both counts which were shared for most of the time with the life-blood of my being, my dear wife, Avril. We'd shared in the serenity of an expanding, widening family and in the thrill of exploring new experiences with equanimity.

But retirement has brought with it also, in recent years, a reawakening of latent love in my first love, Margaret, who has given me a new 'lease of life' beyond my most coveted dreams. My journey with Avril into retirement has come also to embrace a journey with Margaret in search of the ultimate meaning of our lives with a predestined goal in the beyond.

INTO RETIREMENT WITH AVRIL
PIETERMARITZBURG

Pieternaritzburg was new to us. What we knew about South Africa in the past was the Transkei, the Xhosa people, and Red Blankets in former days; and Johannesburg, East London and Durban in passing through. Pietermaritzburg, PMB, 'Maritzburg' in the heart of the Zulu Nation, now KwaZulu Natal, is the home of a proud people with a colourful history, not to be tampered with. Natal of *Little England* imperial settler and rustic Afrikaner Voortrekking days, was all new to us. Touching down, we were at once at the start of a new experience of South Africa. The small internal flight taxied in and came to a standstill. With a dozen others we'd collected our hand luggage and gravitated to the terminal. 'Welcome to Maritzburg!' said Duncan as we caught sight of him and he of us. We last saw him only three years before at Newcastle Airport on his way home with other South African visitors. We'd kept in touch and jumped at the chance of a working visit to his church when his long leave came up. On the way through the city to his home he chatted casually, pointing out landmarks and places with a special story which we'd never remember. Celia, his wife, greeted us with open arms welcoming us warmly to their home that would become our temporary home for the next few weeks. Content just to enjoy the ambience of our surroundings, we quickly settled in.

Drawing the lace curtains aside a chink early the next morning, the warm sunshine crept quickly through the trees and foliage, over the rough grass lawn. At the bottom of the garden, collecting the Sunday paper from the tubular letterbox at one side of the security gate at the entrance to the drive, meandering slowly up the gradient to the house, I caught sight of Duncan, already partly dressed for the service we'd be sharing in an hour or two. I'd be introduced along with Avril and deliver the sermon. He'd conduct his last service before his holidays. In the Congregational Church in Loop Street where the service would be held Avril and I would have an opportunity to meet the combined congregations of Congregationalists and Presbyterians in the final stages of uniting locally to form St John's United Church. At the service everyone gelled. In the car on the way to the airport to see Duncan and Celia off on their epic holiday the next day it was Duncan driving. On the way 'home' it was me. We'd said our farewells. Alone in the house, we'd gone through all the instructions we'd been given. The property was secure. Tired, content, expectant, we were soon asleep in the sultry stillness of our first night alone in PMB.

First thing next morning I unlocked the two cages on either side of our front 'stoep' and tiptoed down the patchy lawn in my bare feet for the paper, then up the warming drive within the reassuring confines of the security fence to unearth the tea bags and the toaster for a 'fly cup' with Avril slowly coming to life. The piercing cries of large grey-green hadedahs of the South African ibis family in the front garden descending from the heights of the tortuous branches of the paper-bark thorn tree and landing clumsily on the front lawn heralded in another day. Familiar now with the layout of the homely home inside, we cast our eyes outside the back door. The pool in the partial shade of lush trees between our garden and our neighbour's was the instant focus of our attention. My instructions had been clear. 'Fish out the leaves and insects on the surface with the net on the end of its long bamboo handle. Scoop out the frogs and millipedes swimming happily in the depths, and pick out any macadamia nuts from the pool and collect those which might have fallen from the overhanging branches in a plastic container to be cracked open and munched later on when dried out. Check the generator, 'off', 'on', in the correct sequence with the lights inside to start the water change and purification system.' '*Chug, chug,*' it spluttered into action, and '*chug, chug*' the cunning 'Creepy Crawly' cleaning device, like a plastic disk on auto', began its rhythmic circulation, devouring the algae gathering on the walls and floor of the pool. Fresh water in one pipe, out another, through the filter system and back, the correct recipe of chlorinated powder stirred into the sump at the poolside, whatever else an attractive trap for unsuspecting frogs, ensuring the sparkling freshness of an ever-ready pool, started to circulate. The dreamland of a tropical pool in a well-stocked garden with grapefruit, oranges, guavas, baby cherries, papaya and macadamia nuts in abundance there for the picking must have got to me for I kept hearing some serpent in me saying:-'*Pick and eat whatever catches your eye in the Eden of the garden.*' And we did.

In the midday heat the brightly coloured, brilliant blue giant gecko was playing on the rooftop. Inside, his smaller brothers and sisters, the common lizard, froze, statue-like, open-mouthed on the walls when under view, darting to another spot when not being watched, seldom seen in motion, catching flies his main aim in life. A phone call from the church forbade us looking near it till the next day. 'Take the time to yourselves,' said Cheryl, the Church Secretary, 'I'll phone again tomorrow.' And we did. Exploring the house, unpacking, settling in, Avril relaxing beside the pool in the cool of the evening, identifying the fruits of the garden, the flowers and shrubs, the singing birds, and the brash barking of the dogs next door brought the day to a close. It had been a good one for us.

Winding our way through the jostling taxi rank the next day, past the somewhat out of place contemporary cathedral in the centre of Pietermaritzburg on Longmarket Street, as instructed, we turned left past the next big building which was our Presbyterian Church and stopped at the end of the alley-way along the side of the church. We rang a bell on a side door and waited. 'Is that you?' said Cheryl's voice through the tannoy, and we replied, 'Yes, it is.' Locks unlocked and doors opened, then the side door creaked open. We stepped in conscious of the mirrors revealing our every movement to suspicious eyes on the inside. In the church office where I was to meet regularly to receive messages and discus the planning of services with Cheryl we learned of her unfortunate experience only a few weeks before. Held up at gunpoint by an intruder who had somehow talked his way through the side door at the busiest time of a working morning, she had held the man in conversation while opening the safe in her office, handed over the petty cash to him and explained that everything else was just church records of no monitory value. Shaking like a leaf but still strangely composed, though terrified at the thought of what might have been, she saw the robber out, alerted the police and church officials, and slumped into an easy chair. 'You've always got to be on the look-out for chancers. There's a lot of violence. It's not quite as bad as Jo'burg, but you're liable to be attacked in your car while stationary at traffic lights or walking on your own in the centre of town.' We got the message and tried not to forget. The very real chance of being accosted and robbed, or knocked down by one of the over-loaded, over-speeding, completely irresponsibly driven 'combies' made walking on the streets or crossing roads hazardous in the extreme. Traditional well-stocked, well-patronised, Little England, departmental stores in the heart of picturesque Pietermaritzburg where you could once go for 'respectable' shopping, to meet your friends for 'tea' or 'coffee' on a Saturday morning, or have a good meal in a good hotel before a concert in one of several theatres or the opera house were being replaced by cheaper, more utilitarian shops to meet the increasing demands of a KwaZulu population gravitating to the centre of the city, displacing white, ex-colonial, influential, commercial enterprise to the periphery.

Yet, in spite of these concerns penetrating to the very heart of white Pietermaritzburg life, we found a church facing the challenges of the day. Struggling still to retain a relevance in a rapidly changing society, the constant exposure to the horrific realities of a not too distant past through the Truth and Reconciliation Commission which was being covered graphically in every minute detail in the local and national media added another painful dimension to a people attempting to come to terms with a new identity in a united church identical, in essence, to the United Reformed Church. With our transient experiences of South Africa over the years and the birth-pains of the URC from its inception, we seemed tailor-made for the role of arbitrator and counsellor. I enjoyed the formality of the form of worship at the imposing Presbyterian Church of Pietermaritsburg which was familiar to both Avril and me from our earliest days, but when the physical move took place in our last few weeks to the much more convenient Congregational Church building in Loop Street, we were equally at home there. Our empathy with the pains and joys of the pilgrim people with whom we served came naturally, prompting me to place our feelings on record in one of the last 'Letters from the Minister' before we returned home to Kelso.

'From the first combined Service I shared with Duncan on the day Celia and he left on their world-wide tour, through the services leading up to Easter at the Gardens Pre-Primary School and the city-centre Church, and the many and varied pre-Easter and Easter services, Avril and I have become more and more part of you. And our affinity doesn't end there. Sharing in Bible Study and Prayer Groups, and taking services in a few 'Age Care Homes' as well as meeting many of you socially and on a personal level, has broadened our perspective of the life and witness of the church here. Coming from the United Reformed Church with its roots in Presbyterianism and Congregationalism, Avril and I can share in your anxieties about the proposed and impending union of your Church with the Congregational Church in Loop Street and we can well appreciate the sensitivity required on all sides, but we can also rejoice with you in the re-energising spirit of awareness which such a union will bring to the glory of God and the benefit of our neighbours'.

In the later weeks, after Easter, Jim and his family arrived. Our eldest son, James, who travelled widely in connection with his work, had business in Pietermaritzburg to attend to and arranged for his family to join him for an extended Easter holiday two weeks of which would be with us. Between our church connections and Jim's friends our social life took off. A game-reserve not far from the city, visits to a nearby water fall in Howick, the Wild Coast south of Durban, a few days in bustling Cape Town including a boat trip to view Table Mountain from the sea accompanied most of the way by a large basking shark, were all unique experiences, but the times together in Duncan's pool and garden, an unbelievable 'tropical breakfast' of all the fruits I could lay my hands on one morning, just savouring the reality of being together so far from home in surroundings we'd made our own, yet in another dream world, were best of all.

At the poolside, in the kitchen and in the garden, and at most places we visited, the conversation spanning our three generations of Avril and me, Jim and Anne, and the three children kept returning to a common question. How did what we were experiencing on our PMB visit compare with the stories of past days which we kept reminiscing on about Sulenkama, the Transkei and Umtata? We wondered and wondered till we started putting out feelers. Our church friends and Jim's work associates were of one mind. 'Oh No!' they said, somewhat alarmed, 'You'd better not go near the Transkei. It's changed from the times you knew it. The roads are badly potholed and reckless, irresponsible drivers make driving a real hazard. And it's not safe. It's as dangerous as Jo'burg, and it's getting worse. The violence is escalating. You're liable to be shot at, robbed or knifed. It's pretty well lawless. Policing and administration have deteriorated. It's virtually all black now. There are very few white faces now. No! Don't go to Umtata even though it would be nice to see Jim's old school again. The road south through the Transkei is so risky now that most people take a wide detour round Lesotho through Harrismith and Bloemfontein to the Eastern Cape.' The message was clear and sound but our daydreams undiminished. Jim prevailed upon a friend to drive us to Umtata in his combi, stay the night with us at the Holiday Inn and return the same way through the dreaded Transkei.

Along the road to Durban, along the Natal coast, to Kokstad and into the Transkei we sped, breathing in the fresh breezes and scenes around us as we did. Our driver took on a more sombre air, unlike the gathering anticipation of his passengers. Along the National road potholes increasing by the

250

mile but negotiated without much difficulty, the panorama unfolded. In the distance blue skies over distant undulating hills and mountain peaks appeared, in the foreground walkers over dongas and along the side of the road, children on their way to school, dogs running wild, occasional skin and bones cattle and a horse or two round a smoking kraal, no red blankets now, over the Tina and the Titsa bridges, past the Sulenkama and the Tsolo road ends, through Qumbu where we took our driving tests when we first went to Sulenkama, and the outskirts of Umtata were in sight. There were not many flowers in the neglected pots between the stone seats around the unkempt grassy square in front of the Municipal Building in the centre of the town.

We stood and stretched and looked around, the children glad of a chance to be out of the van and running around. The hum of the busy town centre was palpable. Some well-shod feet hurried past, others shuffled along, some smiling pearly-teeth faces with sparkling eyes and others scowling, grimacing, almost threateningly came and went, chattering and laughter punctuated by the rising and falling of passing conversation continued into the distance, sweaty arms and bustling bottoms unavoidably brushing past, the crowd glancing only occasionally at us. At the Holiday Inn, checked in for the night, we ventured a smile at the thought of our childish delight at being back in Umtata.

Next morning, before the sun had reached its zenith, our mission had been completed. With the sympathetic understanding of the caretaker, Jim had once again walked through the corridors of his old school, Umtata High School, past the headmaster's door, a transient wince of pain reminding him of the caning he endured, unflinching, as a pupil, reverently saluted the bell still there at the entrance to the school humbled by the mysteries of time, his mother, Avril, on one side to share with him the experience of past years and his son, Andrew, on the other to carry their empathy into the future. The 'Viege house' was no longer a dwelling house but an ambulance depot for the hospital, formally the Sir Henry Elliot Hospital, later and now part of Umtata General Hospital. We went through the shell of the building, typists and clerks busy at their work in the front room once piled high with a new Medical Superintendent's packing cases trapping our baby, Katie, in her pram and blocking our exit from the house. As on a cloud, we drifted through the kitchen now strewn with coke cans, upstairs to one-time familiar bedrooms now offices, offices and more offices, some smiling faces at their desks acknowledging our presence, a few with the trace of a sneer, and, yes, incredibly, through one of the back windows, caught sight of the tree outside from which, one day in years gone by, as the rain came down in buckets so also did our eldest son, Jim, fall clattering through its branches.

Accelerating up the long incline outside the provincial capital, Umtata, our driver seemed to sigh, a sigh of relief not fully expressed until we were outside the Transkei's borders when his passengers fell silent for a while, looking back, at least in their minds, to distant memories of the past. Samples of sugar cane which the children gathered from edges of the cane fields of Natal for a school project at home and a refreshing swim in the rolling surf of the Indian Ocean off the Wild Coast erased the image of the Transkei we had so much wished to see again.

Alone again after the family had left, with only our new friends in the church to confide in, we realised how intimate our relationship with the people had become and our time was almost over. At the farewell service the sermon on Shammah and Absalom which tugged at the heart strings in Ashington did the same in Pietermaritzburg. At the end of the service it seemed only natural for Avril and me to leave together, hand in hand down the central aisle, we and our people together for the last time, singing in unison the words and tune of the exit blessing which touched our hearts more than any other before.

May the Lord, Mighty God,
Bless and keep you for ever;
Give you peace, perfect peace;
Grace for every endeavour.
Lift your eyes and seek his face;
Feel his grace surround you.
May the Lord, Mighty God,
Bless and keep you forever.
(Aaronic Blessing from *Numbers 6:24-26*
Tune: – Edelweiss)

TWO KELSOS

At home in Kelso between our visits to Pietermaritsburg in 1997 and again in 2002 we settled into the tempo of life in the Borders. It was good to know the security of our family home in a part of our native Scotland in which we were coming more and more to feel at home, to love and to cherish. But the name of our house *Abbey Royd* betrayed an inherent greater love of borders in a broader sense. *Royd*, a Yorkshire term implying *a yard* or *clearing*, *my patch* or *my bit* personified our joint concern for life on the edge, on the margins of either side. Finding a spiritual home for ourselves was never easy. In Kelso we gladly joined the congregation of Kelso Old and Sprouston Parish Church and supported it, though often indifferently, as best we could. Avril immersed herself in the Women's Guild and the Abbeyfield Home at 'The Haven'. I took some services in the unusual octagonal Old Parish Church when our minister, Marion Dodd, was ill and she and the people going through anxious times. I was glad to be on the spot to substitute for her at short notice intermittently for almost three months. A usual Sunday routine became almost second nature. A cup of tea in the kitchen at home between the earlier service at the *Sweet-Pea Church* in Sprouston at 10 o'clock and the 11.30 service at Kelso, next door to us, was always a pleasant interlude. Only once was I caught by surprise. Arriving at the Old Parish Church one Sunday morning with five minutes to spare I was greeted with a few anxious faces. 'There are two baptisms! Did you know? The families are in the vestry!', I was informed. I didn't know, but immediately collected my thoughts, composed the elders and myself, jotted down a few names, modified the service a bit and proceeded. Extemporary baptisms sometimes flow as smoothly as the textbook thing.

Then into our world, and into my wardrobe, came a tartan waistcoat. 'We're looking for someone for the Highlander Festival next year,' we heard Frank's quiet American monotone in a lull in the clinking glasses and merry quips at Marion's farewell party for Frank and Betty on their way home to Kelso, WA (Washington State) on the western seaboard of the United States after a short holiday in the Scottish Borders. Frank Wyatt, the pastor of the First Presbyterian Church there and his amiable wife, Betty Mitchell, already knew our Kelso and the Old Parish Church well and just loved everything about Scotland. They'd be away from their home in the States for a month or two over the time of the Highlander event next year, in Scotland, of course, soaking up more of the culture of the Scottish Borders and the workings of the Church of Scotland. But where might they stay in our Kelso during their working holiday, and who might officiate at the Highlander Festival in

Kelso, WA? The questions hung in the air for no more than a split second. 'Over the hedge from here, in our home, *Abbey Royd,*' Avril heard me say, a querulous frown on her brow, and, thrilled at the thought of it, we echoed together, 'We'll come to your Highlander Festival and the Kirkin' o' the Tartan.' The deal was sealed. 'And you'll be wearing your kilt for the Parade as well,' Frank assumed. 'Not me!' I replied in alarm. 'I've never worn a kilt and won't start now.' So the tartan waistcoat was an acceptable compromise.

The long wait at Brussels for a connecting flight and the inhospitable reception at the point of entry to the USA in Detroit, sniffer-dogs and armed police herding aliens along, as well as the poorly serviced internal flight to Portland, were not encouraging. But as we started our descent someone said, 'Have a look down there!' Snow-capped peaks of mountains, Hood, Rainier and St Helens we were told, towered through the clouds to the heavens above. Avril noted in her diary, 'Spectacular!' and followed the comment with 'Filled a sick bag!' as not uncommon turbulence brought up her pre-packed lunch. The sight of a welcome banner, 'First Presbyterian Church & Highlander Festival welcome Rev Bill and Avril Nicol from Kelso, Scotland', and smiling faces were the start of a rare relationship with kindred folk and an unforgettable experience. The drive home to Frank and Betty's was like a drive from Edinburgh to Kelso. A quick look round and we were sound asleep as Frank and Betty were in *Abbey Royd.*

The first few days were like a dream. New home, new friends, thoughtful groceries, imaginative gestures of friendship, introductions to the supermarket, a look round the church and a comprehensive visit to the state of the art hospital with the chaplain, meals at homes here, welcome parties there, a procession to mark the 75thAnniversary of Longview set us up as long-lost friends for life. As in Pietermaritzburg the year before we took every opportunity which came our way to enter into every aspect of life in a part of the world hitherto unknown to us. Each day we grew more and more attracted to our new friends as they became part of us. The church and its visiting pastor and his wife grew in the faith together. Scheduled or unscheduled, we related to everything in the Kelso WA First Presbyterian Church. As temporary official duty hospital chaplain with an authentic identity badge to confirm it staff and patients began to know a little about me, the pastor, and more and more about the two Scottish doctors, Bill and Avril. From visits to well-healed, classy ladies in an up-market retirement home we learnt about the pioneering days of yesterday. From the small Prayer Group that was surprised to see us there we shared the concerns of broken relationships, crime, drugs and alcohol abuse indiscriminately distributed throughout the industrial glue and freight twin towns of Kelso and Longview. Unexpected visits to folk on the breadline in proudly kept homes, flooded repeatedly from the Cowlitz overflowing its banks, and enterprising families in newly constructed houses on fault lines, condemned before they were paid for, spoke of anxieties not far from the surface. A weekly Men's Breakfast Study Group at 6.30 a.m. in an all-night trucker's restaurant over coffee, waffles, eggs and ham and more coffee added another dimension to life. In no time our social life took off. We ate out, dined out, seldom on our own. People popped in for a chat, just to meet us, eager to hear our story, to build on their practice of the faith and feed on the unknown, never inhibited, always attentive and we responded likewise, all to our mutual benefit. I don't think the pastor's home and the people had been so close for ages.

After the Easter Sunday Service celebrating the triumph of life over death, renewal over destruction, it seemed appropriate that a conducted encounter with Mount St Helens would re-enforce the Easter message. Memories of the climactic eruption of the volcano on May 18, 1980, at noon are still etched on the minds of most older Kelso WA people. The maximum height of the ash and gas column was about 12 miles, some of the ash drifting around the globe within about 2 weeks. The scale of destruction from the lateral blast unleashed with the 'unlocking' of the volcano at the moment of eruption, and the resultant pyroclastic volcanic rock and mud flows and floods which followed was colossal. Yet, in a few years, signs of re-birth made their appearance. We could marvel at the destructive power in the nature around us and, at the same time, the wonder of re-creation which followed.

Spellbound by the natural wonders of the countryside around us, our friends responded by showing us more and more every day. There was soon nothing much about the landscape, the people or their heritage we didn't know. A trip to the Columbia Gorge revealed the extent of the timberlands, the vast ranges of tree-covered slopes and the mighty Columbia River associated with Peter Crawford the pioneer from around our Kelso, on the Scottish Borders, who gave his name to the Kelso WA of today. We envied the exhilaration of even the prospect of setting out into the unknown with only the vision of something better as a guide. A more detailed trip exploring the Oregon Trail ended in Astoria, a climb to the top of the impressive Tower and, at last, the sight of the Pacific Ocean.

All too soon our time in Kelso WA had all but come to an end. The razzmatazz of the Parade through the streets of Kelso, the Highland Games afternoon activities including Pipe Bands and Highland Dancers, and the Tartan Ball in the evening over, our last day in Kelso dawned. It was time for the 'Kirkin' o' the Tartan' which had been well publicised. I was particularly pleased to notice that my preamble about the tradition including a request for anyone attending the service 'to be sure and wear your tartan' was extended to include 'or clothing of your ancestral home, proudly'. The service had been extended beyond only Scots folk to everyone from any background, including Native Americans who, along with those originally from Scandinavia, the Philippians and many other localities flocked into the First Presbyterian Church building, some in distinctive dress. Frank, fresh back from his holiday break in Scotland gave a 'Historic Review' of what the whole idea of Kirkin' was about:-

'The ceremony of the Kirkin' o' the Tartan is of American origin, though based on Scottish history and legend. In 1746, following the defeat of the Scots by the English at the Battle of Culloden, April 16, a special Disarming Act was passed, forbidding not only carrying or possessing arms, but also wearing the kilt, plaid or any other tartan garment. This prompted the stubborn Scots to secretly carry with them a piece of their tartan as they went to the Kirk (Church). The minister would then slip a blessing (a Kirkin') into the service for the tartans.

Each clan in Scotland had its own tartan. Clans were gatherings of families for economic and political protection as well as social support. Members of the clans were thus not necessarily related by blood ties. A specific tartan was developed by a clan using local herb dyes. In this way the tartan became the symbol of the wearer's kinship.

Based on this history and legend, the Saint Andrew's Society of Washington, D.C. held a Kirkin' on April 27, 1941 which was led by the late Dr Peter Marshall, the eloquent Scot, then Chaplain of the U.S. Senate and Pastor of the New York Avenue Presbyterian Church. Since that time, Kirkin' o' the

Tartan services have been held with increasing frequency in many churches in the United States.'

Avril then led the congregation in an act of Kirkin' o' the Tartan which included the conclusion:-

'Bless, we pray, these tartans and the memories that each of us have of our native land and our ancestors. May these symbols and our thoughts be a token of the faith of our mothers and fathers and the sign of our service to you. Through Jesus Christ our Lord. Amen.'

Then it was time for my Sermon on 'Identity'. I started with Murdoch Maclean's words:-

> *'Here's to it!*
> *The fighting sheen of it,*
> *The yellow, the green of it,*
> *The white, the blue of it,*
> *The swing, the hue of it,*
> *The dark, the red of it,*
> *Every thread of it!*
>
> *The fair have sighed for it,*
> *The brave have died for it,*
> *Foemen sought for it,*
> *Heroes fought for it,*
> *Honour the name of it,*
> *Drink to the fame of it –*
>   *The Tartan!'*

'The many tartans which we see around us, and have been brought before God and presented for Kirkin', give us an identity which binds our kinsfolk together in the same way that

we are bound together as Christians. Most of us are proud to be associated with one particular tartan or another, which links our ancestors of the past with us here and now, and will be perpetuated in the future. The Scottish ties between this Kelso and the Kelso in Scotland go back, I understand, 150 years or more.

The Tartan, 'the fighting sheen of it, the yellow, the green, the white and blue, the dark and red, the swing and every thread of it, has been sighed for, died for, fought for and honoured' since it first became part of the Highlands and the Highlanders. It has been adopted further afield and is proudly displayed in almost every corner of God's created world now, not least in Kelso here. Originally the tartan was worn as the trews mainly by the chiefs and aristocracy but mostly, and certainly by the common clansman, as the kilt. When the waistcoat was introduced, I don't know, but the one I'm wearing now and had specially made for this occasion, is the Ancient Mackintosh because my wife Avril was a Mackintosh before she became a Nicol, and my mother was a Dallas which is a sept of the Mackintoshes. Avril's sash is the original Mackintosh tartan. So our tartan's bind us together, but as we gather now in this church for the Kirkin' o' the Tartan we're conscious of another, stronger, older, more enduring bond which goes to the very centre of our beings. We all belong to one family of God, and we're made in his image. After he had made the world and all the creatures in it 'God created man in his own image, in the image of God, he created him.' As the weaver weaves a tartan, so did God weave man at the beginning of creation.

Tartan isn't just any checked cloth you can buy in a shop, no matter how pretty and colourful it is. It's carefully woven material, with the stripes of different colours arranged along its length, the warp, the same as those woven across it, the weft. By changing the colours and varying the width and number of stripes, different patterns or 'setts' are produced. The skilful weaver knows exactly how to set the warp and the weft for a particular tartan. The image of all other tartans of the same kind depends on the first sett. The way the warp and the weft are woven gives a particular tartan its identity.

Your minister, Frank, and his wife, Betty, sent us a parcel with maps and guides and posters of Washington State, the State of Oregon, Portland, and the Washington coast-line. They were packed with useful information, and excited us with the thrill of seeing many of the sights you've shared with us in our stay with you. But the most interesting was a simple map of Kelso, marked 'Kelso, you'll love us'. It showed the mighty Columbia River flowing West for endless miles between the States of Oregon and Washington till it turned North and then West again to open into the Pacific Ocean and the Cowlitz River snaking its way North where the Columbia took its final turn West, and the town of Kelso nestling in the curve of the Cowlitz River and its smaller tributary, the Coweeman.

Kelso, in Scotland, nestles, also, in the curve of the longer River Tweed which, in long stretches is the border between Scotland and England and flows eastward to the cold North Sea. Its tributary, the Teviot, bears an uncanny resemblance to the Cowlitz River. The geological similarities are striking but, of course, so are the differences because the Columbia River and the Tweed flow in opposite directions.

In the time that Avril and I have been with you we've been woven into a fabric of respect and understanding, of affection and honest admiration. Like our two Kelsos, we have our similarities and differences. I hope you've seen from us a clearer image of the Scotland of today, people proud of their heritage, but on the threshold of an element of independence we've never known before. We've moved, with our English, Welsh and Irish brothers and sisters, from the centre of the British Empire to nations within nations, struggling to identify ourselves with Europe and retain, at the same time, our loyalties to friends and kinsfolk world wide. We're trying to blend love for our neighbours with justice for everyone. Next year we'll have our devolved Scottish Parliament. We're no longer a caricature of a doll in a kilt, playing the bagpipes, saying 'ma wee dearie'. Like you in this Kelso, we've evolved from an identity with the past, to what we are now. We've all been moulded into the image we identify ourselves with today, by the God in whose image we've been made. Our God is a weaver God who's woven the similarities and differences in each of us into our very fabric, like a weaver fashioning a tartan from the sett on his loom.

Hear now these verses from Kate Compston's 'The Web of Life' in 'A Resource Book' by the United Reformed Church in 1989:-

'Weaver-God, Creator, sets life on the loom,
Draws out threads of colour from primordial gloom.
Wise in designing, in the weaving deft:
 Love and justice joined – the fabrics warp and weft.

Called to be co-weavers, yet we break the thread
And may smash the shuttle and the loom, instead.
Careless and greedy, we deny by theft
 Love and justice joined – the fabrics warp and weft.

Weaver- God, great Spirit, may we see your face
Tapestried in trees, in waves, and winds of space;

Tenderness teach us, lest we be bereft
Of love and justice joined – the fabrics warp
                              and weft.

Weavers we are called, yet woven too we're born,
For the web is seamless: if we tear, we're torn.
Gently may we live – that fragile Earth be left
With love and justice joined – the fabric's warp
                              and weft.'

After references to Shammah and Absalom from my Farewell Sermons in Ashington and Pietermaritzburg I ended my 'Sermon on Identity' in this way:-

'It's my prayer that the warp and weft of the fabric of the tartans we've Kirk'd today, and the warp and weft of the values in our lives, our similarities and our differences, woven by the Master Weaver, God himself, includes above all else, his kind of love and justice, the kind of love and justice Jesus came to show us.'

Our time in Kelso WA was over and the second Millennium drawing to an end. The pace of life was beginning to tell on both Avril and me. I think we both felt it was time for us to draw in our horns, to be content to enjoy our home and each other more, for me to come down to earth, to give my blood pressure a chance. It was then that I heard about the Pilgrimage Against Poverty.

PILGRIMAGE AGAINST POVERTY

'A pilgrimage is,' I learned, 'a journey of faith to a place of spiritual or historical significance. The word describes the kind of life one leads: Christians often refer to themselves as 'pilgrim people' journeying towards God. Inspired and organised by Church Action on Poverty, the 'Pilgrimage Against Poverty' involves Protesting about the persistence and extent of poverty in the United Kingdom, Praying for the needs of those in poverty, and Celebrating the good work of many people to alleviate and eradicate it. We were invited to join the Pilgrimage walk from Iona to London on its epic journey. Along endless country roads and busy highways in order to draw attention to ourselves, relentlessly, for nine weeks, would push body and soul, and feet, to the limits of endurance, but I reckoned I could make it to London. When it was all over I had this to write in the November issue of *Reform:-*

'On 15th *August, 1999, in ancient Iona Abbey, a dozen coy, sensitive, mainly middle-aged oddities set off to walk 670 miles to London on a Pilgrimage Against Poverty. The commissioning words,*

> *'God be with you now*
> *as you start your journey of faith.*
> *May your long walk*
> *be a sign in our land*
> *of the unending walk*
> *of those who are poor,*
> *and the agenda for change they present.*
> *May the companionship*
> *that you find on the way*
> *herald new solidarity*
> *for the marginalised ones,'*

echoed in our minds. A mixed bag of Pilgrims from Established, Conforming, Traditional backgrounds and Disestablished, Non-conforming, Reformed backgrounds, we crossed to Mull and the start of our walk. Whatever our different Christian traditions or our particular political allegiances, we had, from the beginning, one common passion – an anger at the scandal of the degree of poverty in our country the extent of which was later to be described by bishops and politicians, by mayors and provosts, as 'heresy' and even 'blasphemy'. Since 1979 both poverty and inequality have grown markedly. While the richest members of society have seen their incomes grow as never before, the poorest have actually become poorer.

In the early days, the beauty of the Highlands got to us. We were ultra-sensitive to one another. At times we saw God in everything, in the mountaintops and in the glens, in the lochs and in the cool, refreshing rain. It was more difficult to see the same God in blisters and aching feet, in lashing rain and sodden tents or in the midges.

Then we hit Clydebank and the Forth-Clyde industrial belt. Deprivation was there to be seen in the housing estates and city centres, and the sadness in people's eyes. Our assured confidence in what we were doing – 'We're walking to London to see Gordon Brown, the Chancellor of the Exchequer, and tell him about the Agenda for Change based on grass-root input which we're asking him to implement in order to eradicate poverty by 2020' – was now tempered with a note of hope.

As we passed through Glasgow and Edinburgh, crossed the border at Berwick and walked from Newcastle to Jarrow, with vivid memories of the Jarrow March of the years of the depression of the 30s, politics and religion seemed to converge. Politics with an emphasis on the rights of the poor went well with a Social Gospel, Social Responsibility, Justice and Peace and an equitable society. Churches of all denominations played their part in offering us hospitality, providing welcome showers, loos and beds. Sometimes we couldn't help noticing beautiful church buildings set in beautiful surroundings, but cold and out of this world. At other times it was difficult to identify a church as a church for the smell of meals being prepared, children running around, line-dancing and old folk queuing up for games of Bingo, all of this obscuring the worship area which we often slept in. These churches are part of their communities, throbbing with the mixed life of today, which gives hope for tomorrow.

Homelessness was never far away and our prayer about Gary grew in relevance as we walked south. 'My name is Gary. But no one want's to know. I am homeless and everybody's stereotype. Sat in my doorway, I am all things to passers-by. To one I'm a dropout, avoiding life's responsibilities. To another, an alcoholic or a junkie, frightening and disease-ridden. To none am I an individual. I'm not just 'a homeless person', I'm an individual. My name is Gary, but no one....'

Then came comfortable North Yorkshire and later the affluent South. The industrial belt of Leeds-Manchester soon gave way to the densely populated Midlands of Birmingham and Coventry. Though the poverty was obvious and even extensive, there were many stretches of open green lands, prosperity and indulgence. The contrast was startling.

On the streets we were usually well received but occasionally ignored and sometimes challenged with 'There's no poverty in this country!' or 'There's always been and always will be, the poor with us! There's nothing you can do about it'. Our churches in the South have their work cut out encouraging links across the social divides.

Then we were in the outskirts of London. From microchip Slough the sudden change to Southall, a multicultural, multifaith, but deprived, community throbbing with tensions but seizing every opportunity for reconciliation, was striking. The Methodist church we stayed in and its small congregation were a tonic for us all.

At last we were in London on Sunday, 17th October, United Nations Day for the Eradication of Poverty for the climax of the Pilgrimage in Trafalgar Square and a service at St Martin-in-the-Fields. The next day our visit to the Treasury had come and was soon over. We had, as we kept telling everyone we would, seen the Chancellor of the Exchequer and expressed our anger at the state of poverty in our country, explained the content of our Agenda for Change and urged him to take it to heart in order to eradicate poverty from our country by the year 2020.'

HOBKIRK

With the beginning of another millennium came our association with the church at Hobkirk in Bonchester Bridge. The advertisement in *Life and Work* was clear-cut, for a 'locum, part-time, minister at Hobkirk and Southdean.' For the next two years my sole responsibility would be to the united parishes of Hobkirk and Southdean. We'd drive over twenty miles every Sunday morning from Kelso to the church in Hobkirk and back after the service, usually refreshed and satisfied. The sparsely populated countryside around the dominant Ruberslaw was never unimpressive, warm and rustic in the spring and autumn, cold and sometimes bleak, overcast, freezing winds and rain biting deeply, but sometimes crisp, the snow-covered high ground shining in the sunshine beneath a cloudless bright blue sky. My sermons seemed to go down well, Avril's readings even better, and in no time we had found a church we felt at home in, contributing to its spiritual welfare, gathering lasting friendships. Far from being a distraction or disruptive, our Hobkirk connection complemented our life in Kelso. We extracted the best from both. Weekly visits to the Primary School gave me an insight into the children in the community. In practice they were a very real 'Sunday School' through the week. End of term services and school concerts at Christmas or Easter time began to make the church as familiar to parents, pupils and their teachers as the school building itself. Monthly informal services in the residential home at Ween's House proved less predictable. Often a far from captive gathering found the responses to the call of nature more compelling than the promptings of the Spirit. I enjoyed the good nature of my ageing friends, interlaced with good humour, concern for the present, and unspoken contemplation on what lay ahead.

'Keep your eyes open next week!' I slipped into the conversation after the service one week. Though Avril cautioned me, I couldn't keep it to myself any longer. We'd arranged a hot air balloon flight with our two daughters, Ailsa and Kate, as a birthday surprise for them. 'We'll be leaving from the junction of the Kelso road off the Jedburgh-Edinburgh road next Saturday morning, weather permitting.' We waited patiently, then anxiously, and as frustration set in, angrily. Next week came and went; next month came and went; and over a year had passed by. 'Sorry, not yet' was all we could say. Wind and rain, and floods and mud were natural reasons for cancelling pre-arranged dates for the flight. What more unusual was the outbreak of Foot and Mouth Disease which spread rapidly through many parts of the country decimating large numbers of cattle from the disease itself and many more from the debatable culling thought necessary for its control. No animals were lost in the immediate neighbourhood of Bonchester Bridge but our close neighbours were less fortunate. Depression set in. An air of dejection hung over the entire rural community. Every farm was isolated from its neighbours. Coming and going was reduced to a minimum. Smoke from distant culling burns could be seen from time to time and if the wind was blowing strongly in your direction an acrid smell of burnt flesh might be detected. Enormous carcass-filled lorries stalked the country lanes. Eerie deathly silences enveloped many cattle farms affected by the disease, and the sheep around seemed to sense the horror and ceased their bleating. Visiting was discouraged. One Sunday, at its peak, we were advised not to gather for the morning service, but pastoral work was strangely unaffected because phone calls and E-mails proved as affective a means of communication as direct visits. At last the depression lifted. The crisis was over. Everyone had forgotten about our hot air balloon flight until, one Sunday when I broke the news. 'Did you not see us?' I said, excitement mounting, and our friends were good enough to respond with, 'Well done! Not before time!'

Not long after the up, up and away in the hot air balloon it was up again, this time for a trip up the Nile. Transported back in time, the Cairo Museum unveiled the secrets of the Rosetta Stone, restoring to life the deeds, words and thoughts of people from all walks of life, silenced for 5000 years until they were deciphered by Champollio in 1832. As we gazed on the Pyramids I tried to recall the precise dimensions, which I'd read about in the guide-book. The ancient Sphinx and the modern Aswan Dam each held awesome images of the price of human endeavour. A sail in a falluca to a cruise ship which was to give us a touch of the exotic as we disembarked for excursions to the Valley of the Kings, the Edfu Temple consecrated to the god Horas and many wonders I thought I'd never forget but have forgotten in Luxor and Karnak, completed our first and only holiday with Saga. If you're of an age, you can't beat it.

Into the second year in Hobkirk, moves afoot to link the parishes of Hobkirk and Southdean with those of Bedrule, Denholm and Minto, all located round the Ruberslaw began to materialise. No longer would my responsibilities be to Hobkirk alone but to the combined group, which was to be known as The Ruberslaw Churches. No longer would our special relationship with the people of Hobkirk continue. In the process of calling a permanent new minister for all the churches I'd be required to spread myself around, widening my field of interest but at the same time, narrowing my input into any one church. At the same time challenging and satisfying, the changing nature of my work included allaying anxieties, reconciling vulnerable souls to the uncertainties of a changing church in a changing world, preparing minds and hearts for new ministry with a common minister. My task as Interim Moderator in the URC at the churches in Galashiels and Selkirk was moving on in much the same way. The vacancy would soon be filled and a new minister inducted.

Looking back on 2003, our time at the Ruberslaw Churches was coming to an end with the impending arrival of their new parish minister. Hobkirk had been, for us the longest time I had been minister in any one church in all my short ministry. I empathised with the people in the community and they with me because Avril equally empathised with them as they did with her. We were never more at home in any church than there.

At the beginning of the year I closed my right eye to remove a speck of dirt from it, while driving home from

Hobkirk one day and found that I had virtually no vision in the left. Its central vein had been occluded. I could see well enough with one eye but perspective was not so good. As the year progressed I found that I relied more and more on Avril to do the readings for me in church. When it became difficult getting through a wedding ceremony or a funeral service, we realised that my regular preaching days were coming to an end. By my last Sunday at Hobkirk on the first Sunday of Advent, 2003, I was ready to call it a day. *Thank you's* and presentations over, it would soon be Christmas and New Year. One of my tasks would be writing a circular letter to retired URC ministers and their wives or husbands in the East of Scotland, which I had been doing for almost ten years. In recent years the letter had been modified for general circulation and appeared in this form:-

'Christmas 2003.
  Dear...
  Our circular letter is short this year.
  Like you, we've been horror-struck by the scale of terrorist outrages, which seem unlimited, but try not to be too overwhelmed by the ugly side of life. Our grandson, William, and his parents, Kate and Dan, have shown us another side to life, one of beauty and hope. We try to keep things in perspective.
  To see things in perspective, the good and the bad, the wonder and the horror, the beauty and the ugliness, in a watercolour of an artist like John Constable (1776-1837), you need binocular vision, the sight of two co-ordinated eyes in close proximity, a third dimension of depth to an otherwise flat canvas.
  When the central vein of one of my, Bill's eyes 'went' a while ago, an element of perception went with it. Pouring out a cup of tea or filling a glass of water was at first a joke. He'd

give short measure or the cup or glass would overflow. Then he found he was letting go of a mug which he was placing on a table before it was in contact with the surface, or banging it down, unaware that he'd reached the table top so soon. Steps and driving have, so far, been all right, but reading has been a special problem. The average Bible or hymnbook is out of the question now and it's become difficult getting through the Promises at a wedding or the Committal at a funeral. He was glad when his last service was over last week.

So that's him retired now for good - well maybe. He didn't make Nepal last year but... With his limited perception Bill has a problem, but it's nothing with Avril not far away, and there's nothing wrong with her perception. It's her hearing, but his is as acute as ever. You can picture us on Christmas day, all our combined faculties intact, keeping the ugliness of life in perspective; even though one of them might spill his Christmas sherry and the other miss a word or two of the Queen's speech.

It was C. R. Leslie who wrote in his 'Memoirs of the Life of John Constable', the painter, 'There is nothing ugly. I never saw an ugly thing in my life, for let the form of an object be what it may, light, shade and perspective will always make it beautiful.'

May the light, shade and perspective of Christmas transform the ugliness of the picture around you and make it beautiful throughout the Season and into 2004.'

ENDING and BEGINNING AGAIN

Christmas 2003 was one of our best. Every member of our family had reached a phase of contentment in their lives. They'd found companionship. They were able to give affection and to receive it. And because they were at ease and content, so were we. Yes, Christmas 2003 and the New Year were probably our best. 2004 had started all too soon.

The Chest X-Ray showed cancer of the lung. It came out of the blue when Avril went along to our doctor to have a rapid pulse investigated, but we were not surprised. We'd both lived with the fear that one day she'd have the same as her parents before her. What else could I do but stifle any suggestions of guilt, any shameful feelings of 'What have I brought on you and the family?' There was no place for recriminations. 'We've had a wonderful life together,' I mumbled. 'Whenever one of us goes it doesn't matter. What matters is the time we've had together.' We went through the investigations knowing the gravity of the condition, ever hopeful in the early stages, reconciled towards the end. Avril faced the prospects of surgical resection of the tumour confidently, hopeful of a few years longer, if not a complete cure. When I visited her in the High Dependency Unit at the new Edinburgh Royal Infirmary after her operation she looked a poor sparrow of a thing, knees beneath her chin, curled up on a recovery bed, falling to one side. Still not fully recovered from the anaesthetic, all I got out of her was an inaudible sigh and a wry smile. I could have cradled her in my arms and taken her home. She recovered well and came home a week later, everyone hopeful, relieved, grateful for what had been done.

But glands in the opposite axilla were soon detected, then spread beyond. Radiotherapy and steroids kept things under control for a while and we were conditioned to prepare for the worst. Avril began to count the months. Then, at our lowest, when we felt buffeted from one piece of bad news to another, amazingly, things changed when we resolved to take full exclusive control of our situation into our own hands again. Our priorities became clear. Responsibilities, objectives, hallowed conventional and religious rituals fell away. The few services I had lined up in my diary were cancelled. Lifelong commitments fell into perspective. We started to live exclusively for each other and our family. Visits on impulse up and down the country, just to be with the family, were top of our agenda, not least to Sheffield to be part of our grandson, William's baptism.

In late September, 2004, we wrote to all our Christmas circular-letter friends:-

'Now we are at a home-based stage, at peace with ourselves and the world (more or less) and the miracle of it all is that in abandoning the ritual of our traditions, our faith has not been diminished. In fact it's been enhanced. We are no longer tied to any one church. Support from the Church has been international, spanning denominational boundaries and including churchy and non-churchy people alike. Everything has fallen into perspective and, as it's done so, we've become more focussed.
'Now we see only puzzling reflections in a mirror; one day we shall see face to face.'
It's our prayer that you, too, may keep your life in perspective, for in doing so, you'll find you're focussed beyond yourself.
With all our love,
Avril and Bill.'

A few weeks later the family had been and gone at least twice. We all knew and were prepared. Avril died on 20th October 2004. The funeral service in Kelso Old Parish Church was a true reflection of her, just as we planned it, just as she wished. Her ashes were interred at Hobkirk a week before Advent. With the love of my life at rest and our prayer that you, patient reader, might keep your life in perspective, 'for in doing so you'll find you're focussed beyond yourself', the last chapter of my autobiography, *Against the Grain*, I wrote, 'comes to an end. What lies ahead for me is another story.'

THE OTHER STORY

For a year or more I retired into myself struggling to force myself to complete the manuscript I had been happily working on along with the other half of me for many years but was now on my own in a world of memories attempting to breathe life into them. *Abbey Royd* was still *our house, our home,* the place I lived in, but life had lost its heartbeat without Avril. I'd have nothing much to write about in my Christmas letter for 2005, but I did:-

'I've been to many parts of the world as a doctor, and to many others as a minister, but never before, anywhere, as just a pair of hands, until I joined a Rotary Mission Challenge to Sierra Leone last month.

I saw the Aberdeen Clinic and Fistula Clinic at work, comparing the surgical techniques used now to repair a vesico-vaginal fistula resulting from the horrific complications of mismanaged childbirth with my own experiences as a young doctor in a mission hospital in South Africa forty years ago when my wife, Avril, was by my side as an anaesthetist. Looking into the operating room, I was transported back in time to the plaster room in which we first operated in what is now the Orthopaedic Service for the Transkei. I could see, in my mind's eye, a smiling face behind a surgical mask attending unassumingly to our patient.

On the building site next to the Clinic I laboured with my Rotary work-mates alongside local hired workers servicing the builders with cement and breeze blocks, clearing rubble, barrowing heaps of excavated earth from here to there, filling in holes and digging holes. Saturated with sweat and grime, I was not a pretty sight. 'Papa' they called me, and I thought of the Pope until it was pointed out. 'No. Papa! Old Man!' Not far from the surface lurked the reality of extreme poverty in a war-torn land. I was tempted to give advice, medical if necessary, or theological, but resisted both.

It's only when we're stripped of our professionalism and religiosity, when we've been stripped of everything that gives us life itself, that we can stand alongside the poor and work alongside them for change; when we've been reduced to just a pair of hands...'

When completed the book called *Against the Grain* came out in 2006, 'An autobiography of William J. Nicol, Doctor, Surgeon, Minister and Pilgrim with Avril.'

INTO RETIREMENT WITH MARGARET

I thought what had been growing in my mind for some time: 'I wonder how she's doing?'– the sweetheart of my student days in St Andrews, the girl at the bus stop at the top of Wellesley Road in Buckhaven, Margaret Thomson.

So I wrote to her. A telephone call came in reply, and I was on my way. My Renault Megane, its sell-by date well past, seemed to draw on hidden reserves to match its owner's eagerness to reach his former well-known destination. Through Gordon and over Soutra, through Pathhead and Dalkeith we sped, on the still incomplete Edinburgh by-pass, a £1 toll on the south side of the Forth Road Bridge, and I was over the Forth and into the Kingdom of Fife. Past the Dunfermline turnoff, the slip-road to Kirkcaldy soon appeared. I'd be in the 'Lang Toon' before I knew it, and the thought must have prompted a very real diuresis. Behind a hedge on a lay-by provided cover. Sharpened up, glasses cleaned, composed and in control, it was only a few miles to Kirkcaldy and a familiar sign: 'Leven and St Andrews'. Along the Standing Stane Road that I remembered from past days and was reminded of in Margaret's instructions on how to get to her; much sooner than I expected was the turn-off to Coaltown of Wemyss. From then on I was on well-kent ground. As it joined the coast road just beyond the road down to West Wemyss, I glanced to the left but couldn't detect any traces of Venters' building yard where I gathered with my work-mates to labour for a 'brickie' in my student days. Through Coaltown of Wemyss to East Wemyss, past the old St George's Church on the left, and almost as soon, past the graveyard on the right, coast side with the short stretch of road to Buckhaven before me, the only house now on the right a trim cottage, the house where Margaret was born in, 'Rosie Wemyss'. In Buckhaven I missed the turning on to the bus stop which I should have remembered from my student days at the top of Wellesley Road, off an unfamiliar round-about, but two right turns brought me back on course. A hundred yards or so along what I vaguely remembered as Wellesley Road, and my memories of Margaret's home were confirmed. The big iron gate to the drive was open as Margaret said it would be, and I drove in.

Margaret was at the back door. She smiled as I crossed the gravel yard to the spot she signalled me to park in, and as I got out of the car I must have done the same. 'Come in!' she said, 'It's good to see you!'

'It's you all right,' I thought as I looked into her face in the kitchen, and might have said something to that effect. She seemed not to need two looks to see that, yes, it was me. We were happy with what we saw, even though she confessed later that she was a little disappointed that the respectable, accomplished, professional gentleman she expected, had not gone to the trouble of wearing more than a T-shirt and casual chinos for the occasion. Constrained, curious, excited but self-possessed, receptive and at the same time unashamedly transparent, neither of us was in any way surprised at what we felt. In our hearts and minds through the years we'd known that we'd meet again. Our destiny was unfolding. The smart, trim figure was not unfamiliar.

The sparkle in her eyes was still there, like the smiling eyes in the graduation photo on the piano in the sitting room as we moved through from the kitchen. The thick, curly, fair hair was now thinner, no longer almost blonde, but equally startling. Everything about her was tasteful and natural. When she spoke, I recognised her voice and when I spoke, her ears seemed to prick up, the familiar pearl-drop earrings shimmering in response. We started talking about old times, but not for long. It was each other, here and now, we were most concerned with. We sat at the table in the dining room on the same seats we'd sat on for high-tea each Saturday afternoon in our courting days. The familiar lace curtains on the familiar bay window in the mahogany-panelled room with matching doors, and the almost architectural painting of the family home and scenes of old Buckhaven, all the works of Margaret's father, of whom she was justifiably proud, were readily recalled. I was taken back in time to the day I shared my bricklaying labourer's skills with her father, helping to lay a cement incline from the old garage in the back yard, now replaced with a new building concealing our handiwork. We spoke sensitively of the tea we shared at the same table in the dining room with our parents, Margaret's and mine, at the time of our engagement.

In the sitting room, where we moved into for coffee and biscuits, some of the timeless ornaments on the mantelpiece and sideboard were draped in dust sheets in preparation for the painter redecorating the sitting room, which was partly vacated. We exchanged summaries of our families through the years and photos to elaborate on. I gave her a copy of my autobiography, *Against the Grain,* inscribed, 'With fond memories of past days. Much love and every blessing for 2007', which she seemed to hold to herself as though she was cradling my unknown self she wanted to know all about, in much the same way that I wanted to know all about her. I was struck by Margaret's natural interest in Avril. She picked up every nuance of her, from my occasional references and was soon familiar with my extended family from photographs at a Millennium event in Crieff, so dear to Avril's heart. In return I found it easy coming to know her smaller family circle and friends, especially her family tree, including her Sixth Great-grand-uncle, Alexander Selkirk on whom Daniel Defoe characterised his memorable *Robinson Crusoe.*

We talked and listened, and talked more and more, and moved back into the dining room where we sat at the table and talked more, reminiscing on past days which came to life again. Soup and a sandwich, more talking, stories, memories rekindled, laughter and smiles – the time flew past. The 'good luck' seagull droppings on Margaret's shoulder on a day down the Clyde, and a flick of soap suds from washing up the dishes at 234 Kings Park Avenue when my pretentious girlfriend drying up for my strong-willed grandfather returned a half-washed, still partly-dirty plate to be washed again, seemed to have left permanent marks on Margaret. We laughed about them over and over again. I warmed to her lasting appreciation of the ornamental jewellery chest the old man, my one-time-ship's-carpenter grandfather, made for his grandson Willie's

Margaret, of whom he thought so much. But I was thrown by the musical box she brought from her room to show me. 'You'll remember this,' she said with certainty, and she was right. Opening the gift I'd given her so long ago in our time together, the chimes of 'The Merry Widow's Waltz' rang out as clearly as in former days. They were Margaret's and mine, but they were also Avril's and mine for the same tune was set to the words, 'Cinderella, Cinderella, we love you', at a Christmas pantomime at Bridge of Earn in 1959 when Avril was the front end of a horse and I was an ugly sister. The refreshing blend of sad reflections and profound happiness is a rare experience, one to be treasured, as we have since done at a performance of 'The Merry Widow' in the Tait Hall in Kelso a few years ago. Tender, secret, loving emotions have since stirred our souls.

Supper still at the table in the dining room, still talking animatedly, the day was drawing in. It was time for me to go. Whatever else, we both agreed that we'd been comfortable in each other's company. There was no hint of recriminations, no suggestion of bitterness or deprivation. We'd both fulfilled our separate lives and were now on the cusp of something else. No fixed plans were made for the future but one thing was mutual. 'It would be a pity if we never met again.' I gave her a friendly pat on the shoulder in the kitchen as I left.

Over the next few weeks we dwelt in our own thoughts. Impulsive me, I was carried away. We'd be up the aisle in next to no time. Practical Margaret was cautious, even bluntly honest. Her articulated feelings were what lay smouldering in the deepest recesses of my mind too. Marriage commitment for two strong, quite different personalities recognised fifty years ago and, no doubt, still palpable today, with fulfilling and continuing lives behind them, could never be a reality. We acknowledged this but couldn't help feeling that 'it would be a pity if we never met again.'

So we met again, and it was more than a friendly pat on the shoulder in the kitchen that we exchanged. In spite of the delay of a succession of visitors at *Abbey Royd,* a series of cardiac investigations for me, and painting and carpet laying in Buckhaven, we've met regularly since and are now a recognised entity. Our families have met and gelled. Everyone, family, friends and observers knew something from the day we met up again. We behave as though we belong to each other because we do belong to each other. In spite of ourselves we can't help ourselves.

THE SERMON ON THE HIP JOINT

It was time for the sermon, 'The Sermon on the Hip Joint'. In the central pulpit in Trinity Church, Hawick, backed by the impressive organ and no less impressive organist and choir swallowing me up in its tones whenever it burst into songs of praise, my notes carefully displayed before me, aware of a reasonable congregation in the pews surrounding me, beneath me in the main body of the kirk as well as in front of me, around me and to my right and left, it was the reassuring smiles of my three supporters, Joe and Debbie who had brought Margaret with them, a few rows back from the front, that caught my eye. This was the first service that Margaret had come especially to share in, with me taking it. We were both conscious of this, and, though we'd said nothing about it, we knew that we were expecting something different, personal, inspiring for everyone in the church but with an undertone of understanding amounting to commitment to each other as tangible as many a service of 'I dos!'

We'd read the Scripture Readings from Genesis 32, v. 22-32 about Jacob wrestling with God and Mark 6, v. 1-6 about Jesus being rejected at Nazareth, from the *Good News Bible*, and my words of introduction needed no script. I knew them backwards because they had been my life for many years.

'The hip joint is a ball and socket joint. It's normally a good, strong, stable joint. The smooth, round ball or head fits snugly into a deep socket, allowing it to move around easily. (A fist on one side and a cupped palm on the other demonstrates this.) But sometimes the ball slips out of the socket. That's a dislocation. There are three causes of dislocation of the hip joint.

First, Congenital Dislocation of the Hip, CDH. Some babies are born with one or both hips out of joint, or dislocated, and they end up waddling around when they get on to their feet, and that's not very good. The incidence of CDH is high in Native Americans and other people who carry their babies around with their legs bandaged together in papooses, because the newly formed joints are dislocated in this position. It's easy for a mother to hang her baby in a papoose on a maple tree while she gets on with her work and pick it up at the end of the working day, but the penalty is untreated CDH. If, on the other hand, you go to many places in Africa where mothers carry their babies around on their backs with their hips splayed out, you'll not find any dislocated hips, because this is the way to treat dislocations in children. Putting babies in a frog plaster or something like that until the hips have developed normally is an easy and effective method of treatment. But later on, if nothing is done in childhood, there can be big problems as an adult.

The second cause of Dislocation of the Hip Joint is Trauma. If you're sitting in the front passenger seat of a car with your legs crossed, chatting to the driver, driving down a

Motorway, you're asking for your hip to be dislocated when the car comes to a sudden stop at a sharp bend or in a collision. (Most ladies in the congregation sit up and uncross their legs at this point.) The head of the femur, or ball of the joint, is forced out the back of the socket. Not a nice thing. So no more crossed legs in the front seat of your cars.

And the Third cause of Dislocation of the Hip Joint is from Wrestling with God.

You'll remember the story about Jacob cheating his father, Isaac, and his brother, Esau and so receiving his father's blessing. When he was found out, Jacob had to flee into hiding, and he went to stay with his mother's brother, his uncle, Laban.

When Jacob arrived at Laban's house and met his two daughters, Leah and Rachel, it was Rachel he fell in love with, but he had to work for seven years only to be tricked into marrying Leah, and another seven years to get Rachel, and then six years to cheat his uncle out of the best of his flock of sheep. After twenty years Jacob decided to take his wives and his flock and all his possessions and return to his father's home and face his brother, Esau. On his way home he had his hip dislocated when he wrestled with God.

Though Abraham was the patriarch who was specially noted for his trust in God, it was Jacob, the stubborn, wilful, self-reliant, man-of-the-world, cheat who cheated his brother out of his birthright – it was Jacob who eventually came to terms with God when he wrestled with him and had his name changed from 'Jacob', meaning 'cheat' to 'Israel' meaning 'he who wrestled with God'. When Jacob wrestled with God it was God who initiated the struggle which ended in the defeat of the old Jacob. It was God, as we heard, and is quoted in some translations as, 'struck Jacob in the hollow of his thigh so that his hip was dislocated as they wrestled'. It was God who first rendered Jacob helpless, but from that point on, it was Jacob

283

who grappled with God, and clung on to him until he had received a blessing. Then Jacob limped away, a new man, having seen God 'face to face'. From then on, Jacob was bound to God.

As Israel, the Hebrew people, the chosen people, wrestled with God throughout the years, a covenant relationship developed. Initially it was God who wrestled with the Israelites on his terms. But later on the people clung on to God as they became more and more dependent on him.

A few years ago a friend of mine visited several countries to try to see what problems the churches faced in them. When he came back after his tour, which included South Korea, Zambia and one of the poorest parts of Bangladesh, what he had to say was what most of us have to face in our everyday lives. In Korea, he told me that everyone was polite and courteous. The people he met, told him about their churches, their schools, their culture and their customs – everything else except what must have been uppermost in their minds, 'when were the North Koreans going to invade the South and threaten the whole country?' In Zambia, he heard about the growing churches there and was inspired by the open, uninhibited worship of the poorest of poor people struggling for survival. The people he met liked talking about all these things and asked about how people lived in this country – talking about everything and anything except the scourge of the country, haunting everyone's life, AIDS. In Bangladesh it was the same. The enthusiasm of everyone he met to tell him everything except what must have been foremost in their minds – recurring flooding and the thousands of lives lost from drowning and disease which followed in its wake, stood out in his memory. When we, like Jacob, wrestle with God, we should not be afraid to allow God to initiate the wrestling, with concerns pertinent to our lives and those of our vulnerable *neighbours and not content ourselves with superficial small-talk until we've grappled with God and clung on to him.*

I continued in my 'Sermon on the Hip Joint' in 2006:–

'It's over seven years now since the horrific outrage of 11 September in New York when the twin towers were blown up and flattened. And since then more and more suicide bombings have become almost part of life. (As I go to Press now at the beginning of 2017 outrages in Paris, Germany, Brussels and on our doorsteps in our own country have unfolded compounding the unending carnage in the Middle East centred on Syria and Iraq throwing our political systems into chaos with one humanitarian crisis after another crying out for respite.) *If the whole episode of 11 September has taught us nothing else, it is that the issues of global terrorism, anger and injustices, retaliation and retribution, are out in the open now. People are talking about these issues now, not least the chaotic financial crisis which is crippling, in its own way, almost every country in the world. Nations are talking more and more than ever before to one another about real issues, not shying clear of facing up to differences because of vested interests. Long may this continue and deeper may we all delve into the most sensitive feelings we all harbour.*

It was the same with Jacob. He'd jogged along, on the make, his self-interest uppermost in his mind for years, till he was challenged by God; till he grappled with issues he'd never faced before; till he met his match in God who started the wrestling; who dislocated Jacob's hip and brought him to his senses. May the world be changed like Jacob, and that includes each of us, Arab, American, Muslim or Christian, professing nothing or anything, Russian, Chinese, English, Scots, Irish or Welsh. Important people on the world scene are being brought up with a start. They're wrestling with God in their own way.

First Ministers, Prime Ministers, Presidents, Chancellors, good leaders and bad leaders, dictators and despots alike, are having to face the music.

Every now and again some national personality takes a stand on some issue, like the Moderator of the General Assembly of the Church of Scotland a while ago on a Long Walk from Faslane to Edinburgh to protest against the nuclear deterrent. You're in good company whenever you feel you're wrestling with God.

And now the change in my life from that of a doctor, from one of Orthopaedic Surgery to the Ministry, pastoral work and Sunday Services. A big change, most of my friends imagined, and in many ways they were right. But putting a good hip joint into someone is not all that different from carpentry, making a good dove-tail joint. In our second reading we heard about Jesus' visit to his hometown, Nazareth. Many people were there; and when they heard him they were all amazed. 'Where did he get all this?' they asked. 'What wisdom is this that he has been given? How does he perform miracles? Isn't he the carpenter, the son of Mary, and the brother of James, Joseph, Judas and Simon? Aren't his sisters living here?' And so they rejected him.

The people in his own hometown can recognise Jesus' wisdom all right, but they will not take the next step of accepting the message of the Kingdom of God. They were not expecting this kind of Messiah. Jesus is too familiar, as one who worked like them and whose family they knew. They were expecting something more spectacular. We shouldn't be surprised at this because the history of Israel is full of examples of prophets who were rejected because their message challenged the acceptable understanding of God. In Nazareth the people couldn't bring themselves to see God working through one of their own town's folk, the carpenter, or the son of the carpenter, they were familiar with. And if they couldn't recognise God in the humanity of the man, Jesus, who they were familiar with, how could they grasp the idea of a divine dimension? 'And so they rejected him. He was not able to perform miracles but he placed his hands on a few people and healed them.'

'How different is Orthopaedics from the Ministry? Not much! They're both helping people along the road. A new hip joint is just a piece of carpentry. What I'm doing now, in the Ministry, is what we're all doing, following the carpenter of Nazareth.

Amen.   Let us pray,
'Wrestle, gracious God, with each of us
that we may cling on to you'.

A REFLECTION ON REMEMBRANCE

I've worn my General Service Medical with clasp 'Malaya' on only a few Remembrance Sundays in recent years, the last time on Sunday 11 November, 2007 when Margaret, the renewed well-stream of my life now, was by my side. It was a time of particular poignancy for both of us united again after almost fifty years apart with our busy, active lives dictating every minute of every day.

This is from the Remembrance Day Service at Hobkirk Parish Church on 11 November, 2007:-

'On either side of the river stood a tree of life, which yields twelve crops of fruit, one for each month of the year. The leaves of the trees serve for the healing of the nations.' (Revelation, Ch. 22 v 2. New English Bible.)
'The leaves of the trees are for the healing of the nations.'

Did any of you see the Royal British Legion Festival of Remembrance in the Royal Albert Hall on T.V. last night? Probably most of you – and at the end, the red poppy petals fluttering down from the roof, first only a few, then more and more, until they were raining down on all the uniforms below, and on to the floor. That part of the Festival is always one of the most touching parts.

Autumn has past and winter has started. Almost all the leaves from the trees have fallen now, and most branches are bare. John, the writer of Revelation, gives a similar image, or a vision, of the River of the Water of Life, sparkling like crystal, and coming from the throne of God and from the Lamb, and flowing down the main street of the new Jerusalem and on either side of the river a Tree of Life with its leaves for the healing of the nations. He doesn't tell us whether all the leaves are still on the trees, or whether some have fallen on to the ground below, over the nations of the earth. But I like to think of some of the leaves having fallen, some in the process of falling, fluttering down like the poppies in the Albert Hall last night, and some still left to fall. I see in the Tree of Life, the leaves that have been shed for the healing of the nations in the past, some falling on the conflicts of life at this very moment for the healing of the discords of the nations today, and some still left for the healing of the nations tomorrow.

Why do leaves fall from trees anyway? I know that if it's blowing a gale or you shake the branch of a tree, the leaves might fall off, but looking out of our front window at the beautiful copper beech tree in our garden last week, on a still day, with no breeze in the autumn air, and no rain, the leaves were falling from the branches like a gentle shower of rain – you could hear the rustle as they fell. I went back to my early student days and looked up a book on 'Biology and Physiological Regulation' and found that the cells at the end of a leaf, where it joins the branch of a tree, have something special about them. They swell up on one side more than the other in response to light shining in one direction or another, and the leaf turns towards the light. The cells contain minute particles of a remarkable pigment called 'photochrome' which absorbs red light of only one particular wave-length and is activated to promote growth at the base of leaf stalks. When there's sufficient light of this highly selective wavelength for a critical duration of time each day, the leaves adhere strongly to the branches of the tree, but, as summer gives way to autumn and the days shorten, and the particular wave bands of light disappear, the cells at the base of leaves no longer adhere to one-another, and the leaves fall off. Light, and a very critical type of light, is essential for the life of the cells at the base of the leaves.

The first few verses of the Bible tell us that 'In the beginning of creation, when God made heaven and earth, the earth was without form and void, with darkness over the face of the abyss, and a mighty wind swept over the surface of the waters. God said, 'Let there be light,' and there was light.' God must have known about 'photochrome' and the need of light for life, as well as knowing about the Tree of Life, 'which yields twelve crops of fruit, one for each month of the year, and that its leaves are for the healing of the nations.'

Today, on this Remembrance Sunday, we are especially conscious of all those who lost their lives in wars in the past. God is often used as a scapegoat for his warring children and has his work cut out to make any meaning of the passionate causes they die for. I'm sure we all remember the story about the First World War, when the British and German soldiers stopped fighting one Christmas Day in France, had a chat, a cigarette, and even in some places, played a game of football together, only to start killing one another again the next day. J.C. Squire wrote about it:-

'God heard the embattled nations sing and shout;
'Gott strafe England.' – 'God save the King!' –
'God this' – 'God that' – and 'God the other thing' –
'My God,' said God, 'I've got my work cut out!'

It's tempting to look back on wars in past years, and remember the dead, and to imagine that they died for us in the future, which is now, today. And it's tempting for us to look to the future with hope, and to dream dreams and see visions. But it's the present in which we live, the world around us as it is now, and it's in the world now that God is alive. There are very real dangers in dwelling too much in the past, and waiting too long for, and leaving too much to, the future.

Memories bind us to the past which is no longer. Hope casts us upon a future, which is not yet. We remember having lived, but do not live. We remember having loved but do not love. We remember the thoughts of others, but do not think for ourselves. And it's much the same for hope in the future. We hope to live, but do not live now. We hope to be happy one day, but miss out in happiness today. We're never, in our memory of the past and hope for the future, wholly ourselves and wholly in the present. They can, if we let them, cheat us of the eternal presence of God, so that we can't see God active and present in our lives today.

But though memories and hopes may have their dangers, they are both, at the same time, essential for a full understanding of the present, because there's much more to life than just the present, even with a God of the present.

The 'now', the 'today', the 'present' of the New Testament isn't an eternal present going on and on. It's a 'now, this very instant', an 'all of a sudden' in which the newness of a promised future is lit up and seen in a flash – the kind of flash many of the lives we remember today experienced at the height of hostilities in past wars which fed them with a purpose, which *drove them to their destiny. The past which we remember today wasn't an eternal present but a glimpse of a better eternal future.*

So, what can we learn from our memories of the past that will help us today to build a better future tomorrow?

We can learn to ' love our enemies and pray for those who persecute us', to look with compassion on those in need around us and put ourselves out to help where help is needed, for it's only then that we can hope for lasting peace, for war-free life. 'The leaves of the 'Trees of Life' are for the healing of the nations.'

Amen.

TWO CRUISES AND A ROCK

Ever since first learning what 'white horses' in the Atlantic Ocean were – when returning home from British Guiana as a boy towards the end of the Second World War, beef-juice and crackers on deck, wrapped in a blanket on a deck-chair; what kipping down on a three-tiered, hinged, canvas bunk, all my possessions carefully packed in a kit-bag and rucksack on a troop ship with open toilets affording no privacy and a wash-room floor awash with sick and excreta in stormy weather, but also the inviting smell of cooking and canteen food which never failed to excite me on the mess deck, on the ways to and from National Service in Singapore and Malaya as a young conscript in the Army; a return trip with our family of three boys on the British India Line up the west coast of Africa from Durban in South Africa, the *thump, thump, thump* of copper bars being loaded on at Beira, some of the roughest seas I've ever experienced in the Mediterranean, picking up our eldest son, Jim, aged four, from the bottom of a stair-well he'd been thrown down in an unexpected especially violent roll that seemed to roll on and on before eventually correcting itself; the journeys on the Mail Ships *Oranje* and *Edinburgh Castle* from Southampton to East London in South Africa and back ,the hearts and minds of their passengers a mix of profound sadness, anxious expectancy, relief and unrestrained joy – ever since these encounters with the oceans of our planet, I've associated an ocean-going voyage with coming from one stage in life or going to another, a challenge ahead or a dream behind, a mix of exhilaration and apprehension, which is the balanced fuel of my very being.

A sea voyage in an ocean liner journeying from one point in life to another has caught my imagination, thrilled me to the core, renewed my curiosity in my surroundings, my interest in my affinity for humanity, love for friends and family and country, endearment to those closest to me. I like nothing better than the fresh wind in my face on deck, a roughish sea around me, the bow of the ship cleaving the waters ahead of it, the stern churning out a pathway to an immediate past in its wake. A two-week cruise, especially with Margaret, the life-blood of my renewed life now, would, I thought, be much the same, and, in some ways, it was, but in many others it was quite different.

Not pictured in all its splendour sailing home with the white cliffs of Dover on the horizon as in the Photo Gallery , but no less spectacular, nestling in the port of Dover, bathed in the summer sunshine of July 2008, our first sight of the *Balmoral* was breathtaking. My oldest son, Jim, had driven Margaret and me from his home in Westley, near Bury St Edmunds, where we'd stayed overnight having travelled south from Fife the previous day. The excitement was mounting. Plans for our Fred Olsen Cruise were about to materialise. Like children waiting for the magic appearance of *Co-Co* or some other clown or celebrity at a birthday party, the moment for the start of our cruise had arrived. In no time we were through the town, at the docks and in the Departure baggage check-in bay alongside our majestic cruise liner, the *Balmoral*. 'Have a good trip,' said Jim to Margaret, and to me, 'Keep the heid, Dad,' 'Enjoy yourselves. I wish I was going with you' – and he was off and we were up the gangway having our 'Welcome on Board' photo taken, our hands sanitised, and exploring the ship. The cabins were nothing like those of any ship I'd sailed on before. The traditional porthole, the focal point in the cabin, was replaced by a curtained window, the bunk beds by trim divans, the luxury of the 'Superior Outside Cabin with Window' completed by a well-appointed en-suite bathroom with shower. No longer, it appeared, was there any need to run along to a toilet block at the end of a corridor or wait for a seawater bath to be filled for ablutions at sea. By the time we sailed in the evening we had a good layout of our floating hotel, notably where the main dining hall was on the deck above us.

Boarding a cruise liner like the *Balmoral* poses immediate pressing calls on the priorities of life we all take for granted from day to day. Casting off, the massive bulk of a floating city edging away from the stability of a motionless land mass, the *Balmoral* leaving Dover and the white cliffs receding into the setting sun, heading off from the English Channel into the North Sea, exploring the five-star surroundings, checking on the ship's standing orders outlining the recommended routine for safety procedures, social programmes like cultural talks and mini lectures on places and events which lay ahead, were all of equal significance for me but in no way approached my top priority, namely the sight of and expectancy of the dining hall, the smell and taste of good food and good wine.

A Fred Olsen cruise is top drawer. The almost ceremonial procession to or from a meal, especially a formal evening dinner; the strict observance of hygienic hand sterilisation with some kind of foam spray like that with which we were welcomed on board and were to accept unquestioningly for the entire voyage; the table which Margaret, my always tastily colour-coded dress conscious partner and soul-mate, and I were to share with a most congenial seasoned cruising couple; the happy meals which we enjoyed, well served by respectful waiters and stewards made the formality of an appropriate dress code tolerable to my non-conforming nature which Jim, my conforming-when-he-wants-to son, was probably aware of in his veiled warning to 'Keep the heid' as we boarded the *Balmoral.*

As though by magic we had negotiated the entrance to the North Sea and the approaches to the German coastline by the end of our first formal meal and were well into the Keil Canal by the end of our first night at sea securely docked at Warnemunde ready for our first full day tour to Berlin. A chain of enormous floating hotels, cargo-laden transporters, oil tankers and ocean-going liners interspersed with more normal, easily recognised, private yachts and nondescript ships in what seemed a hair's breadth of another similar chain passing in the opposite direction traversed miles of industrial and residential land masses, stretches of forestation and grassy landscapes, endless miles of sandy desert or barren rocky mountains reduced, I'm sure, many an awe-inspired spectator like me lining a deck rail to a speck floating on an endless sea of land wondering, drinking in the marvels of man's ingenuity married to the majesty of creation, a combination out of this world. The man-made miracle of a strategic canal like the Suez, which I've seen several times, and now the Keil Canal, never fail to excite my imagination. I'd love to walk on the Great Wall of China before I die, but above all other longings, to traverse the Panama Canal, to sail from the Caribbean Sea to the Pacific Ocean.

A full day tour of the spectacular sights of Berlin from Warnemunde dispelled for short periods the tragically ingrained images of war years on the Western Front and post-war Communist days. Some bitter memories of dying generations are encouragingly being replaced with more hopeful signs in their children and grandchildren.

Tired but informed from our first tour, it was good to head into the Baltic Sea the next day and address ourselves to a Finnish perspective on life at our next port of call in Helsinki. The pattern was set. Cruising in the luxury of our home from home, the *Balmoral,* with a few quiet days at sea to relax and savour, but mainly one tour after another, each with its own fascination, giving a glimpse of another way of life in another culture, left little time for reappraisal. After Helsinki came Saint Petersburg, the most western seaport in the mighty Russian Empire of Peter the Great of a former glory era, its grandeur betraying the contrasting opulence of an inordinately wealthy, self-indulgent aristocracy and the abject poverty of an unrecognised serfdom. The gardens, palaces, cathedrals and most ornate, heavily gold-embossed paintings held me spellbound, but it was posing with Margaret for a photograph in front of a battle cruiser, *The Aurora,* from which the sound of a single canon shot proclaimed the start of The Great October Revolution of 1917 which fired my imagination as much as it warmed the hearts of the proletariate of the day. Tallinn, in independent Estonia bordering Russia, proved the most relaxing port of call. Then on to Copenhagen in Denmark and Oslo in Norway. Our comprehensive tours completed, home to Dover and the end of an excellent cruise.

THE SHETLAND and ORKNEY ISLANDS

The following year, in May 2009, it was not another Fred Olsen cruise on the *Balmoral* which attracted us but an equally enlightening, informative and satisfying, enriching and heart-warming, lower-key, ferry-coach, comfortable and homely, tour of Shetland and the Orkney Islands with Cupar–based Brightwater Holidays that appealed to us. Northlink Ferries overnight from Aberdeen to Lerwick, and Kirkwall to Aberdeen, and the short but roughest passage from the outermost Shetland Islands to the Orkneys were mini-cruises in themselves. Windswept Shetlands included a trek to the now derelict Sumburgh Head lighthouse to catch a certain view of every tourist's dream, a mass of colourful puffins in flight only to find that all the elusive birds had flown, and the oil indulged Orkneys, home of Scapa Flow and Scara Brae, salutary reminders of our ancient heritage, proudly proclaimed patriotism for Norway at least equal to that for Scotland and, in many hearts, much more than for Westminster. On the coach from Aberdeen to our pick-up point in Kinross, Margaret and I were both conscious of our roots in the Kingdom of Fife, in the Scotland of our birth, an integral part of the United Kingdom of Great Britain and Northern Ireland of today, proud of our past enhanced, now, by our new-found affinities for the Shetlands and the Orkneys. Almost back home, a glimpse of the coastline and the mouth of the Firth of Forth beyond, in a brief, precious moment, infinitely thankful for the gift of our beings, we were conscious also of the Bass Rock in our minds' eyes.

A silent sentinel at the mouth of the Firth of Forth, the Bass Rock can be seen equally well on a clear day from Margaret's home-town of Buckhaven and mine in West Wemyss a few miles south-east along the Fife coast. Gazing almost due east over the sheltered waters of the Firth to the restless North Sea beyond, the Rock is, in one sense, a barrier, an impenetrable protection proclaiming the security of home in the Kingdom of Fife. In another it's a stimulus demanding the quest of what cannot be seen on the other side, a magnet to exciting seas beyond, the God-goal of our lives. The same Bass Rock that we viewed from our student-day homes in Buckhaven and West Wemyss aroused different emotions in each of us, Margaret and me, then, and still does.

NEW TESTAMENT TURKEY

'McCabe Pilgrimages' offer to visit 'New Testament Turkey' with the Revd John Robinson from 22 May to 1 June 2014 – to spend 11 days visiting the Seven Churches of Revelation, imbibing the busy day and night life of Istanbul and soulfully contemplating the 'Gentlemen's War ' of the Gallipoli Campaign of 1915 – was one neither Margaret nor I could resist. Our tour would, we were assured, 'provide an introduction to the classical world of Greek and Roman architecture and culture, alongside the realities of life in a secular state, with the predominant religion being Islam'. But for the Christian pilgrim there would be much more – 'a journey to the origins of our faith and a window into the history of our Church'.

The in-flight Turkish red wine went down well on the flight from Heathrow to Istanbul and the full day city tour the following day concentrating on the splendours of the city including the underground Justinian Cisterns and the architecturally superb Blue Mosque proved, indeed, spectacular, as did the Egyptian Spice Market, the Byzantine Church of St Saviour with stunning mosaics and frescoes, an out-of-this-world sail on the Bosphorus and the purchase of an authentic Turkish Carpet after being bewitched at the Grand Bazaar another day.

The first three days of our Turkey tour over, the remaining days, devoted more to the sites of ancient days from which the 'Seven Churches of Revelation' sprung, were yet to come. The day between, a Sunday, 24 May, was quite different from either. We drove from Istanbul to Gallipoli to visit, as our 'Daily Programme' informed us, 'some of the battlefields and the British memorial at Cape Helles and recall the events of the First World War, when thousands of Allied and Ottoman troops perished.' The sheer scale of the senseless slaughter of Turk, British, Australian, New Zealand and French men hardly out of their boyhood days was palpable. Crossing the Dardanelles Strait by ferry from the Gallipoli peninsula was sobering, giving added poignancy to an act of worship as a token of repentance.

The most spectacular ruins we were introduced to were in Pergamum. The great Hellenistic city towers 1000 feet above the modern city of Bergama. Of particular interest to me was the impressive ancient medical centre of Asclepion on the lower slopes of the ancient city adjacent to the Grand Theatre and a restored library, but try as hard as I could, scrambling over endless monumental ruins in the scorching heat of the midday sun with Margaret at my heels hat in hand for my beaming scalp, I could find no traces of the Greek god of Medicine in any of the still-standing rows and rows of granite pillars and rubble. With lunch at the Kardesler Restaurant to revive us for the rest of the day we were off on our coach south to view the Temple of Artemis, a Roman gymnasium and elaborate mosaics in a mosque, stopping briefly at Philadelphia before arriving for two days at Pamukale (Hierapolis) with its unique white terraces and warm calcium pools.

One sometimes familiar, sometimes anything but, ancient ruins of bygone centuries after another replaced by modern towns then invaded our tranquil musings. Hierapolis and Laodicea, a scheduled Eucharist out of the blazing heat of the day, Aphrodisias with its fine stadium and extensive ruins, and on the penultimate day of our tour perhaps the prize, but not especially for me, a visit to Ephesus, brought our pilgrimage to a conclusion. It was salutary to realise that Paul had been there, in Ephesus for some years, long before us and that it is one of the most impressive archaeological sites in the world. The day came to an end with a Eucharist shared with a local church. Homeward bound the next day, the pilgrimage was over.

And so, dear, patient reader, has this saga of my life been enriched beyond measure by the two loves of my life, Avril and Margaret, and by my extending family and friends from far and wide, all of whom have, in their own ways, given me glimpses of the kind of love revealed in a baby in a manger a long time ago.

CHRISTMAS 2016

William J Nicol,
Abbey Royd,
Bridge Street,
Kelso, TD5 7JE.
Tel. 01573225052

Dear

'I feel a sermon coming on.' That is what a dear ministerial friend of mine kept saying every time we met and got talking. You've read many of my Christmas letters over the years and are excused from assuming 'the same again' from me this year, another sermonising Christmas letter. So no mention of world affairs and petty tittle tattle and you can get the state of my eyes in a combined re-edition of *Against the Grain* and *Another Story* which should come out early next year as *Never a Home of my Own.*

My life with Avril has been a Pilgrimage, with Margaret a journey to an unknown future. When the Pilgrimage was over and the Journey not yet started I was at a low point till I met up with Margaret again and was given a 'New lease of life'. Since then I've had a few new leases of life, first with my partial knee replacement, then, in more recent years, a cataract operation on my remaining good eye and a re-run in the form of laser beam intervention followed by alarming almost complete blindness which fortunately turned out to be a transient aftermath. I can, therefore, in some small measure, sympathise with John Milton writing 'On his Blindness':-

When I consider how my light is spent,
Ere half my days, in this dark world and wide,
And that one Talent which is death to hide
Lodged with me useless, though my Soul more bent
To serve therewith my Maker, and present
My true account, lest he returning chide;
'Doth God exact day-labour, light denied?'

I've been, then, several times reduced to 'They also serve who only stand and wait' –but can still see to read and see to write just now.

My sermonising blessing sent to you this Christmas season with all my love and Margaret's, is this Aaronic Blessing from *Numbers 6:24-26*:

May the Lord, mighty God,
bless and keep you for ever;
grant you peace, perfect peace,
courage in every endeavour.

Lift up your eyes and see his face
and his grace for ever;
may the Lord, mighty God,
bless and keep you for ever.

(Goes well to tune 'Edelweiss')

FINIS

Lightning Source UK Ltd.
Milton Keynes UK
UKHW020630181220
375367UK00012B/2385